Criteria and Guidelines for Quality Continuing Education and Training Programs:
The CEU and Other Measurement Units

International Association for Continuing Education and Training

KENDALL/HUNT PUBLISHING COMPANY
4050 Westmark Drive   Dubuque, Iowa 52002

These copyrighted logos of the International Association for Continuing Education and Training are reserved for use only by organizations that have been reviewed and approved by IACET.

ORDER FROM:

International Association for Continuing Education and Training
1200 19th St., NW
Suite 300
Washington, DC 20036-2422

Phone: (202) 857-1122
Fax: (202) 223-4579
E-mail: IACET@DC.SBA.COM
URL: WWW.IACET.ORG

Table of Contents

Table of Contents

Table of Contents

Table of Contents

Criteria and Guidelines for Quality Continuing Education and Training Programs: The CEU and Other Measurement Units

Purpose of this document

Marking the thirtieth anniversary of the CEU, this publication serves a number of purposes:

- Refines the criteria and guidelines for awarding the IACET CEU.
- Defines the IACET CEU--a uniform, internationally-recognized unit of measure for continuing education and training.
- Defines a systematic means for program development and delivery.
- Identifies criteria by which the quality of learning activities are judged.
- Identifies criteria by which education/training providers are evaluated.
- Provides a systematic means to document learning across a variety of delivery formats. . . . .
- Testifies to the commitment of hundreds of individuals and their organizations who have volunteered their service on committees, projects, the IACET Board of Directors, and the Authorized Provider Commission. Their role in refining and enhancing the practice of continuing education and training is gratefully acknowledged.

Section 1

The International Association for Continuing Education and Training (IACET)

The International Association for Continuing Education and Training (IACET)

Vision	IACET is the internationally recognized organization for standards and certification for continuing education and training.
Mission	Promote and enhance quality in continuing education and training through research, education, standard setting, and certification.
Goals	• Promote IACET standards and certification world-wide. • Promote and conduct research on effective practices in continuing education and training. • Publish, disseminate, and promote the use of research-based standards for enhancing quality in continuing education and training. • Develop and disseminate educational programs and materials for the continuous improvement in continuing education and training.
Strategic objectives	• Promote IACET standards as the benchmark for quality program delivery and certification. • Develop standards and procedures for certifying organizations. • Establish educational programs and resources on IACET's standards for providers of continuing education and training. • Sponsor research projects aimed at enhancing standards of good practice in continuing education and training.

The International Association for Continuing Education and Training (IACET)

History

We celebrate the thirtieth anniversary of the CEU in 1998. Just as the CEU has evolved from the generic CEU to the IACET CEU, the Association has evolved from the original organization with a limited mission to an organization with an international mission:

- A voluntary national task force was created to devise the CEU in 1968.

- The task force created a non-profit, membership organization called the Council on the CEU in 1977 to continue the task force's work.

- The Council changed its name to the International Association for Continuing Education and Training (IACET) in 1990 to reflect its expanding mission and membership. The CEU is widely used in North and South America, as well as in other parts of the world. Multinational corporations, the professions, and governmental agencies use the standards upon which the CEU is based to develop, implement, and evaluate continuing education and training.

Membership

Over 650 organizations and individuals committed to continuous quality improvement in continuing education and training programs constitute the IACET. The membership includes individuals, associations, businesses, industries, higher education institutions, government agencies, health organizations, regulatory agencies, proprietary schools, and others.

Transition period

January 1998 marks the beginning of a transition period for IACET. Standards are being raised to promote IACET's mission of promoting and enhancing quality in continuing education and training through standard setting.

The International Association for Continuing Education and Training (IACET)

Continued

New categories
There will be two membership categories (individual and organizational) and one approval category.

Individual membership
- **Individual membership** will be for any person who is interested in continuing education and training and who supports the mission and activities of the Association. The individual member will have full voting rights. There will be no authorization to use IACET or IACET CEU logo. The individual membership cost will be $100 annually.

Organizational membership
- **Organizational membership** will be for any group that is interested in continuing education and training and which supports the mission and activities of the Association. The organization will have one vote to be cast by one designated person. The organizational membership cost will be $300 annually.

Authorized Providers
- **Authorized Providers** will consist of all organizations that award the IACET CEU based on IACET criteria.

  — These organizations submit materials for review by the IACET Authorized Provider Commission, receive a site visit for verification from a trained site visitor, and sign a letter of agreement to adhere to IACET criteria.

  — Authorized Providers are authorized to use both the IACET and Authorized Provider logos.

  — The organization pays a non-refundable application fee of $350, $150 honorarium for the site visit, site visitor's expenses, and annual fees of $600. The approval period is five years.

  — Reapplications after five years require a nonrefundable fee of $300.

  — Authorized Providers are entitled to one vote to be cast by one designated person.

The International Association for Continuing Education and Training (IACET)

Continued

Authorized Provider (cont.)

— Any organization which is currently a Certified Provider or Authorized CEU Sponsor will be required to meet the new standards and to submit a new application at the time of its next regularly scheduled renewal date. If the organization's certification expires between January 1, 1998 and April 30, 1999, the expiration date will be extended so that all organizations have at least a year's notice to comply with the new standards.

Increasing emphasis on quality

● As caretaker of the CEU, the Association continually refines and publishes *The Criteria and Guidelines for Quality Continuing Education and Training Programs: The CEU and Other Measurement Units.*

● IACET has undertaken several research projects leading to enhancements in the criteria and guidelines for the use of the CEU. These projects produced three additional publications:

— *Principles of Good Practice in Continuing Education*

— *A Practical Handbook for Assessing Learning Outcomes in Continuing Education and Training*

— *Guidelines for Distance Education*

(See Appendix B for instructions for ordering IACET publications.

● The Association also restricts use of the IACET logo to those providers which are authorized by IACET as adhering to the criteria and guidelines.

Section 2

The Continuing Education Unit (CEU)

The Continuing Education Unit (CEU)

Purpose

The Continuing Education Unit (CEU) was created to:

- provide a standard unit of measure,
- quantify continuing adult education and training activities, and
- serve the diversity of providers, activities, and purposes in adult education.

Definition

One CEU = **ten contact hours** of participation
in **organized continuing education experience**
under **responsible, qualified direction and instruction**.

Ownership and use of the CEU

The International Association for Continuing Education and Training (IACET) is the caretaker of the CEU. IACET assumes responsibility for refining and disseminating information about the CEU. Through its programs, publications, research, and technical assistance, the Association assists organizations in correctly utilizing the criteria.

The CEU is in the public domain. Use of the CEU is voluntary and no permission or approval is required. The decision to award the CEU is made by the provider and should be based on a thorough review of the provider's capabilities in meeting the IACET CEU criteria.

Any organization can offer the traditional CEU. Unfortunately, there are organizations which award the CEU which do not adhere to the standards developed by the IACET. This has led to consumer misunderstanding and distrust of the value of the CEU. Therefore, IACET has taken steps to ensure the credibility of the IACET CEU.

Authorized Providers

To ensure quality in continuing education and training programs and to increase the consumer's confidence in those organizations which adhere to the standards, IACET established the Authorized Providers Program. This program provides recognition for providers who adhere to the criteria and are willing to have their programs assessed by the Authorized Providers Commission. (See page 3-7 for application details.)

The Continuing Education Unit (CEU)

IACET CEU   To distinguish between the generic CEU and the CEU granted by IACET Authorized Providers, the Association restricts the use of its IACET CEU and Authorized Provider logos to providers which are certified as "Authorized Providers" by IACET.

Criteria for Awarding the IACET CEU

12 Criteria

The criteria represent a systematic approach to cause learning to occur. Each of the 12 criteria contains guidelines to assist organizations which award the CEU in interpreting and applying the standard. Each criterion is related to each of the other criteria. For example, Criterion #6 Needs Identification is an integral part of all other activity, course, or program criteria. Information gathered and analyzed In Criterion #6 is used in each succeeding criterion through Criterion #12 Evaluation.

Criteria 1-5 (organization)

Criteria 1-5 refer to the organization.

1. Organization: The provider must have an identifiable continuing education or training unit or group with assigned responsibility for administering continuing education and/or training activities, courses, or programs.

2. Responsibility and Control: The provider, through its continuing education or training unit, ensures certification criteria are followed.

3. System for Awarding the Continuing Education Unit: The provider has a system in place to identify learners who meet requirements for satisfactory completion.

4. Maintenance and Availability of Records: The provider maintains a complete, permanent (at least 7 years) record of each learner's participation and can provide a copy of that record upon request.

5. Learning Environment and Support Systems: A learning environment and support services appropriate to the continuing education or training goals and learning outcomes is provided.

Criteria 6-9 (activity, course, or program development)

Criteria 6-9 refer to the activity, course, or program development.

6. Needs Identification: Each activity, course, or program is planned in response to identified needs of a target audience.

Criteria for Awarding the IACET CEU

Continued

Criteria 6-9 (activity, course, or program development) (cont.)	7. Learning Outcomes: The provider has clear and concise written statements of intended learning outcomes (e.g., behavioral or performance objectives) based on identified needs for each continuing education and training activity, course, or program. 8. Activity, Course, or Program Planning and Instructional Personnel: Qualified personnel are involved in planning and conducting each activity, course, and program. 9. Content and Instructional Methods: Content and instructional methods are appropriate for the learning outcomes of each activity, course, or program.
Criteria 10-12 (evaluation)	Criteria 10-12 refer to evaluation activities. 10. Assessment of Learning Outcomes: Procedures established during activity, course, or program planning are used to assess achievement of the learning outcomes. 11. Requirements for Satisfactory Completion: The provider assures that satisfactory completion requirements are established for each activity, course, or program and are based on the purpose and learning outcomes. 12. Post-Activity, Course, or Program Evaluation: Each learning activity, course, or program is evaluated.
Detailed explanation of criteria	The criteria, with guidelines and required practices, can be found beginning on page 2-6.

Criteria, Guidelines, and Required Practices

**Criterion 1
Organization**

The provider must have an identifiable continuing education or training unit or group with assigned responsibility for administering continuing education or training (CE/T) activities, courses, or programs.

Guidelines

Providers which are eligible to award the IACET CEU include those that are chartered, incorporated, or a recognized proprietorship or governmental unit. The eligible providers will have a well-defined organizational structure in which the authority and responsibility for administering continuing education or training activities is assigned to a particular unit, group, or individual which can ensure each of the IACET CEU criteria are met.

Large, complex providers whose continuing education is conducted by various parts of the organization may choose to specify those divisions, departments, colleges, or units that are responsible for specific CE/T activities, courses, or programs.

The provider's continuing education group or unit is clearly identified within the organizational structure. The activities of the group/unit must support the organization's mission. This support must be evidenced by the group/unit's own mission statement or similar document that defines the group/unit's responsibilities.

**Required
practices**

1.1 The unit or group with responsibility for continuing education or training is clearly identified within the organization.

1.2 Assigned responsibilities of the educational or training unit/group support the provider's mission.

1.3 The unit/group administers education/training activities, courses, or programs.

Criteria, Guidelines, and Required Practices

**Criterion 2
Responsibility
and Control**

The provider, through its continuing education or training (CE/T) unit, ensures certification criteria are followed.

Guidelines

Internal policies should clearly show the CE/T unit has authority and responsibility to establish and implement review procedures that ensure CE/T activities meet current IACET CEU criteria. In jointly sponsored activities, courses, or programs, i.e., those which are co-sponsored by an Authorized Sponsor and one or more organizations which are not Authorized Providers, the Authorized Provider is responsible for ensuring that the criteria are met.

The provider must designate one person from the organization as the CE/T administrator who is responsible for ensuring that all IACET CEU criteria are followed. The professional designated by the provider as the CE/T administrator must be qualified by experience or training to ensure that all requirements and procedures are followed.

**Required
Practices**

2.1 Internal policies clearly indicate a review process that adheres to the criteria.

2.2 The review process is conducted by individual(s) who have been trained and/or have experience in the criteria.

2.3 Authority and responsibility for adherence to the criteria are clearly vested in the appropriate individual(s) responsible for the review process.

2.4 The review process incorporates the latest revisions in the criteria.

Criteria, Guidelines, and Required Practices

Continued

**Criterion 3
System for
Awarding the
Continuing
Education Unit**

The provider has a system in place to identify learners who meet requirements for satisfactory completion.

Guidelines

A designated official of the continuing education or training organization, usually the coordinator or instructor, verifies and reports that each learner has (or has not) met the specified requirements for satisfactory completion and is (or is not) awarded CEU or other measurement units. The criteria for successful completion is compatible with the learning outcomes of each activity, course, or program.

When partial credit is awarded to learners who do not attend the entire activity, course, or program, the provider has a system to track, calculate, and award variable credit.

The provider has a process for calculating the IACET CEU which includes the provision that there be no retroactive granting of the CEU (e.g., before the provider was authorized). If units other than the IACET CEU are awarded, the process will include a conversion formula or explanation so that the equivalent IACET CEU can be determined. Permanent individual records are established indicating the number of CEU awarded to each learner. Only learners who successfully complete a activity, course, or program are awarded CEU or other units.

**Required
practices**

3.1 A systematic process is used for identifying individuals who satisfactorily complete a activity, course, or program.

    3.1a When learner attendance is part of the requirements for awarding CEU, the provider has an appropriate system in place to track and monitor learner attendance.

    3.1b When partial credit is awarded to learners who do not attend the entire activity, course, or program, there is a system to track, calculate, and award variable credit.

Criteria, Guidelines, and Required Practices

3.2 A process is in place for calculating the number of IACET CEU available for each learning activity, course, or program.

Criteria, Guidelines, and Required Practices

**Criterion 4
Maintenance and
Availability of
Records**

The provider maintains a complete, permanent (at least 7 years) record of each learner's participation and can provide a copy of that record upon request.

Guidelines

The provider is responsible for maintaining permanent records of all IACET CEU earned and must have a written policy on retention and releasing of such records that ensures the privacy and security of its learners' records. The provider is expected to maintain a permanent record for each learner who successfully completes a activity, course, or program and to record the number of IACET CEU earned. Cumulative records of all IACET CEU earned are to be available for a minimum of 7 years and are to be issued as an official permanent record upon request by the learner.

The permanent record may be maintained by the provider or a contracted service; however, the provider bears primary responsibility for maintenance and availability of permanent records.

A permanent record is an official cumulative record or file issued by the Authorized Provider that documents an individuals' participation in the Authorized Provider's CE/T activities. This individual record should include:

- Provider name and address
- Learner name and social security number (or other numerical identification)
- Activity, course, or program title (title should be as descriptive as possible)
- Completion date of the activity, course, or program
- Number of CEU awarded (If units other than the IACET CEU are awarded, the transcript will include a conversion formula/explanation so that the equivalent CEU can be determined.

Additional information, such as current address, telephone number and assessment scores may be included at the option of the provider.

Criteria, Guidelines, and Required Practices

Guidelines
(cont.)

The permanent record may be a computer-generated, typed, or handwritten listing or may consist of a cumulative file of activity, course, or program completion documents that can be reproduced at the learner's request.

IACET provides an International Registry for Continuing Education and Training for those providers wishing to contract the service. This registry assures that a permanent record is maintained and individuals can be provided transcripts of their CE/T activities.

Providers may choose to issue a certificate of completion to each learner who completes the activity, course, or program. Certificates are to be used in addition to, not in lieu of permanent records. Authorized Providers may display the IACET CEU logo and/or the Authorized Provider logo on the certificates.

Required practices

4.1 A permanent record system for learner records is operational.

4.2 Permanent records contain information referenced in the guidelines.

4.3 The permanent record information is presented in a manner which a third party can readily interpret (i.e., no codes or codes explained).

4.4 Records are kept up-to-date.

4.5 A system is in place to issue a copy of a permanent record to a learner or others authorized within six weeks or less.

4.6 A written policy is operational to ensure that the privacy and security of learners' records.

4.7 A written policy is operational on retention and releasing of records.

Criteria, Guidelines, and Required Practices

**Criterion 5
Learning
environment and
support systems**

A learning environment and support services appropriate to the continuing education or training goals and learning outcomes are provided.

Guidelines

The provider includes determination of resources, to include financial resources and administrative support, the learning environment, and support systems (e.g., technology, facilities, library or reference materials, access to instructors and advisors, and instructional aids and equipment), and means of ensuring the availability of these resources to support the learning outcomes in planning of each learning experience.

The design and use of facilities should facilitate teaching and learning. For example, lighting, sound, seating, visuals, reference materials, and other needed resources should be appropriate and available to enhance learning.

In distance learning formats such as correspondence study and computer-assisted instruction, the provider may not be able to control the learning environment. In such cases, the provider should include ways to support learners and facilitate learning in the planning process.

**Required
practices**

5.1 The organization has a process for determining the resources, to include financial resources and administrative support, required to support the learning outcomes and ensuring that the resources will be sufficient/available to maintain the activity, course, or program through to completion.

5.2 The physical environment (i.e., light, sound, seating, etc.) is appropriate for the learning activities.

5.3 Access to the facilities, equipment, learning experiences, and resource materials is in compliance with Americans with Disabilities Act (ADA).

5.4 Educational services and technical support are provided to instructors and learners.

Criteria, Guidelines, and Required Practices

Required Practices (Cont.)

5.5 Instructors and/or advisors are available to provide assistance and support to learners.

Criteria, Guidelines, and Required Practices

Continued

**Criterion 6
Needs
identification**

Each activity, course, or program is planned in response to identified needs of a target audience.

Guidelines

The purpose of identifying learning needs is to identify the difference between an existing condition and a desired condition. The gap between the existing and desired condition is the foundation for any education or training activity, course, or program. Multiple information sources, including learners, are tapped to identify needs.

Needs represent a shortage/deficit condition or a required enhancement in contrast to interests or wants, which usually represent personal preferences. Needs may be identified within a society, profession, community, organization, or individuals. Needs may arise from a variety of reasons such as new legislation or regulations; new performance expectations or deficiencies; changes in information, skills, attitudes, processes, systems, organizations, occupations, and professions. The process should identify who is affected by the need; that is, who the potential learners should be. Each activity, course, or program does not require a separate needs assessment; however, the rationale and planning for each activity, course, or program should be the result of needs which have been identified and documented by some assessment method(s). Some methods for assessment include: focus groups, questionnaires and surveys, participants' comments and suggestions, records and reports, tests or self-assessments, print media, observations, and work samples.

Once needs have been identified, they must be analyzed to determine if an educational or training solution is appropriate. Some identified needs require a form of intervention other than an educational/training intervention. For example, a need in an organization might be corrected by changing policies or procedures, a disciplinary action, or feedback, rather than by a training activity, course, or program.

**Required
practices**

6.1 An established process provides objective needs assessment data which is the basis for activity, course, or program planning and development.

Criteria, Guidelines, and Required Practices

Required practices (cont.)

6.2 Potential learners and/or multiple sources of information are tapped for needs assessment.

6.3 Needs assessments are systematically documented and updated.

6.4 Activity, course, or program topics and content must originate from identified needs.

6.5 The provider defines the potential learners/target audience and any prerequisites for each continuing education activity, course, or program and includes this information in promotional efforts.

Criteria, Guidelines, and Required Practices

Criterion 7 Learning outcomes

The provider has clear and concise written statements of intended learning outcomes (e.g., participant behavioral or performance objectives) based on identified needs for each continuing education and training activity, course, or program.

Guidelines

Learning outcomes, commonly referred to as participant behavioral or performance objectives, are written statements which:

- Provide a framework for activity, course, or program planning;
- Are the basis for selection of content and instructional strategies;
- Describe to learners exactly what knowledge, skills, and/or attitudes they are expected to accomplish/demonstrate as a result of the learning activity, course, or program;
- Are the basis providing periodic feedback, measuring progress, and final assessment of learning.

The provider assures that learning outcomes are developed from identified needs. The learning outcomes must be clear, concise, and measurable. Learners should be informed of these intended learning outcomes prior to and during the activity, course, or program.

Required practices

7.1 Planned outcomes are based on identified needs.

7.2 Written learning outcomes which reflect what learners will achieve are established for each activity, course, or program. When learning outcomes are established for a program, each activity or course within that program must be keyed to one or more of the program outcomes.

7.3 The number of planned outcomes is appropriate for the learning activity, course, or program.

7.4 Outcome statements are clear, concise, and measurable.

7.5 Learners are informed of intended learning outcomes.

Criteria, Guidelines, and Required Practices

**Required
practices**
(cont.)

7.6 Learning outcomes are established for large events such as
conferences or conventions. Each session within that event has its
own learning outcomes or is keyed to one or more of the overall
event outcomes.

Criteria, Guidelines, and Required Practices

**Criterion 8
Activity,
course, or
program
planning
and
instructional
personnel**

Qualified personnel are involved in planning and conducting each activity, course, or program.

Guidelines

The provider assures that qualified individuals are directly involved in determining the activity, course, or program purpose, and planning, designing, developing, conducting, and evaluating each learning experience. Continuing education activity, course, or program development may require a team approach involving the provider's continuing education administrator, development experts, and content experts. The continuing education administrator has oversight responsibilities and should be directly involved in this phase of activity, course, or program development.

The quality of a continuing education activity, course, or program and its value to the learner rests heavily on the planners, the instructor(s)' competence in the subject matter, and the ability of both to communicate and facilitate learning. It is the joint responsibility of the provider, the planner(s), and the instructor(s) to ensure that the learning experience results in the learners achieving the learning outcomes.

Decisions made about activity, course, or program planning and development should be made by individuals who are:

- Competent in the subject matter;
- Understand the activity, course, or program purpose and learning outcomes; and
- Have knowledge and skill in instructional methods and learning processes.

Criteria, Guidelines, and Required Practices

Guidelines
(cont.)

Individuals who participate in a CE/T activity, course, or program have the right to know of any commercial interest an instructor may have in a product or service mentioned during an activity, course, or program. The provider is required to disclose each instructor's proprietary interest in any product, instrument, device, service, or material discussed in the activity, course, or program as well as the source of compensation related to the presentation. This information must be made available to the learners prior to the activity, course, or program and may be conveyed through promotional materials, a written handout, or an announcement prior to the commencement of the training.

**Required
practices**

8.1 Individuals involved in activity, course, or program planning and instruction are qualified by virtue of their education and/or experience.

8.2 Expertise in subject content and instructional methodologies is used in developing learning activities.

8.3 Individuals involved in activity, course, or program planning understand and utilize learning outcomes in planning and development.

8.4 Instructors are reasonably and consistently effective in meeting learning outcomes and learner expectations.

8.5 Instructors are provided feedback on their performance.

8.6 Instructors demonstrate high standards of professional conduct and do not discriminate against learners on the basis of gender, age, socioeconomic or ethnic background, sexual orientation, or disability.

8.7 The provider discloses, in advance of the activity, course, or program, any instructor's proprietary interest in any product, instrument, device, service, or material discussed during the activity, course, or program, and the source of any compensation related to the presentation.

Criteria, Guidelines, and Required Practices

**Criterion 9
Content and
instructional
methods**

Content and instructional methods are appropriate for the learning outcomes of each activity, course, or program and provide opportunities for learners to participate and receive feedback.

Guidelines

Both learners and instructors must understand the learning outcomes and how they will be achieved. The provider assures that the selected content logically supports learning outcomes. Content is organized in a logical manner, proceeding from basic to advanced levels.

Instructional strategies are just as important as content. Each learning outcome dictates a level of performance which is to be carefully planned and organized to ensure the learner's attainment of the outcome. Instructional methods should appeal to the diverse learning styles of each audience. The methods used should provide opportunities for learners to be actively involved, interact with the instructor(s) and materials (as well as other students, where applicable), process what they have learned, and receive feedback that reinforces learning.

The provider must take steps to protect of intellectual property rights, i.e., ownership, faculty compensation, copyright, and the utilization of revenue derived from the creation, production, and use of materials produced for the educational activity, course, or program.

**Required
practices**

9.1 Subject matter and content are directly related to learning outcomes.

9.2 Instructional methods are consistent with learning outcomes.

9.3 Instructional methods accommodate various learning styles.

9.4 Content is organized in a logical manner.

9.5 Learner interaction and assessments are utilized throughout the activity, course, or program to reinforce learning, monitor learner progress, and to provide feedback to learners on their progress.

Criteria, Guidelines, and Required Practices

Continued

Required
practices
(cont.)

9.6 The provider has established policies and procedures to address intellectual property rights.

Criteria, Guidelines, and Required Practices

Criterion 10
Assessment of
learning
outcomes

Formal processes or procedures established during activity, course, or program planning are used to assess achievement of the learning outcomes.

Guidelines

Formal assessment of learning outcomes refers to specific process(es) through which learners demonstrate the attainment of learning outcomes. In every activity, course, or program for which CEU are awarded, the provider has the obligation to require learners to demonstrate that they have attained the learning outcomes.

How learners will demonstrate their attainment of the outcomes should be an integral part of activity, course, or program planning. The assessment procedure, its timing, and its application are part of the planning process.

Learner demonstrations serve many purposes for learners and instructors. Assessments actively involve the learners and provide them a basis for refining their knowledge and skills. Learner demonstrations should be used throughout an activity, course, or program as instructional strategies to help keep learners actively involved, reinforce learning, monitor learner progress, and to provide feedback to learners on their progress. Assessments may also be made at the conclusion of the activity, course, or program, or after some elapsed time following the learning experience.

Learning outcomes dictate the nature of learner demonstrations. Assessments may take diverse forms, such as performance demonstrations under real or simulated conditions, written or oral examinations, written reports, completion of a project, self assessment, or locally or externally developed standardized examinations. Because the assessment method depends on the intended learning outcomes, they must be measurable or observable, clearly stated, and focused on the performance of the learner.

Assessment of learning outcomes must be a part of a activity, course, or program and the methods of the assessment procedure must be made known to the learners. Learners should be advised in advance what will be required of them.

Criteria, Guidelines, and Required Practices

Guidelines
(cont.)

The utility of the CEU allows providers to choose whether individual scores should be assigned for learner demonstrations. Whether or not scores are provided for each learner depends on the intent of the learning activity, course, or program. In an activity, course, or program where individual proficiency is a goal, demonstrations by each individual should be required. The assignment of individual scores would be appropriate. In an activity, course, or program where individual proficiency is not a specific goal, group demonstrations, i.e., planned group activities which provide a means of determining whether participants have achieved the learning outcomes, may be appropriate.

Required practices

10.1 Assessment procedures are established during activity, course, or program planning.

10.2 Assessment methods measure achievement of learning outcomes.

10.3 Learners are informed in advance that learning outcomes will be assessed.

Criteria, Guidelines, and Required Practices

**Criterion 11
Requirements
for satisfactory
completion**

The provider assures that satisfactory completion requirements are established for each activity, course, or program and are based on the activity, course, or program purpose and learning outcomes.

Guidelines

Satisfactory completion requirements are established prior to the beginning of the activity, course, or program.

Requirements for performance levels should be based on the intended learning outcomes. When learner attendance is part of the satisfactory completion, attendance requirements should be high and documented on rosters, sign-in sheets, or other methods for tracking attendance.

Learners should be informed of requirements prior to their participation in the learning activity, course, or program. Learners should be informed that only those who meet those requirements will earn IACET CEU.

**Required
practices**

11.1 Well-defined requirements for satisfactory completion are established for each planned activity, course, or program.

11.2 Learners are informed of the satisfactory completion requirements prior to the activity, course, or program.

11.3 Learners are notified if they have not met satisfactory completion requirements (e.g., IACET CEU will not be awarded).

Please continue on page 2-26.

Criteria, Guidelines, and Required Practices

Continued

**Criterion 12
Post-activity, course, or program evaluation**

Each learning activity, course, or program is evaluated.

Guidelines

Activity, course, or program evaluation is a measurement of the quality, or determination of the worth of the activity, course, or program as a whole. Evaluation is a coordinated process that examines all parts of the activity, course, or program planning and delivery process. It consists of gathering data about the activity, course, or program based on established criteria and observable evidence. Evaluation includes an analysis of the results of learning assessments or measurements of learners' attainment of the learning outcomes, but activity, course, or program evaluation is much more encompassing.

In planning for an activity, course, or program, the provider assures that an evaluation process is established to examine various aspects of the activity, course, or program, such as the needs assessment, logistical and instructional planning and execution, selection and preparation of instructors, operations, and the extent to which learning outcomes were achieved.

Using only learner reaction surveys, i.e., end-of-course evaluations which are not clearly based on the learning outcomes, will not yield the data needed for an adequate evaluation of learning experiences. Any surveys utilized as a part of the activity, course, or program evaluation should be designed to capture specific information that will allow providers to make continuous improvements in their offerings.

Required practices

12.1   Post-activity, course, or program evaluation procedures are established during planning.

12.2   Evaluation methods are comprehensive.

Criteria, Guidelines, and Required Practices

Required practices (cont.)

12.3   Summative evaluations are prepared and analyzed based on the following minimum components:

- 12.3a   Did the learning experience and the instructional methods used result in individual behavioral or performance change (i.e., the learning outcomes)?

- 12.3b   Did the learners indicate that the learning outcomes were appropriate for the stated activity, course, or program purpose and for the learners involved?

- 12.3c   Was activity, course, or program execution effective and efficient?

12.4   Evaluation results are incorporated into activity, course, or program improvements.

Calculating the CEU

Definition: CEU	One CEU = **ten contact hours** of participation in **organized continuing education experience** under **responsible, qualified direction and instruction**

Definition: contact hour

Contact hour = **one clock hour**
of **interaction** between: **learner and instructor**
OR
learner and materials which have been prepared to cause learning

Contact implies a connection between a learner and a learning source. For the purposes of the CEU, that connection is two-way. The instructor or learning source must monitor the learner's progress and/or provide some form of feedback to the learner. This definition applies for face to face interaction as well as distance learning programs.

What can be counted

The following learning activities are examples of types of activities to include when calculating contact hours for CEU:

- Classroom or meeting session time led by instructor and/or discussion leader.
- Activities in which a learner is engaged in a planned activity, course, or program of learning in which the learner's progress is monitored and the learner receives feedback. Examples include independent study, computer-assisted instruction, interactive video, web site learning, and planned projects.
- Field trips, projects, and assignments which are an integral part of a activity, course, or program.
- Learner assessment and activity, course, or program evaluations.

Calculating the CEU

**What
CANNOT
be
counted**

The types of learning listed below can produce worthy learning and are occasionally recognized by the professions and licensing boards; however, they do NOT meet the IACET criteria and should be quantified with units of measurement other than the CEU.

- Unplanned
- Unsupervised
- Non-sponsored

The following activities are not intended to receive the CEU. These activities may be worthwhile learning experiences; however, they should be measured and documented by some form of measurement other than the CEU.

- Academic credit courses: CEU may be awarded for academic credit courses which meet the CEU criteria; however, individual participants should not receive both CEU and academic credit.

- Association membership and leadership activities: Holding membership or serving in some leadership capacity in an association or society do not qualify for the CEU.

- Committee meetings: Participation in committee meetings and activities do not qualify for the CEU.

- Entertainment and recreation: CEU may not be awarded for attendance at cultural performances, entertainment, or recreational activities unless they are an integral part of a planned course which meets the CEU criteria.

- Individual scholarship: CEU may not be awarded for independent writings such as articles, books, research reports, or presentation of papers outside of a planned, directly supervised continuing education experience that fulfills the CEU criteria.

Calculating the CEU

**What
CANNOT
be
counted**
(cont.)

- Mass media activities, courses, or programs: Activities, courses, or programs delivered through the mass media (e.g., television, radio, newspaper) do not qualify for CEU, unless these presentations are an integral part of a planned activity, course, or program which meets the CEU criteria.

- Some meetings, conventions, exhibitions: meetings, conventions, and exhibitions which attract large numbers of participants, involve different activities, and are conducted primarily for information sharing purposes generally do not qualify for the CEU. Planned learning activities within such events which meet the criteria are eligible for CEU.

- Travel: Travel or participation in a travel-study program does not qualify for CEU, unless the educational component of travel-study program meets the CEU criteria.

- Unsupervised study: Individual, self-directed study or other form of independent learning experience which is not planned, directed, and supervised by a provider does not qualify for CEU.

- Work experience: On-the-job training and other work experiences do not qualify for CEU unless the work experience is structured as part of a planned and supervised continuing education experience that meets the criteria. CEU are not to be awarded for life or previous work experience.

- Youth programs: CEU are not to be awarded for participation in programs designed primarily for ages below adulthood.

**Minimum
hours**

CEU should not be granted for a activity, course, or program that is less than one hour in length. Sessions within an activity, course, or program may be of any length. An activity, course, or program of short duration, one or two hours, often do not warrant the degree of planning required by the criteria. Caution should be exercised with shorter length Activity, course, or program to ensure their adherence to the criteria.

Calculating the CEU

Counting minutes in the contact hour

The 60-minute hour is the current standard for awarding CEU.

The 50-minute hour is commonly used in a number of professions and by state licensing boards. The IACET accepts the 50-minute hour as the measurement unit for a contact hour for providers of education or training for these professions; however, 50 minutes was not intended to be the standard for every contact hour of instruction.

No credit may be counted for the ten-minute differential between the 50- and 60-minute hour. The 10-minute increments may not be accumulated to form additional contact hours. Example: Using the 60-minute hour, a activity, course, or program from 9:00 AM until 12:00 noon would be counted as three contact hours for CEU calculation. Using the 50-minute hour would also result in the same three contact hours calculation, since the 10 extra minutes in each of the three hours cannot be totaled as 3 and one-half contact hours for CEU calculation.

Calculating the CEU

- Determine the number of contact hours per instructions above.
- Divide the number of contact hours by 10. The result will be the number of CEU.
- CEU may be expressed in tenths of a CEU (i.e., 17 contact hours equate to 1.7 CEU; 3 contact hours equate to .3 CEU).
- Providers may use hundredths to express a one-half hour increment. For example, a course of three and one-half hours may be expressed as .35 CEU. Hundredths are not to be used to express any portion of an hour other than a half-hour.
- When the fractional part of an hour is at least 5/6 (50 minutes or more), the fractional portion should be counted as a whole hour. Any portion of an hour between 30 and 49 minutes should be counted as 30 minutes. Any part of an hour less than 30 minutes should be discarded.

Miscellaneous

Relationship with other continuing education regulatory or certifying bodies

Some licensing boards, certifying bodies, and regulatory agencies require providers to obtain approval from that agency before the provider's CEU will be recognized. Such approval usually involves the provider submitting activity, course, or program materials to the approving agency for review against some established criteria.

Some providers find that their CEU are more readily acceptable when recognized as an IACET Authorized Provider. The application process to become an IACET Authorized Provider is explained on page 3-7 of this publication.

IACET continues to work with state licensing boards and other organizations who approve continuing education and training activities, courses, or programs to establish reciprocity for those organizations which follow IACET's standards; however, IACET cannot compel organizations to offer reciprocity.

Locating help in implementing the CEU

The IACET Headquarters office may be able to identify an organization which you can contact in your area that is using the CEU. Other publications are offered by IACET which are excellent references for any organization planning or using the CEU. (Appendix B contains a list of publications, ordering information, and various means to contact IACET Headquarters.)

NO retroactive award of CEU

IACET CEU CANNOT be awarded retroactively. A determination has to be made before an activity, course, or program is conducted that it meets the criteria and has been approved by the provider's internal review process.

Miscellaneous

Continued

Maintenance of records

The maintenance of permanent records is the responsibility of the Authorized Provider which provides the activity, course, or program and awards the CEU. These records must be maintained separately from attendance records and, in most cases, from personnel records. This service can be contracted. The International Registry for Continuing Education and Training; (202) 939-9432, is one agency which provides this service through a contract.

Use of CEU records

Activity, course, or program participants who need documentation of their learning activities for submission to organizations such as licensing boards, certification agencies, professional associations, and employers use the CEU records. The CEU can also be added to a professional's resume or portfolio.

Relationship between the CEU and college credit

The CEU was developed for learning activities, courses, or programs, usually of short duration, which are not part of an academic degree program. The CEU cannot be offered for training or education for which college credit is granted. The CEU, however, when included in an individual's portfolio along with work experience, may be evaluated by some colleges and universities who have the ability to assess prior learning activities.

Calculating CEU for Distance Education and Other Alternative Delivery Methods

Introduction

The growing trend to deliver an activity, course, or program in nontraditional methods demands guidance for calculation of CEU for a distance education and training activity, course, or program.

Self-paced programs

Self-paced programs include activities or courses in which learners progress at their own pace. The provider should establish a standard number of contact hours based on an average number of hours required of several representative learners to complete the program. A provider desiring to introduce a new self-paced activity, course, or program might select a representative sample from the intended audience--the larger the audience, the better--to complete the activity, course, or program. Each member of the sample records the actual amount of time spent completing the activity, course, or program. The total hours spent by all members of the sample is totaled, averaged, and divided by 10.

Example

Course A is a self-paced home study course with a posttest. Interaction with the instructor is by mail or phone. To arrive at an average time for completion of the course, five individuals were selected to complete a pilot course. Each participant recorded the actual amount of time spent completing the course:

Student 1 - 16 hours   Student 4 - 12 hours
Student 2 - 10 hours   Student 5 - 14.5 hours
Student 3 - 8.5 hours   Total - 61; Average - 12.2 hours

The average is rounded off to 12 hours and becomes the standard contact hours for the course. 12 divided by 10 (1 CEU = 10 contact hours) yields 1.2 CEU to be awarded to those who satisfactorily complete the course. Satisfactory completion might be based on the satisfactory completion of all assignments, including an 80% score on the posttest.

Calculating CEU for Distance Education and Other Alternative Delivery Methods

Continued

Continuing validation

Providers should continue to monitor the amount of time it takes learners to complete the activity, course, or program. The standard should be adjusted, if necessary. This continuing validation provides credibility to the provider's established standard.

Field experiences

Field experiences provide learners opportunities to gain practical and realistic experiences which cannot be acquired in a classroom setting. Such activities may or may not be highly structured; may vary in duration from one learner and location to another; and may not be readily calculated into contact hours. Therefore, providers often view field experiences in terms of tasks to be accomplished rather than the amount of time involved. Because of the unstructured nature of many field experiences, providers may choose to use some form of checklist to record the accomplishment of certain specified tasks.

If the field experience hours are to be counted, the provider must first determine whether the experience meets the CEU criteria. If so, a standard number of contact hours could be determined by calculating the average time spent by several learners in different field experiences as discussed on page 2-34 under Self-Paced Programs.

Laboratory assignments

Laboratory assignments tend to be an integral part of a planned activity, course, or program and are generally structured. Since the conditions for learning are rather consistent and the amount of time for assignments is fairly even for all learners, the provider may count each hour of lab time as a contact hour. If there is considerable variation in lab conditions and time required for the completion of assignments by different learners, the provider should consider establishing a standard number of contact hours based on the average time utilized by a number of learners. The lab assignment must, in any case, meet CEU criteria before any CEU credit can be awarded.

Calculating CEU for Distance Education and Other Alternative Delivery Methods

Continued

Homework assignments

Providers may choose one of two options when making outside assignments of learners. Such assignments may be considered a requirement of the learning with no contact hours granted for the assignment or the provider may choose to calculate a standard number of hours using the averaging method discussed in Self-Paced Programs on page 2-34. If contact hours are assigned for the purpose of calculating CEU, the provider is responsible for validating that each learner completed the assignment.

Additional resource

A new IACET publication, *Guidelines for Distance Education*, is a good resource for determining whether a learning activity, course, or program qualifies for CEU.

Section 3

Authorized Provider Certification Program

Authorized Provider Certification Program

Introduction

This chapter is for organizations seeking Authorized Provider status.

Purpose of certification

The purposes of the IACET Authorized Provider Certification Program are to:

- promote quality and consistency in continuing education and training;
- review educational processes used by organizations, not the content of activities, courses, or programs;
- monitor providers against established criteria;
- recognize providers that adhere to the effective practices found in the criteria.

Application process

Organizations applying for Authorized Provider status must:

- file an application;
- sign an agreement to adhere to established criteria;
- undergo a site visit;
- participate in periodic monitoring requirements; and
- pay application and annual membership fees.

Program administration

The Authorized Provider Certification Program is administered by the Authorized Provider Commission, an autonomous unit of the International Association for Continuing Education and Training (IACET).

Transition period

Beginning July 1, 1998, new applicants must adhere to the criteria and complete the application contained in this manual. Current Certified Providers and Authorized CEU Sponsors will be required to adhere to the criteria in this manual as of the renewal date of their current authorized period and will be given one years notice to do so.

Section 3

Authorized Provider Certification Program

Authorized Provider Certification Program

Introduction   This chapter is for organizations seeking Authorized Provider status.

**Purpose
of
certification**

The purposes of the IACET Authorized Provider Certification Program are to:

- promote quality and consistency in continuing education and training;
- review educational processes used by organizations, not the content of activities, courses, or programs;
- monitor providers against established criteria;
- recognize providers that adhere to the effective practices found in the criteria.

**Application
process**

Organizations applying for Authorized Provider status must:

- file an application;
- sign an agreement to adhere to established criteria;
- undergo a site visit;
- participate in periodic monitoring requirements; and
- pay application and annual membership fees.

**Program
administration**

The Authorized Provider Certification Program is administered by the Authorized Provider Commission, an autonomous unit of the International Association for Continuing Education and Training (IACET).

**Transition
period**

Beginning July 1, 1998, new applicants must adhere to the criteria and complete the application contained in this manual. Current Certified Providers and Authorized CEU Sponsors will be required to adhere to the criteria in this manual as of the renewal date of their current authorized period and will be given one years notice to do so.

Authorized Provider Certification Program

Continued

Organizations that qualify for certification

Any organization that offers continuing education and/or training programs may apply for certification if it:

- is chartered, incorporated, a recognized sole-proprietorship, or a government unit;

- has a well defined organizational structure in which the authority and responsibility for administering continuing education and/or training activities, courses, or programs is assigned to a particular department or unit; and

- has its educational activities, courses, or programs administered by an individual or group that can ensure that each criterion is met.

Certification of units or programs within organizations

Large complex organizations in which continuing education and training is conducted by various parts of the organization may choose to seek certification for specific divisions, departments, colleges, schools or units rather than for the entire organization.

Applicants may choose to apply for certification for certain programs or categories of programs within their organization. For example, a community college that offers a broad range of continuing education programs may seek certification only for its health related programs. An automobile manufacturer may choose to apply for certification of its dealership training programs only.

Whenever applicants seek certification for one or more units or specific programs, it is the responsibility of the applicant to clearly identify the units or programs and their relationship to the entire organization or total program offerings. The applicant may need to attach additional information to the application. As a rule, the Commission does not review individual course offerings except as representative samples of an organization's ability to adhere to the criteria.

Authorized Provider Certification Program - Organization

**Administrative
structure**

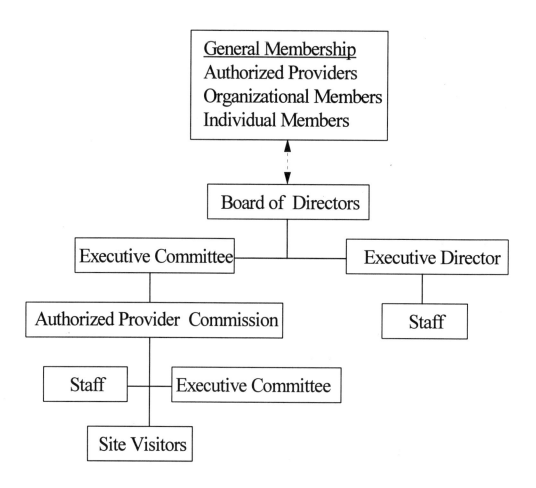

General Membership
Authorized Providers
Organizational Members
Individual Members

Board of Directors

Executive Committee

Executive Director

Authorized Provider Commission

Staff

Staff

Executive Committee

Site Visitors

Authorized Provider Certification Program - Organization

Relationship between the Commission and the IACET Board of Directors

The role of the IACET Board of Directors is to:

- Appoint members to the Authorized Provider Commission;
- Budget adequate funds and resources for the Commission to carry out its mission;
- Serve as an appeals body when there is a dispute regarding an organization's application or certification status;
- Maintain a role of non-interference with the review and decision-making process of the Authorized Provider Commission; and
- Oversee the Commission's activities.

Authorized Provider Commission membership

The certification process is governed and administered by a fifteen-member Authorized Provider Commission. Of the Commissioners, approximately 60% are selected from Authorized Provider organizations, and at least 20% from other membership category of IACET. Commissioners from outside IACET membership may comprise no more than 10% of the total commission membership.

The Authorized Provider Commission makes recommendations for Commission members to the IACET Nominating Committee. The Nominating Committee reviews the recommendations before they are submitted to the IACET Board of Directors for final approval. This is to prevent duplication of membership on the APC and IACET Board of Directors in accordance with the bylaws. No member of the IACET Board shall serve concurrently as a member of the Commission; however, the Commission Chair shall serve as a nonvoting, ex-officio member of the IACET Board of Directors.

Authorized Provider Certification Program - Organization

Continued

**Role of
Authorized
Provider
Commission**

The role of the Commission is to:

- Establish criteria and policies for certification, subject to approval by the IACET Board of Directors, and assume responsibility for procedural and management decisions;

- Review applications for initial and continuing certification;

- Determine whether applicant should be granted or denied certification;

- Systematically monitor Authorized Providers' activities for compliance with Authorized Provider criteria and take appropriate action as necessary;

- Publish a list of Authorized Providers annually as part of the IACET resource directory;

- Provide training on the certification process;

- Identify and train site visitors;

- Promote quality and consistency in continuing education and training programs;

- Recognize providers that adhere to the effective practices defined by the criteria.

Authorized Provider Certification Program - Certification Process

Applying for certification

Each applicant must follow these steps when applying for certification:

- **Review this manual** thoroughly before completing the application. The Certification Criteria, pages 2-6 through 2-27, specifies the requirements for certification. The application, pages 4-4 through 4-21, clarifies which materials should be attached to the application and page 4-23 specifies which materials must be available on site for review by the site visitors.

- **Conduct a self-assessment** of the applicant's program processes, resources, and effectiveness. The certification criteria provide an excellent guideline to evaluate the program. Although the primary purpose of a self-study is to help the program become more effective, it also helps the program to assess the extent to which it meets the Authorized Provider criteria and is ready to submit the application.

- **Complete the application.**

  — A copy of the application form is included with this manual (page 4-4 through 4-21). Additional copies may be obtained from the Commission administrative office by calling (202) 857-1122, faxing (202) 223-4579, or e-mailing, IACET@DC.SBA.COM.

  — Five copies (5) of the completed application and supporting materials must be sent to the Commission office along with a check for the initial application fee. This initial payment is non-refundable (refer to fee schedule, page C-2). Each copy of the application <u>must</u> be accompanied by copies of supporting materials as indicated. Representative samples rather than voluminous materials are requested (as indicated in the application).

- **Sign the Authorized Provider Agreement.** Applicants are required to sign an agreement form that details specific obligations of the applicant. This form is included with the application form.

**Review
of
application**

● **Preliminary review.** Upon receipt of the $350 non-refundable application fee, completed application, and required materials, the Commission headquarters staff will make a preliminary review for completeness and inclusion of necessary attachments. The staff will contact the applicant if further information is needed.

● **Review of the Application.**

— The staff selects the review team next in line to receive an application and forwards one application and attachments to each of the two reviewers. The staff indicates deadline for the Commission review team to return their completed Commissioner's Criteria Checklists and the team's Consensus Worksheet. The staff forwards one copy of the application to the Chair, retains one copy for the site visitor, and files one copy for reference purposes.

— The review team members review the application and complete the Criteria Checklist and Team Consensus Worksheet. Forms are returned to staff with recommendation whether a site visit should be conducted. If a team determines that more information is needed, the staff is notified to obtain the information from the applicant.

— If the team cannot reach consensus on its recommendations, the Chair will review the application and make the decision.

— When the staff receives notice to proceed from the team or the Chair, the staff notifies applicant of approval of site visit.

Authorized Provider Certification Program - Certification Process

Continued

**Purpose
of
site visit**

The purpose of the site visit is to:

- verify the accuracy of the information provided on the application

- review all materials and information required to show compliance with the Authorized Provider criteria.

**Site visitor
selection**

When the Commission Headquarters staff receives notice to schedule the site visit, a site visitor is selected who meets as many of the following guidelines as possible:

- Approved by Certified Provider Commission (**required**)

- Has received training as a site visitor (**required**)

- Has no conflict of interest (**required**)

- Represents an Authorized Provider Organization

- Has some knowledge or exposure to the type of organization being visited

- Lives within the geographic region of the site to be visited

In the event that the IACET staff and Commission determine that a situation warrants more than one site visitor, additional visitors may be appointed. This decision will be made after a review by the Commission and discussion with the applicant organization. One of the site visitors will be designated Chair of the visitation team. The fees for the additional site visitor will be the responsibility of the applicant in accordance with the fee schedule in Appendix C.

Authorized Provider Certification Program - Certification Process

Continued

Scheduling the site visit

When the applicant is notified by the Authorized Provider Commission staff that a site visit has been approved, the staff member and the applicant will determine a mutually agreeable date for the site visit. The one-day visit, designed to be as non-intrusive as possible, should not involve more than a few people within the applicant organization. The applicant will receive written notification of the site visit.

**Conducting
the
site visit**

Prior to the visit, the applicant should make sure all on-site materials that are requested in the Authorized Provider Application are readily available for the site visitor. (See Section 4-23 for list of materials.)

Upon arrival, the applicant organization should describe the organization and its purpose and role in continuing education/training. A brief tour of the facility is considered appropriate. The site visitor will review the two-fold purpose of the visit: to verify the accuracy of the application information and to discuss the responsibilities of an applicant and a Authorized Provider.

The site visitor has been trained to gather data and clarify the criteria. The site visitor will review the application question by question and ask the applicant to verify with evidence the response to the question. The visitor may ask for additional examples of materials. These additional examples may be included in the on-site materials which the applicant has already gathered. The applicant must keep in mind that the visitor is attempting to ascertain whether the organization is following the certification criteria.

It is quite appropriate for the site visitor to meet and talk with others in the organization. Such contacts and meetings should be brief and informal in order to allow the site visitor to complete the assignment. Site visitors may not advise or consult with the organization during the certification process.

The visitor is prohibited from receiving any free gifts or services. Modest meals and refreshments, however, are appropriate.

Upon the conclusion of the visit, the site visitor usually meets one-on-one with the organization's contact person--preferably the same person the visitor started out with at the beginning of the visit. The site visitor will offer general impressions and comments about factual matters, but not offer interpretations and opinions about possible actions the Authorized Provider Commission might take.

**After
the
site
visit**

The site visitor must complete a report of findings and forward it to the Commission within two weeks of the site visit. The report will be forwarded to the initial pair of Commissioners for review and for recommended action by the Commission.

The applicant is responsible for the site visitor's expenses and an additional $150 site visitor honorarium fee. Site visitor and honorarium fee expenses will be billed to the applicant by the Commission Office upon completion of the visit.

The Commission is eager for the applicant's input on the Site Visitor Evaluation Form. The applicant should complete it as soon as possible and mail it to IACET so that the system for certification can be continuously improved.

**Commission
actions
regarding
applications**

Upon receipt and assessment of all certification application materials, the Commission will make any one of the following decisions:

- **Award Certification:** Full certification is granted for a period of four years to programs that are judged to be in compliance with certification requirements.

- **Defer Decision:** Certification is deferred for up to six months when compliance with certification requirements has not been clearly demonstrated and the Commission determines that compliance can be demonstrated within six months or less. The decision to defer may not be appealed by the applicant.

  Proof of compliance after a defer decision may consist of:

  — Completion of appropriate portions of the application

  — Letters of documentation to support previously submitted application and attachments

  — A follow-up site visit (follow-up site visit expenses in accordance with the fee schedule in Appendix C will be the responsibility of the applicant organization.)

Commission actions regarding applications (cont.)

— The Commission will review the additional evidence provided and vote to grant or deny certification. If the applicant does not submit the necessary evidence in the time required, the Commission will deny certification. If the Commission has not received a response from the applicant 30 days after the due date, the application is then considered inactive. The applicant may reapply after a one year period from the date of the Commission's denial action or inactive status by submitting a new application and fee.

- **Deny Certification:** Certification is denied when the Commission, after a full review of the applicant's program, determines there is noncompliance with the Authorized Provider requirements and that the deficiencies cannot be corrected within six months or less. The reasons for denial will be specified in a written report to the applicant. Upon denial of certification, the applicant may appeal this decision to the Commission as outlined in the Appeals Process. If the Commission has not received a response from the applicant 30 days after the due date, the application is then considered inactive.

  The applicant may reapply after a one year period from the date of the Commission's denial decision. If the applicant wishes to again seek APC status, a new application and fee must be submitted.

Notification of actions taken

When the Commission awards certification, the IACET President will send a letter to the Chief Administrative Officer of the applicant organization with a copy furnished to the liaison person listed in the application. Only the Chair will send letters of denial or deferral. Copies of the appeals process will be included with these letters.

Authorized Provider Certification Program - Certification Process

Continued

Steps in the application process

Applicant	1. Submits 5 copies of application. 2. Makes application fee payment.
Staff	3. Reviews application for completeness. 4. Forwards application to Commission reviewers.
Commission reviewers (2)	5. Review application. 6. Notify staff whether site visit is authorized.
Staff	7. Contacts APC Chair to review application if reviewers disagree. 8. Notifies applicant of site visit approval. 9. Arranges site visit.
Site visitor	10. Contacts applicant. 11. Makes travel arrangements. 12. Conducts one-day visit. 13. Completes site visit report for APC staff. 14. Submits expense report to IACET.
Staff	15. Sends site visit report to Commission reviewers. 16. Bills applicant for site visitor's expenses and honorarium.
Commission reviewers (2)	17. Review site visit report. 18. Recommend approval/disapproval. 19. Forward recommendation to staff.
APC	20. Approves or disapproves the application. 21. Notifies applicant of Commission action. 22. Sends plaque if approved.
Staff	23. Bills applicant for first year annual membership dues. 24. Mails applicant site visitor evaluation form.

Authorized Provider Certification Program - Certification Process

**Flowchart
of application
process**

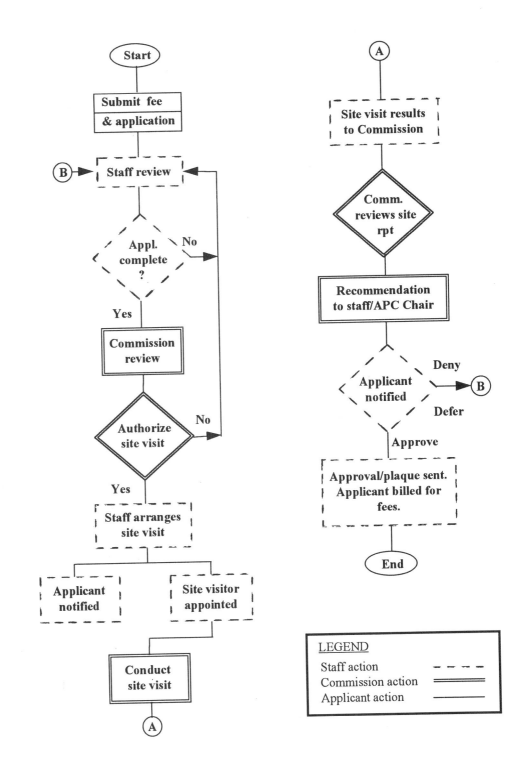

LEGEND

Staff action	– – – –
Commission action	═══════
Applicant action	───────

Authorized Provider Certification Program - Certification Process

Confidentiality and disclosure

Each application and the entire review process of that application should be treated as a confidential matter by staff, site visitors, Commission and Board members. All materials shall be stamped "CONFIDENTIAL" when they are mailed by the IACET staff.

In response to inquiries about a provider's application, an acknowledgment may be made only that an organization has applied for certification. No reference is to be made to anyone or any organization outside IACET about the status of an application during the review process.

IACET seeks to maintain the integrity of the certification process by respecting the confidentiality of information provided by the applicant and simultaneously releasing essential information to the public. The following information about Authorized Providers may be released by IACET and the Commission.

- names of applicant organizations

- names of Authorized Providers, including dates of certification period

- names of Authorized Providers whose certification has been withdrawn

- names of former Authorized Provider organizations that voluntarily withdrew from certification status

- names of Authorized Providers that were denied recertification (not initial certification)

Conflict of interest

The integrity of the certification process must be preserved. It is imperative to avoid conflicts of interest or even the appearance of a conflict of interest that might interfere with a fair and objective review. Commission members and site visitors must not be influenced in any way that would interfere with objectively reviewing, evaluating, approving, and/or disapproving any applicant organization. The Board of Directors, while preserving the high standards of the Commission, must guard against any undue pressures that would affect the role of the Commission.

Conflict of interest (cont.)

A conflict of interest may exist if there is a personal, financial, or professional relationship between the applicant organization and those who are charged with responsibility for reviewing that organization's application. An apparent conflict of interest is a circumstance in which others could reasonably infer that a conflict of interest exists even when the person in question has no actual stake in the outcome and is confident that his or her objectivity would not, in fact, be compromised.

Site visitors, commission reviewers, and commission members should not participate in certification procedures in which a real or apparent conflict of interest exists. In particular, they should not participate in the evaluation of applications whose outcome might, in any way, affect the interests of an organization or institution with which the reviewer, an immediate family member, or a close personal associate is an employee, consultant, officer, director, trustee, partner, or has a financial interest, current or prospective.

Site visitors, commission reviewers, and commission members are therefore expected to decline to participate in deliberations or actions on any application that they believe presents a real or apparent professional, personal, or financial conflict of interest. The same standards apply to Board of Directors members who should abstain from participating in appeal proceedings concerning organizations with whom they have some connection or relationship that could be construed as a real or apparent conflict of interest.

Authorized Provider Certification Program - Certification Process

Continued

Certification application fees

The IACET Board of Directors shall be responsible for determining all fees related to the certification process. (See fee schedule on page C-2.) The fees include all costs related to the review of the application by the Authorized Provider Commission except for direct expenses of the site visitor and the site visitor honorarium.

First year's dues

When the applicant is certified by the Commission, a bill for the first year's annual fees will be sent to the applicant. Fees will be according to the current fee schedule. (See fee schedule on page C-2.) Fees will be prorated, if necessary, to bring a new provider up to the annual billing cycle which is the same for all categories of membership.

Authorized Provider plaque

Each Authorized Provider will receive a plaque. The plaque will indicate the beginning and ending dates for the certification period. Additional plaques may be ordered through IACET headquarters for an additional fee.

Authorized Provider Logo and Statements

**Use of
Authorized
Provider
logo**

Authorized Providers are encouraged to use the Authorized Provider logo and/or the CEU logo on their continuing education marketing or promotional materials for those units or programs of the organization that are certified. Each provider will be given camera-ready copies of the logos for their use. Logos are also available in an electronic file. Use of the logos requires an accompanying statement (see next section).

**Approved
statements
to be used by
Authorized
Providers**

Upon approval, the provider will be assigned the most appropriate of the following statements for use on their promotional materials. The statement must be used when the logo is used.

- When approval is granted for the **entire organization**:

  "The (*organization*) **meets the Criteria for Certification established by the Authorized Provider Commission of the International Association for Continuing Education and Training, 1200 19th St., NW, Suite 300, Washington DC 20036-2401."**

- When approval is granted for **one unit of an organization**:
  "The (*unit*) **of** (*name of organization*) **meets the Criteria for Certification established by the Authorized Provider Commission of the International Association for Continuing Education and Training, 1200 19th St., NW, Suite 300, Washington DC 20036-2401."**

- When approval is granted for **certain programs**:
  "The (*program name*) **of** (*organization*) **meets the Criteria for Certification established by the Authorized Provider Commission of the International Association for Continuing Education and Training, 1200 19th St., NW, Suite 300, Washington DC 20036-2401."**

Authorized Provider Monitoring Process

Provider monitoring process

A sustained level of high quality programming is essential to maintain Authorized Provider status. IACET Authorized Providers are regulated as a condition of recognition and must be recertified every five years. IACET reserves the right to monitor compliance with the criteria and to investigate complaints of possible violations. A site visit will be conducted at least once every ten (10) years, and an interim site visit may be scheduled if there is evidence of substantial changes within the provider organization or possible non-compliance with the criteria.

Monitoring techniques

The Commission may utilize a variety of monitoring techniques. Providers may be chosen randomly for periodic review or if information is received about possible violations of the criteria or provider agreement. When an Authorized Provider is selected for review, the Commission will notify the provider in writing. The method(s) of review will be determined by the Commission and conveyed to the provider in writing. The Commission may choose to use any or all of the following techniques.

- Review of records required in the Authorized Provider Agreement. Records may be reviewed at the provider's location, IACET office, or another location determined by IACET.

- Review of documentation (e.g., materials related to needs assessments, planning, learning and instruction, assessment, evaluation, record keeping, advertising, policies and operations) deemed essential for compliance with the criteria. Records may be reviewed at the provider's location, IACET office, or another location determined by IACET.

- Visits and assessments of specific programs.

- Investigation of complaints or information regarding alleged violations of the criteria or provider agreement.

- Self-assessment conducted by the provider.

Authorized Provider Monitoring Process

Continued

Post-monitoring action

When the review has been completed, a written report will be forwarded to the provider by the Commission for action.

Complaints

The Commission has an obligation to assure that any Authorized Provider is conducting its educational/training activities in compliance with the criteria and in an ethical and honest manner.

- Program participants may file complaints in writing to the Authorized Provider Commission, IACET, 1200 19th St., NW, Suite 300, Washington DC 20036. They must provide details such as date, activity, course, or program, name of provider, location of activity, course, or program, the participant's name, address, phone number, and the nature of the complaint.

- Complaints from other program providers, organizations, faculty, or the public must also be in writing and shall contain details as outlined above.

The Commission will determine the appropriate steps needed to gather further information. If the Commission decides the complaint(s) warrants attention, they will contact the provider for a response.

If the complaint cannot be resolved to the satisfaction of the Commission, the Commission may choose to place the provider on probation until the matter has been resolved to the Commission's satisfaction.

Probationary status

An Authorized Provider may be placed on probation for failure to comply with the APC Criteria and/or adhere to the Authorized Provider Agreement.

Prior to placing a provider on probation, the Commission shall notify the provider in writing of concerns or issues that are being reviewed by the Commission. The provider will be granted a specific period of time not to exceed sixty (60) days to make necessary corrections or clarify situations to the satisfaction of the Commission. If the provider's situation has not been resolved by the end of period, the provider will be placed in a probationary status.

Authorized Provider Monitoring Process

Probationary status (cont.)

The provider has ninety (90) days from the date of the Commission's probationary decision to take corrective action and/or to show cause why it should not remain on probation. If at the end of the ninety (90) day period the provider's probationary status has not been removed by the Commission, the Commission may withdraw the provider's certification. The provider may appeal the Commission's decision. The procedures for appeal are outlined in the appeals section. The provider has thirty (30) days from the date of postmark on the decision letter to appeal the decision.

Withdrawal of certification

The Commission reserves the right to withdraw certification if a provider:

- provides false information on the application;

- fails to conduct educational/training activities in compliance with the Authorized Provider Criteria;

- fails to comply with the conditions listed in the Authorized Provider Agreement on the application form;

- fails to maintain the organizational requirements necessary for certification; and/or

- fails to remove its probationary status.

In most instances a provider will be placed on probation prior to having certification withdrawn. The probationary period should give the provider sufficient time to make necessary changes for full compliance.

When the Commission withdraws the certification status of a provider, that decision will be forwarded to the provider in writing and will indicate the Commission's reasons for withdrawing certification. The provider will have thirty (30) days from the date of postmark on the decision letter to appeal the decision. The procedures for the appeal are outlined below.

Authorized Provider Monitoring Process

Appeals process

If the decision of the Authorized Provider Commission is to deny or withdraw certification, or to place a provider on probation, the provider may appeal that decision. The first level of appeal is a request for reconsideration by the Commission. If the Commission sustains its negative decision, the provider then may appeal the decision to the Board of Directors of the International Association for Continuing Education and Training (IACET).

Request for reconsideration

Upon receipt of notification of the Commission's decision to deny or withdraw certification, or to place a provider on probation, the provider may request the Commission to reconsider its decision. The request for reconsideration must be made in writing to the Commission within thirty (30) days from the date of postmark on the decision letter. The right to request reconsideration shall be waived if such request is not made within the thirty (30) day period. During the reconsideration procedure, an Authorized Provider shall retain its certification status.

In the request for reconsideration, the provider must provide evidence that:

- the Commission committed an error or violated its procedures;

- the Commission made an oversight in its decision-making process; or

- matters have arisen in the activity, course, or program since the on-site visit or the Commission decision that might indicate current compliance with the criteria.

Should the provider wish to make a personal appearance before the Commission, it should be so stated in the written request for reconsideration.

The Commission will review the request for reconsideration no later than its next meeting. The Commission shall notify the provider of the time, date, and location of the meeting in order that a representative of the organization may appear.

Authorized Provider Monitoring Process

Continued

Notification of Commission's decision on reconsideration request

The Commission shall notify the provider of its reconsideration decision by registered or certified mail within ten (10) days after the decision has been reached. If the decision of the Commission is to affirm the initial decision to deny or withdraw certification, or to place the provider on probation, notice of the right to appeal the decision to the IACET Board of Directors will be sent with the decision letter.

Appeal

Upon receipt of notification of the Commission's decision after reconsideration, the provider shall have thirty (30) days from the date of postmark on the decision letter within which to appeal the decision to the IACET Board of Directors. The appeal request must be in writing and sent by certified or registered mail to the IACET office. If such appeal is not made within the thirty (30) day period, the right of appeal shall be waived. An Authorized Provider shall retain its certification status until the appeal is decided.

Issues on appeal must derive from the record of the Commission's reconsideration decision. No new information may be introduced during the appeal (e.g., developments, plans, or improvements made after the Commission review and action). All supporting materials must be submitted with the request for appeal.

The Board of Directors will review the appeal at its next regularly scheduled meeting. The appellant provider shall be notified of the time and place of the scheduled appeal hearing. A representative(s) of the appellant organization and the chair of the Commission (or a designated representative) shall have the right to attend the hearing to present a statement in support of or in opposition to the appeal.

During the appeal hearing, the appellant program shall be afforded a thirty (30) minute opportunity to be heard. Finally, the appellant provider shall be afforded fifteen (15) minutes to present a closing statement.

Authorized Provider Monitoring Process

Hearing transcript

If the provider desires to have an official transcript of the proceedings of the hearing, it will arrange and pay for a transcriber to be present. The provider will supply one (1) copy of the transcript to the Commission at the appellant's expense.

Hearing travel expenses

The appellant provider will be responsible for travel expenses of its own representative(s).

IACET Board of Directors' final decision

The IACET Board of Directors will reach its decision in closed sesson by majority vote. The decision may be to (a) uphold the Commission's decision or (b) reverse the decision and award certification or remove probation. The president of IACET shall advise the appellant program of the Board of Director's decision by certified or registered mail within ten (10) days after the appeal hearing. The decision of the IACET Board of Directors shall be final.

Authorized Provider - Miscellaneous

Continued

Listing of Authorized Providers

The Commission will make public and publish annually a listing of Authorized Providers indicating the beginning and ending dates of each provider's certification. This listing will be included in the IACET general resource directory.

Official Authorized Provider representative

Each organization shall designate one official representative as the liaison to the Authorized Provider Commission on the application. This person is responsible for the program administration and assuring that the organization and its instructors adhere to the Authorized Provider criteria. The representative is expected to attend IACET meetings and vote on all matters of official business that relate to the certification process, as well as all other matters of IACET business. IACET should be notified as soon as possible if the official representative changes.

Section 4

Authorized Provider Application

AUTHORIZED PROVIDER APPLICATION INSTRUCTIONS

Procedure   Organizations applying for certification should:

1. **Review the *Criteria and Guidelines for Quality Continuing Education and Training Programs: The CEU and Other Measurement Units.*** The Criteria, Guidelines, and Required Practices located on pages 2-6 through 2-27 in this document explain the requirements that providers must meet in order to be certified as an IACET Authorized Provider. Applicants will want to refer to this information as they complete the application.

2. **Complete the application.**

A copy of the first pages of the application are included on pages 4-4 through 4-5 for applicants who wish to complete this portion of the application using a typewriter. Applicants who wish to complete the application using a computer may either retype pages 4-4 through 4-5 in the same format as shown or download the application from IACET's website on the Internet (http://www.iacet.org).

Information required by the remaining portion of the application should be tabbed and clearly identified according to the criterion. For example, all information requested for Criterion 1 should be placed behind a tab marked "1". Each question should also be clearly marked. For example, information required for Question 1.1a should be placed behind Tab 1 and marked Question 1.1a. Stating the question prior to beginning the response would be useful for the applicant and the reviewing commissioners.

Prepare the original application and four copies (5 copies total), as well as five copies of all attachments. Each copy should be assembled exactly as the original.

AUTHORIZED PROVIDER APPLICATION INSTRUCTIONS

Continued

Procedure
(cont.)

3. **Submit a check for $350 for the nonrefundable application fee with the five copies of the application and attachments to:**

    IACET
    Authorized Provider Commission
    1200 19th Street
    Suite 300
    Washington, D.C. 20036-2422

Assistance

Further assistance is available by calling IACET administrative offices at (202) 857-1105.

AUTHORIZED PROVIDER APPLICATION

1. **APPLICANT ORGANIZATION:**

2. **APPLICANT SEEKS CERTIFICATION FOR**:

   If for unit(s), name of unit: _____
   If certification is for certain categories or programs only, specify title and topic of program(s) and briefly describe content.

   _____

   _____

   _____

   _____

3. **The organization or unit is:** (check one):
   - ____ Chartered by the state
   - ____ Incorporated
   - ____ Accredited
   - ____ Governmental agency
   - ____ Other (explain) _____

   _____

   _____

4. **Number of years applicant organization has been conducting continuing education/training:** ____ years

5. **Total number of continuing education/training activities conducted during the past fiscal, calendar, or academic year by the applicant (organization, unit, or program):**

   ____ Year   ____ # activities   ____ # participants

IACET Authorized Provider Application

6. **Are your continuing education or training programs currently accredited or approved by another agency (ies)?** Yes _____ No _____

   If yes: Specify the agency (ies): _____

   _____

   _____

7. **Has accreditation, certification, or approval of your continuing education or training program or activities ever been denied or removed?** _____ Yes _____ No

   If yes: Indicate the agency and the year that denial or removal occurred.

   Agency _____ Year _____

8. **The individual listed below agrees to:**

   - be available to answer questions about the application
   - ensure applicant adheres to all Authorized Provider criteria;
   - be the liaison to the Authorized Provider Commission (APC) and the International Association for Continuing Education and Training (IACET);
   - receive all correspondence from the APC and IACET and respond as required.

   Name: _____

   Title: _____

   Organization: _____

   Mailing Address: _____

   City/State/Zip/Country: _____

   Phone/FAX (include Area Code): _____

IACET Authorized Provider Application

Instructions: Place the responses requested below behind the appropriate tab and include as attachments to your application. Be sure to identify responses by question number.

TAB 1:

Criterion 1 - Organization: The provider must have an identifiable continuing education or training unit or group with assigned responsibility for administering continuing education and/or training programs.

1.1 The unit or group with responsibility for continuing education or training is clearly identified within the organization.

Question 1.1a: **Explain briefly the nature, role, and purpose of applicant entity (organization, unit, or specified programs).**

Question 1.1b: **What is the title of the identifiable unit or group in your organization which is responsible for administering continuing education and training?**

Question 1.1c: **Attach an organizational chart of the continuing education and training unit/group showing its relationship to the overall organization.**

1.2 Assigned responsibilities of the educational or training unit/group support the provider's mission.

Question 1.2a: **Describe how the responsibility of the continuing education/training unit supports the overall organization's mission.**

Question 1.2b: **Attach the mission statement.**

1.3 The unit/group administers education/training programs.

Question 1.3: **Attach a representative listing (3-4 programs) of your education or training programs (copies of promotional materials are preferred).**

IACET Authorized Provider Application

TAB 2:

Criterion 2 - Responsibility and Control: The provider, through its continuing education or training unit, ensures certification criteria are followed.

2.1   Internal policies clearly indicate a review process that adheres to the criteria.

Question 2.1: Describe how your organization's internal review process addresses all of the criteria. Attach samples of any documents that are created as a result of this process. (Examples: policies, procedures, etc.)

2.2   The review process is conducted by individual(s) who have been trained in and/or have experience with the criteria.

Question 2.2a: State the name and title of the person(s) responsible for the review process.

Question 2.2b: Describe the qualifications of the person(s) responsible for review of the criteria.

2.3   Authority and responsibility for adherence to the criteria are clearly vested in the appropriate individuals responsible for the review process.

Question 2.3: How does the organization ensure that the person(s) listed above is (are) clearly responsible for assuring adherence to all criteria?

2.4   The review process incorporates the latest revisions in the criteria.

Question 2.4:   Describe how you ensure changes in the criteria are incorporated into your review process.

TAB 3:

Criterion 3 - System for Awarding the Continuing Education Unit: The provider has a system in place to identify learners who meet requirements for satisfactory completion.

3.1   A systematic process is used for identifying individuals who satisfactorily complete a course or program.

Question 3.1: Describe your process used to verify satisfactory course/program completion by each learner.

3.1a: When learner attendance is part of the requirements for awarding CEU, the provider has an appropriate system in place to track and monitor learner attendance.

Question 3.1a: Describe your system for tracking and monitoring learning attendance.

3.1b: When partial credit is awarded to learners who do not attend the entire activity, there is a system to track, calculate, and award variable credit.

Question 3.1b: Describe your system for tracking partial attendance and calculating and awarding variable credit for that partial attendance.

3.2   A process is in place for calculating the number of CEU available for each learning activity.

Question 3.2a: Describe the quantitative unit of measure (e.g., CEU, clock hour, point system) you currently use to record the extent of learner participation.

Question 3.2b: Describe the process your organization will use to calculate CEU once you become an IACET approved provider.

Please continue on page 4-10.

IACET Authorized Provider Application

TAB 4:

Criterion 4 - Maintenance and Availability of Records: The provider maintains a complete, permanent (at least 7 years) record of each learner's participation and can provide a copy of that record upon request.

4.1 A permanent record system for learner records is operational.

Question 4.1: Briefly describe the system for maintaining permanent records for a period of at least 7 years for learners who successfully complete your courses/programs.

4.2 Permanent records contain information referenced in the guidelines.

4.3 The permanent record information is presented in a manner which a third party can readily interpret (i.e., no codes or codes explained).

Question 4.2/3: Attach a sample of a completed permanent record.

4.4 Records are kept up-to-date.

4.5 A system is in place to issue an up-to-date copy of a permanent record to a learner or others authorized within six weeks or less.

Question 4.4/5: Describe your system for ensuring records are up-to-date and can be issued within six weeks or less.

4.6 A written policy is operational to ensure the privacy and security of learners' records.

Question 4.6: Attach a copy of your written policy on ensuring the privacy and security of learner records.

4.7   A written policy is operational on retention and releasing of records.

Question 4.7: Attach a copy of your written policy on retention and release of permanent records.

IACET Authorized Provider Application

TAB 5:

Criterion 5 - Learning Environment and Support Systems: A learning environment and support services appropriate to the continuing education or training goals and learning outcomes is provided.

5.1 The organization has a process for determining the resources, to include financial resources and administrative support, required to support the learning outcomes and for ensuring that the resources will be sufficient/available to maintain programs/courses through to completion.

Question 5.1: Describe your process for determining what resources are required to support the learning outcomes and for ensuring that the resources will be sufficient/available to maintain programs/courses through to completion. Also, describe the types of learning support your organization provides.

5.2 The physical environment (i.e., light, sound, seating, etc.) is appropriate for the learning activities.

Question 5.2: Describe your process for determining that the learning environment is appropriate for the continuing education/training goals and learner outcomes.

5.3 Access to the facilities is in compliance with the Americans with Disabilities Act (ADA).

Question 5.3: Describe your policy on accessibility of facilities per the Americans with Disabilities Act (ADA).

5.4 Educational services and technical support are provided to instructors and learners.

Question 5.4: Briefly describe the educational services and technical support you provide to instructors and learners.

5.5 Instructors and/or advisors are available to provide assistance and support to learners.

Question 5.5: Briefly describe your policy for instructors and/or advisors providing assistance and support to learners.

TAB 6:

Criterion 6 - Needs Identification: Each program or activity is planned in response to identified needs of a target audience.

    6.1   An established process provides objective needs assessment data which is the basis for program planning and development.

    6.2   Potential learners and/or multiple sources of information are tapped for needs assessment.

        Question 6.1/2: **Describe the process used by your organization to identify the training needs of potential learners. Include the primary sources of information. Attach sample forms or data-gathering instruments used to document the process.**

    6.3   Needs assessments are systematically documented and updated.

    6.4   Program topics and content must originate from identified needs.

        Question 6.3/4: **Describe how needs assessment data are used to plan programs/courses.**

    6.5   The provider defines the potential participants/target audience and any prerequisites for each continuing education activity and includes this information in catalogs and promotional efforts.

        Question 6.5: **Attach copies of two entries in offerings catalog or promotional efforts which show the identification of the target audience and any prerequisites.**

IACET Authorized Provider Application

TAB 7:

Criterion 7 - Learning Outcomes: The provider has clear and concise written statements of intended learning outcomes (e.g., behavioral or performance objectives) based on identified needs for each continuing education and training program.

7.1   Planned outcomes are based on identified needs.

   Question 7.1:   Describe how your organization uses needs assessment information to develop learning outcomes.

7.2   Written learning outcomes that reflect what learners will achieve are established for each course or program. When learning outcomes are established for a program, each course within that program must be keyed to one or more of the program outcomes.

7.3   The number of planned outcomes is appropriate for the learning activity.

7.4   Outcome statements are clear, concise, and measurable.

   Question 7.2/3/4:   Attach a sample set of learning outcomes from two of your courses/programs.

7.5   Learners are informed of intended learning outcomes.

   Question 7.5:   Describe the process you use to inform learners of the intended learning outcomes (e.g., list outcomes in promotional materials, distribute list of outcomes at the activity, etc.). Attach a sample of any distributed material.

TAB 7 (cont.):

7.6 Learning outcomes are established for large activities such as conferences or conventions. Each session within that activity has its own learning outcomes or is keyed to one or more of the overall activity outcomes.

Question 7.6: Describe your organization's process for establishing learning outcomes for large activities such as conferences or conventions, as well as for each session within the agenda. Provide samples of learning outcomes for two large activities.

TAB 8:

Criterion 8 - Program Planning and Instructional Personnel: Qualified personnel are involved in planning and conducting each activity.

8.1 Individuals involved in program planning and instruction are qualified by virtue of their education and/or experience.

8.2 Expertise in course content and instructional methodologies is used in developing learning activities.

8.3 Individuals involved in program planning understand and utilize learning outcomes in program planning and development.

Question 8.1/2/3: **Describe the process you use to identify and screen potential planners/instructors and to determine they are (a) competent in the subject matter; (b) aware of the activity's purpose and learning outcomes; (c) knowledgeable and skilled in instructional methods appropriate for adults; and (d) able to communicate to participants at the appropriate level.**

8.4 Instructors are reasonably and consistently effective in meeting learning outcomes and learner expectations.

8.5 Instructors are provided feedback on their performance.

8.6 Instructors demonstrate high standards of professional conduct and do not discriminate against learners on the basis of gender, age, socioeconomic or ethnic background, sexual orientation, or disability.

Question 8.4/5/6: **Describe your specific procedures used to monitor and provide feedback to instructors.**

IACET Authorized Provider Application

TAB 8 (cont.):

8.7   The provider discloses, in advance of the activity, any instructor's proprietary interest in any product, instrument, device, service, or material discussed during the activity and the source of any compensation related to the presentation.

Question 8.7:   **Provide your written policy for disclosure of any instructor's proprietary interest in any product, instrument, device, service, or material discussed in the activity and the source of any compensation related to the presentation.**

TAB 9:

Criterion 9 - Content and Instructional Methods: Content and instructional methods are appropriate for the learning outcomes of each activity.

9.1   Subject matter and content are directly related to learning outcomes.

9.2   Instructional methods are consistent with learning outcomes.

9.3   Instructional methods accommodate various learning styles.

9.4   Content is organized in a logical manner.

9.5   Learner interaction and assessments are utilized throughout the programs to reinforce learning, monitor learner progress, and to provide feedback to learners on their programs.

9.6   The provider has established policies and procedures to address intellectual property rights.

Question 9.1/2/3/4/5:   For two of your courses/programs, provide documentation that shows the interrelationship between the learning outcomes, the course content, and the instructional methods used.

Question 9.6:   Provide your organization's policies and procedures to address intellectual property rights.

TAB 10:

Criterion 10 - Assessment of Learning Outcomes: Procedures established during program planning are used to assess achievement of the program's learning outcomes.

10.1   Learning assessment procedures are established during program planning.

10.2   Learning assessment methods measure achievement of learning outcomes.

Question 10.1/2a: Describe the methods of learning assessment most commonly used in your programs/courses.

Question 10.1/2b: For each of the two examples provided in Tab 9.1/2/3/4, provide documentation to show the relationship between the assessment methods and the learning outcomes.

10.3   Learners are informed in advance that learning outcomes will be formally assessed.

Question 10.3:   Describe how and when your organization notifies participants prior to the activity, course or program about methods for assessing learning outcomes.

IACET Authorized Provider Application

TAB 11:

Criterion 11 - Requirements for Satisfactory Completion: The provider assures that satisfactory completion requirements are established for each activity and are based on the activity's purpose and learning outcomes.

11.1 Well-defined requirements for satisfactory completion are established for each planned course or program.

Question 11.1: Provide the specific completion requirements for the two examples documented in Question 9.1/2/3/4.

11.2 Learners are informed of the satisfactory completion requirements prior to the course or program.

Question 11.2: Describe how and when your organization notifies participants about course or program requirements for successful completion.

11.3 Learners are notified if they have not met satisfactory completion requirements (e.g., IACET CEU will not be awarded).

Question 11.3: Describe your method for notifying learners who have not satisfactorily met completion requirements.

TAB 12:

Criterion 12 - Post-Program Evaluation: Each learning activity is evaluated.

12.1 Post-program evaluation procedures for each learning activity are established during program planning.

12.2 Evaluation methods are comprehensive.

Question 12.1/2: **Describe how your organization develops the program/course evaluation process during the initial program planning phase.**

12.3 Summative evaluations are prepared and analyzed based on the following minimum components:

12.3a Did the learning experience and the instructional methods used result in individual behavioral or performance change (i.e., the learning outcomes)?

12.3b Did the learners indicate that the learning outcomes were appropriate for the stated course/program purpose and for the learners involved?

12.3c Was program execution effective and efficient?

Question 12.3: **Attach the course/programs evaluations for the courses/programs used as examples in Question 9.1/2/3/4.**

12.4 Evaluation results are incorporated into program improvements.

Question 12.4: Describe how your organization uses course/program evaluations to make continuous improvements in the continuing education/training activities. Provide any attachments you feel might be helpful.

IACET Authorized Provider Application

MATERIALS TO HAVE AVAILABLE FOR THE SITE VISITOR: The site visit process can be enhanced if these suggested materials are readily available for the site visitor. **DO NOT** submit these materials with your application.

---

1. A written statement that confirms the organization's status as answered in Question #3.

2. Vitae of primary program administrator(s) directly involved with ensuring adherence to the certification criteria.

3. Complete schedule of continuing education and training offerings.

4. If continuing education and training programs are specifically accredited/approved by another agency, a copy of criteria or standards used by that accreditation approval agency.

5. Evidence of record keeping system, how privacy and security are provided, and policy on retention and release of records.

6. Needs assessment documentation including methods used for three (3) courses other than those submitted with the application.

7. Sample course materials from the three courses listed in #6 above including:

    a. Learning outcomes
    b. Courses/curriculum outlines
    c. Instructor credentials
    d. Instructional methods used in each course
    e. Method(s) of assessment and evaluation
    f. Summary of assessment and evaluation results
    g. Promotional materials for each course/program

8. Evidence of how satisfactory completion by participants is confirmed.

9. Other materials you feel help describe your program.

IACET Authorized Provider Application

Authorized Provider Agreement

As an applicant for certification as an IACET Authorized Provider, our organization agrees to:

1. Provide accurate and truthful information to IACET in all transactions to the best of our knowledge.
2. Conduct our operations, courses, and programs in an ethical manner that respects the rights and worth of the individuals we serve.
3. Provide full and accurate disclosure of information about our programs, services, and fees in our promotions and advertising.
4. Use only the IACET approved statement without any modifications when referencing our Authorized Provider status.
5. When the Authorized Provider logo is used on continuing education marketing or promotional materials for those units or programs of the organization that are certified, the approved statement also will be used.
6. Report to IACET within thirty (30) days any major organizational or program changes that impact the role and mission of the administrative unit on which certification is currently based.
7. If accredited or approved by another agency, notify IACET within thirty (30) days if our organization is placed on probation or has its accreditation/approval withdrawn for other than voluntary reasons.
8. Accept IACET designated monitors in any programs we provide for purposes of monitoring compliance with the criteria and to waive registration fees for such monitors.
9. Furnish requested information, work cooperatively with IACET, and pay fees on a timely basis.
10. Operate within the certification criteria and the terms of this agreement or relinquish our certification status after due process.
11. Upon notification from the Authorized Provider Commission, abide by any revision of the certification criteria or inform the Commission of intentions to withdraw.
12. Pay such sums as the court may adjudge for reasonable attorney fees and pay all costs and disbursements incurred in the event a lawsuit is filed on behalf of IACET to obtain compliance by our organization to cease and desist use of the approved statement of certification if such certification is withdrawn by IACET.

_____ hereby agrees with all of the foregoing terms and conditions.

Applicant Organization

_____   _____
Signature: Applicant's Chief Administrative Officer   Title of Chief Administrative Officer

_____   _____
Printed/Typed Name   Date

Appendix A

Definitions and Terms

APPENDIX A - Definitions and Terms

Introduction

The following terms are defined for the reader's use with this publication.

Activity

Event(s) planned to cause learning; often used synonymously with the terms "course" to indicate planned learning experience(s); would include seminar. See "course".

Authorized Provider Commission (APC)

The unit within IACET responsible for certifying that providers are in compliance with the IACET criteria and guidelines; formerly the Certified Providers Commission.

Contact

Interaction between a learner and instructor or between a learner and materials which have been prepared to cause learning. Contact implies two-way communication in order for the learner to receive feedback to monitor and assess learning.

Contact hour

One clock hour of interaction as defined above under "contact". A clock hour may be 60 or 50 minutes, depending on the profession concerned.

Continuing education and/or training (CE/T)

Structured educational and/or training experiences for personal or professional development in which participants are assumed to have previously attained a basic level of education, training, or experience.

Continuing education unit (CEU)

Ten (10) contact hours of participation in an organized continuing education experience under responsible providership, capable direction, and qualified instruction.

Appendix A - Definitions and Terms

Course	The terms "course", "program", and "activity" are often interpreted differently and yet used interchangeably. **For purposes of this document**, "course" means a defined curriculum usually dealing with one issue or subject, such as *How to Prevent Back Injuries*, that has a beginning and ending time. A course may be taught in different time frames such as one hour, one day, one week, one month, or over a period of days, weeks, or months.
Criteria	Standards, requirements, or rules that define acceptable practices.
Demonstration	An activity in which participants provide evidence that they have learned what was intended in the stated learning outcome(s).
Delivery formats	Methods used to deliver instruction, including, but not limited to, on-site workshops, computer-based instruction, video-conferences, self-paced workshops via Internet, audio tapes, video tapes.
Distance education and learning	The acquisition of knowledge and skills through mediated information and instruction, encompassing all technologies and other forms of learning at a distance. Normally, distance education is characterized by the following: • Separation of place and/or time between instructor and learner, among learners, and/or between learners and learning resources • interaction between the learner and the instructor, among learners, and/or between learners and learning resources conducted through one or more media. • Processes may employ a multiple set of delivery methods in the learning experience such as written correspondence study, interactive audio and/or video, computer, and other electronic technologies. Each of these may be used alone or in combinations. Use of electronic media is not necessarily required; technology is a tool to aid the delivery and provision of educational opportunities.

Appendix A - Definitions and Terms

Distance education and learning (cont.)	Processes may be in "real time" interaction between learners and instructors, or "asynchronous" involving the access of instructors and materials by learners at any time.[1]
Education	A process for acquiring knowledge whereby individuals learn to think and reason beyond the level of application.
Evaluation	A process for measuring discrete elements or the overall success of courses including such elements as learner satisfaction, benefits, results or outcomes, learning achievement, and impact.
Instructional methods	Methods used by an instructor to cause learning to occur. Examples include, but are not limited to, lectures, questions, discussions, visuals, exercises, summaries, case studies, electronic simulation, demonstrations, practical hands-on exercises, and virtual reality sessions.
Learner	An individual participating in an activity for the purpose of acquiring knowledge, skills, or attitudes.
Learning need	The gap between a learner's current level and some desired level of knowledge, skills, attitudes, or performance, generally stated as a problem or issue. For example, consider the *problem* of excessive back injuries to employees. The *learning need* is for information and skills required to correctly lift heavy objects.

[1]Adapted from the Southern Regional Education Board, Educational Technology Cooperative *Survey Report of SREB State Regulations as They Apply to Distance Learning*, April 1997; *Guiding Principles for Distance Learning in a Learning Society*, published by the American Council on Education, 1996; and the Commission on Institutions of Higher Education--North Central Association of Colleges and Schools *Guidelines for Distance Education*, approved March 1997.

Appendix A - Definitions and Terms

Learning outcomes

Statements which define the solution to the problem or issue identified in the assessment of learning needs. Each outcome statement explicitly lists what learners will know and/or be able to do as a result of a course. Outcome statements are expressed in measurable and observable terms such as: "Learners will demonstrate the five key rules for preventing back injuries."

Needs assessment

An organized and planned process for identifying learning needs; a process that identifies the gaps between a learner's current level and some desired level of knowledge, skills, attitudes, or performance.

Permanent record

A record of an individual's continuing education participation which is maintained by a provider. Frequently referred to as a learner record or transcript, the provider must provide a copy of the individual's record upon request of the individual.

Program

Program is viewed as an umbrella term covering a series of activities or courses.

Provider

The organization responsible for the design and/or delivery of an education or training activity, course, or program.

Satisfactory completion

Having met the provider's established requirements for completion of a activity, course, or program.

Summative evaluation

Evaluation conducted at the end of an activity, course, or program to determine its effectiveness and worth.

Training

Planned learning experience(s) in which individuals learn to perform a specific skill; generally interpreted as being more narrowly focused than the term "education".

Appendix B

IACET Publications

APPENDIX B - IACET Publications

Guidelines for Distance Education

(1997). This publication addresses a growing concern to define and maintain quality in distance education programs. These guidelines build on previous work and present a practical approach for assuring quality in distance delivery of continuing education and training courses and programs. Available through IACET Headquarters.

The Continuing Education Guide: The CEU and Other Professional Development Criteria

(1994). The first book ever written which explores in-depth how to interpret and use the continuing education unit or other criteria used for continuing education programs. This guide is a reference source complete with sample forms, charts, checklists, and everything you need to plan, develop, and evaluate your continuing education program. Available through IACET Headquarters.

A Practical Handbook for Assessing Learning Outcomes in Continuing Education and Training

(1991). This easy to use innovative guide leads the reader through a series of steps to help select an assessment plan which will work for any organization. The handbook has an appendix that includes sample participant feedback questionnaires, a plan of action form, description of common assessment techniques, and a useful bibliography. The price includes a copy of the *Practical Guide to Assessment Plans*. Available through IACET Headquarters.

Principles of Good Practice in Continuing Education

(1984). This statement of principles consolidates elements from many sources into a single statement of principles for the field placing a pervasive emphasis on learning outcomes for the individual learner. The statement also provides amplification and interpretation of the *Criteria and Guidelines for Quality Continuing Education and Training Programs: The CEU and Other Measurement Units* as well as a brief discussion of the major principles. Available through IACET Headquarters.

Appendix B - IACET Publications

How to order IACET publications

IACET publications may be ordered from IACET Headquarters by forwarding VISA or MasterCard prepayment via:

- Mail: IACET Headquarters
  1200 19th Street NW, Suite 300
  Washington, D.C. 20036-2422

- Phone: (202) 857-1122

- FAX: (202) 223-4579

- E-mail: IACET@dc.sba.com.

- WWW: An order form for all of IACET's publications is available on the IACET Web Page: www.iacet.org.

Purchase orders may also be faxed to: (202) 223-4579.

Appendix C

Fee Schedule

APPENDIX C - Fee Schedule

Members

- Individual: **$100 annually** (1 Jul - 30 Jun)

- Organizational: **$300 annually** (1 Jul - 30 Jun)

Authorized Providers

- Application fee: **$350** submitted with application; nonrefundable

- Site visit fees: **Site visitor expenses PLUS $150 honorarium** for the site visitor. The site visitor expenses vary according to the visitor's travel expenses. The expenses and the honorarium are invoiced after the completion of the site visit. (The Approved Provider Commission attempts to select a site visitor who is close in location to the applicant organization in order to reduce travel expenses. However, the site visitors who are available at a given time can vary, as well as their locations, and therefore, the expenses vary.)

- Annual fees: **$600** (includes one organizational membership) (1 Jul - 30 Jun). The applicant will be invoiced upon acceptance as an Authorized Provider. The fees will be prorated according to the quarter if the first year as an Authorized Provider is only a partial year.

- Recertification fee: **$300** submitted with recertification application

International Association for
Continuing Education and Training
1200 19th Street, NW
Suite 300
Washington, DC 20036-2422
IACET@DC.SBA.COM
WWW.IACET.ORG

the Book of
Texas Lists!!

the Book of Texas Lists !!

Edited by Anne Dingus

★

Texas Monthly®Press

Texas Monthly Press, Inc.
P.O. Box 1569
Austin, Texas 78767

A B C D E F G H

Library of Congress Cataloging in Publication Data

The Book of Texas lists.

   1. Texas—Miscellanea. I. Dingus, Anne,
1953–
F386.B73   976.4   81-8907
ISBN 0-932012-17-5   AACR2

Book Design by The Composing Stick

Contents

the Book of
Texas Lists !!

★ I N T R O D U C T I O N ★

The alphabet is a list. So is the Bill of Rights. So are the laws of thermodynamics. Lists are everywhere, and always have been: consider the Ten Commandments, the Three Musketeers, the Seven Seas. Something in human nature favors the list: it is short and concise; it reassures the disorganized and inspires the tidy. By its very form a list can render palatable subject matter that might discourage a reader if it were presented in great gray blocks of type.

Irving Wallace and David Wallechinsky started the list craze in 1977 with *The Book of Lists.* Since then, the idea has joined the ranks of hula hoops and hot pants as a national fad. There have been books of lists of all sorts: movie lists, food lists, lists about women, lists about wars — in short, lists about almost every field of interest. Hence *The Book of Texas Lists,* for Texas is, all by itself, a field of interest. It is one of the very few states with a life and a history broad and varied enough to produce an entertaining assortment of lists. Texas has almost everything: the good (rock 'n' roll and fine art), the bad (murderers and natural disasters), and the ugly (venomous snakes and cactus). It is full of people with keen minds and towns with dumb names, and its Texans and tales are often equally tall. Texas has coined words and money, and raised cotton, cattle, and hell.

Some Texas lists are obvious (the Six Flags of Texas); some might come as a surprise (Real Names of Famous Texans). Some may clear up misconceptions (Five Things That Were *Not* Invented in Texas), and others reiterate popular state brags (Battles Only Texans Would Have Fought). The lists vary in length from one item (Texas Colleges That Won the GE College Bowl) to fifty (Major Movies Made in Texas), and the length of individual items on a list ranges from a single word to a full page. All together, there are 310 Texas lists.

All sorts of people contributed to *The Book of Texas Lists*. A host of celebrities generously donated lists about their own particular worlds. U.S. vice president George Bush took time out from his 1980 campaign to send not one but two lists. Heart surgeon Denton Cooley contributed, as did former Dallas Cowboy Roger Staubach, actress Farrah Fawcett, gossip columnist Liz Smith, Baptist preacher W.A. Criswell, entrepreneurs Stanley Marcus and Roger Horchow, and attorneys Richard "Racehorse" Haynes and John L. Hill. Dozens more notables also heeded the call.

From less famous folks came even more lists—hundreds of them. *Texas Monthly* subscribers who had read ads for *The Book of Texas Lists* began to deluge us with submissions. Entries came from all over Texas, from eight other states, and even from Guam. Some were, to put it bluntly, boring ("Why I love Texas" was a popular theme). But others were brilliant, and among those were the five winners of the Great Texas List contest promoted in *Texas Monthly*. The grand prize winner, Randolph Polk of Fort Worth, got a sterling silver platter topped with a Texas-size steak for his outstanding contribution of five examples of architectural plagiarism in the state. Close behind him were the four runners-up, who each won a sterling silver fork for their enjoyable efforts: Charles Edward Turner II of Dallas, who listed his city's worst street names; A. Ruff of Bellaire, who came up with the least-known heroes and heroines in the state; Charles Steger of Longview, who gave us the burial sites of famous and infamous Texans; and J.M. Braffett of San Marcos, who submitted a list of early Texas jazz greats.

Thanks are due to those five and to the many other contributors whose lists appear throughout the book, as well as to the state agencies, city halls, universities, sports clubs, and other institutions that cheerfully provided information. Credit is due to four individuals in particular: Patrick D. Redman, Kati Redman, Lorraine Atherton, and Lisa Farrell. And we could list many more.

All and Sundry:
A Texas Miscellany

EPONYMS: NAMES THAT BECAME WORDS

1. From the name of Samuel A. Maverick, an early Texas lawyer and pioneer, we get our word meaning unbranded stock. It has since come to mean a nonconformist, which the original Maverick himself was.

2. Alamo hero Jim Bowie lives on through the bowie knife, a hefty weapon that Jim made famous but that his brother Rezin actually designed.

3. The blocker was a commonly used lasso loop popularized by Texas cattleman John Blocker. When correctly thrown, the huge loop was as good for showing off as it was for roping. As with the Bowie brothers, some people credit John's brother, Ab, with creating the blocker loop. (Ab did design the XIT brand.)

4. Poinsettias were named after Joel Poinsett, who served as special minister to Mexico in the 1840s. While living in Texas during his tenure in office, he took a liking to the large, showy flowers; when he later introduced them in Washington, they were given his name.

5. "Texas" itself became a common noun, a term for the officers' cabins on a Mississippi steamboat as well as the deck the cabins were on. Traditionally, cabins on the ships were named after states and, obviously, the officers' cabins were the largest.

6. A texas leaguer in baseball is a fly that sails too far out to be snagged by an infielder but too far in to be caught by an outfielder. No one knows why it was named after our own minor league.

7. "Pecos" became a verb meaning to rid oneself of an enemy by killing him, slitting open his body, stuffing it with rocks, and then tossing the corpse in a river. It was a popular method of disposal along the Pecos River.

8. Oscar, the Academy Award statuette, was named for a Texan, Oscar Pierce, whose niece worked in Hollywood for the Academy of Motion Pictures Arts and Sciences. When she saw the gold statuette, she supposedly said, "Why, that looks just like my Uncle Oscar!"

NICKNAMES OF FAMOUS TEXANS

1. Sam Houston, first president and first governor of Texas, was given the name "the Raven" by the Cherokee Indians with whom he lived in Tennessee. He was adopted by a chief of the band, who chose the name because of the bird's powerful medicine in Cherokee mythology.

2. "Bum" Phillips, former coach of the Houston Oilers, has had his nickname since childhood, when a younger sister couldn't pronounce "brother." Real name: Oail. Honestly. No wonder he's better known as "Bum."

3. "Racehorse" Haynes, like Bum Phillips, is better known by his sobriquet than by his given name of Richard. Supposedly Haynes got his nickname in junior high when, while playing football, he veered toward the sidelines as he ran, whereupon his coach asked him if he thought he was a racehorse.

4. Lady Bird Johnson, born Claudia Alta Taylor, was given her nickname as a term of endearment by Alice Tittle, her nursemaid. Charmed by the brown-eyed infant, Alice exclaimed, "Why, she looks just like a little lady bird!"

5. John Nance Garner, vice president for two terms under Franklin Delano Roosevelt, was called "Cactus Jack" because, during an early term as a mere state legislator, he urged the adoption of the cactus as the state flower.

6. W. Lee O'Daniel, former governor, was usually referred to as "Pappy," but that name itself was a shortened form of "Pass the biscuits, Pappy," a phrase that stuck on him because of his longtime association with a Fort Worth flour mill.

7. Cattle baron "Shanghai" Pierce, yet another Texan whose nickname is better known than his real name (Abel), no doubt acquired the moniker when, as a youth of twenty, he stowed away on a ship. Discovered by the crew, he was shanghaied into working as a common sailor for the duration of the trip until the ship docked at Indianola, Texas.

8. "Jinglebob John" Chisum, Texas cattleman, was so nicknamed by his cowboys because of the particular earmark he used on his stock, a deep slit. His ranch was also called "the Jinglebob."

9. Erastus Smith, famous scout and Texas revolutionary, was nicknamed "Deaf" because he was.

10. Robert M. Williamson, lawyer and frontier judge, was better known as "Three-Legged Willie." One of his legs, crippled in a childhood accident, was withered and drawn up at the knee; the feisty judge wore, from the knee down to the floor, a wooden peg on which the shorter leg rested.

11. John W. "Bet a Million" Gates, barbed-wire tycoon of the 1870s, got his name by risking his fortune on the chance that barbed wire would change the course of the Texas frontier. It did.

12. Mabry "Mustang" Gray, a drifter who fought in the Battle of San Jacinto as well as in the Mexican War, got his name after being stranded on the plains when his horse threw him and ran. Undaunted, Gray supposedly lassoed a wild mustang, tamed it, and rode it home.

13. John Ireland, elected governor in 1882, earned the name "Oxcart John" because of his continuing opposition to the federal subsidization of railroads.

14. William A. "Bigfoot" Wallace was an Indian scout who had, you guessed it, big feet.

TEN BIG TEXES: PEOPLE WHO BEAR THE NAME OF THE LONE STAR STATE

1. Tex Ritter, country and western great.
2. Texas Guinan, sexy blonde singing star of the twenties.
3. Tex Schramm, president of the Dallas Cowboys.
4. Tex Maule, sportswriter.
5. Tex Watson, a member of the murderous Manson family.
6. Tex McCrary, journalist and radio and TV commentator.
7. T. Texas Tyler, singer and songwriter.
8. Tex Williams, singer, songwriter, actor, bandleader.
9. Tex Rickard, boxing promoter.
10. Joe Tex, soul singer.

ALIAS SMITH OR JONES: REAL NAMES OF FAMOUS TEXANS

1. Frances Octavia Smith (Dale Evans).
2. Baldemar G. Huerta (Freddy Fender).
3. Lucille LeSueur (Joan Crawford).
4. Tula Ellice Finklea (Cyd Charisse).
5. Juanita Dale Slusher (Candy Barr).
6. Florencía Bisenta de Casillas Martinez Cardona (Vikki Carr).
7. Josephine Cottle (Gale Storm).
8. Marvin Lee Aday (Meat Loaf).
9. Ponce Cruse Evans (Heloise II).
10. Mission San Antonio de Valero (the Alamo).
11. *Dasypus novemcinctus* (the armadillo).

NUMBER OF SMITHS IN 1980 CITY PHONE DIRECTORIES

1. Amarillo: 671.
2. Austin: 1862.
3. Corpus Christi: 528.
4. Dallas: 6138.
5. El Paso: 650.
6. Fort Worth: 3837.
7. Houston: 9375.
8. San Antonio: 1907.

MOST COMMON NAMES FOR BABIES BORN AT PARKLAND MEMORIAL HOSPITAL IN DECEMBER 1980

Boys:
1. Dewayne.
2. Lynn.
3. Roderick.
4. Ray.
5. Michael.

Girls:
1. Marie.
2. Nicole.
3. Dawn.
4. Michelle.
5. Renee.

SOURCE: *Parkland Memorial Hospital, Dallas.*

MOST COMMON NAMES FOR BABIES BORN AT JEFF DAVIS HOSPITAL IN DECEMBER 1980

Girls:
1. Nicole.
2. Marie or Maria.
3. Erica or Ericka.
4. Monique.
5. La Kisha.
6. La Shawn.
7. La Toya.
8. Guadalupe.
9. Mary.
10. Rebecca.
11. Dawn.
12. Rose or Rosa.
13. Francisca.
14. Shontell.
15. Yvette.
16. Yvonne.
17. Yolanda.

Boys:
1. Antonio.
2. Michael.
3. James.
4. Eric or Erik.
5. Jermaine.
6. Shawn.
7. Demond.
8. Guadalupe.
9. José.
10. Juan.
11. Javier.
12. Richard.
13. Charles.
14. Edward.
15. Francisco.
16. Robert or Roberto.
17. Daniel.

SOURCE: *Jefferson Davis Hospital, Houston.*

AS THEY SAY IN TEXAS . . .

1. "G.T.T." was nineteenth-century shorthand for "Gone to Texas," a quick way for people to let their families know that they'd headed for greener grass. Eventually, though, so many men headed to Texas to escape the clutches of the law that "G.T.T." came to mean "on the lam."

2. "Come and Take It" was a legend that appeared on a flag flown at Gonzales in 1835, referring to a cannon that the defiant Texans refused to surrender to the Mexican army. The cannon was the first to fire a shot in the Texas Revolution.

3. "Remember the Alamo!," the battle cry at San Jacinto, is often attributed to Sam Houston but was actually coined by Colonel Sidney Sherman.

4. "One riot, one Ranger," an expression aptly describing the noted ability of a Texas Ranger to break up even the wildest dispute, has been in use for more than a century.

5. "Take it away, Leon," said by Bob Wills or vocalist Tommy Duncan to steel guitarist Leon McAuliffe, always preceded an instrumental interlude.

6. "Gig 'em." You aren't a Texan if you don't know where that one's from.

CLEAN SPANISH WORDS AND PHRASES EVERY TEXAN SHOULD KNOW

1. Cerveza.
2. Frijoles.
3. Gringo.
4. Dinero.
5. Picante.
6. Baño.
7. Sí.
8. Adiós.
9. Vaya con Dios.
10. Amigo.
11. Jefe.
12. Número uno.
13. Guero.

MAXINE MESINGER'S LIST OF TEXAS' BEST CONVERSATIONALISTS

Maxine Mesinger is a columnist for the *Houston Chronicle.*

1. John Connally, lawyer and former governor.
2. Nellie Connally, wife of John.
3. Stanley Marcus, Mr. Neiman-Marcus.
4. Lady Bird Johnson, former first lady.
5. Liz Carpenter, former press secretary to above.
6. Leon Jaworski, lawyer and Watergate prosecutor.
7. Tommy Thompson, author (*Blood and Money*).
8. Philip Warner, *Houston Chronicle* editor.
9. Robert Sakowitz, department store magnate.
10. Denton Cooley, heart surgeon.
11. John McCutchen, physician.
12. Richard "Racehorse" Haynes, lawyer.
13. Red Adair, oil well firefighter.
14. Robert Herring, energy company executive.
15. Oscar Wyatt, energy company executive.
16. Robert Strauss, Democratic party bigwig.
17. Eugene Cernan, former astronaut.

TWELVE COMMON EXPRESSIONS USED BY EAST TEXAS GOOD OL' BOYS

1. I hear you cluckin' but I can't find your nest.
2. I had it in me big as a horse.
3. That's useless as teats on a boar hog.
4. He's nervous as a whore in a church house.
5. He's wettin' on my leg, but it feels good.
6. I don't care if syrup goes to a dollar a sop.
7. She's ugly as homemade sin.
8. He's poor as a lizard-eating cat.
9. She raised hell and stuck a chunk under it.
10. He was knee-walkin', commode-huggin' drunk.
11. I feel like I been rode hard and put up wet.
12. He was like a one-eyed dog in a smokehouse.

CONTRIBUTOR: *Bob Bowman, Lufkin.*

PEOPLE WHO COULD NEVER BE MISTAKEN FOR TEXANS

1. Pope John Paul II.
2. Mao Tse-tung.
3. David Bowie.
4. David Niven.
5. Idi Amin.
6. Andy Warhol.
7. Miss Piggy.
8. Woody Allen.
9. Truman Capote.
10. Henry Villechaize (Tattoo).
11. Sophia Loren.
12. John Travolta.

CONTRIBUTOR: *Ben Anderson, Irving.*

MISS AMERICAS FROM TEXAS

1. Jo-Caroll Dennison, Tyler, Miss America 1942.
2. Phyllis Ann George, Denton, Miss America 1971.
3. Shirley Cothran, Fort Worth, Miss America 1975.

TEXANS WHO WERE HELD HOSTAGE IN IRAN

1. Robert Engelmann, Hurst, Navy attaché.
2. Johnny McKeel, Jr., Balch Springs, guard.
3. William Royer, Houston, cultural affairs officer.

FAMOUS EAGLE SCOUTS

1. William P. Clements, governor.
2. Lloyd Bentsen, U.S. senator.
3. H. Ross Perot, businessman.
4. Walter Cronkite, newsman.
5. Ernie Banks, former Chicago Cub.
6. Maynard Jackson, mayor of Atlanta.
7. Dolph Briscoe, former governor.
8. Charles Whitman, killer.

FAMOUS SISTERS

1. Lynda Bird and Luci Baines Johnson, daughters of the late president Lyndon Baines Johnson, grew up under the prying eyes of millions. The girls gave Americans the thrill of two state weddings and provided countless gossip items such as Lynda's Academy Awards date with actor George Hamilton.

2. Adelaide and Julia Germain, sisters kidnapped by the Comanche chief Grey Beard in 1873, were two of the few captives recaptured quickly enough to be successfully returned to white civilization. The girls, ages nine and twelve when they were taken, were kept for over a year; at one point the Comanche abandoned them in the desert but later returned and recovered them. One of the men in the Germain girls' rescue party was Bat Masterson.

3. The Finnigan sisters, a trio of strong-minded Houstonians, began the first real women's suffrage movement in Texas. In 1903 the three women, Annette, Elizabeth, and Katherine, organized the Houston Suffrage League. Annette later served as president of the statewide league.

4. Ura and Wera Hogg, famed sisters of millionaire philanthropist Ima Hogg, do not exist. Miss Ima had only three brothers. Though she died in 1975, the legend of her sisters lives on.

5. The Twin Sisters, two hefty iron cannon, were gifts to the fledgling Republic of Texas from the city of Cincinnati, Ohio. Sent down the Mississippi to New Orleans, the cannon were moved by barge to Galveston and then hauled overland to San Jacinto, where they totally overwhelmed the Mexican artillery during the decisive battle on April 21, 1836. Removed to the Texas Capitol after the revolution, the Twin Sisters disappeared sometime during the Civil War.

TEXAS HEROES WHO WERE FREEMASONS

1. Sam Houston.
2. William Barret Travis.
3. James Bowie.
4. James Bonham.
5. Almaron Dickenson.
6. Davy Crockett.

CONTRIBUTOR: *Frank W. Latham, Jr., Waco.*

SHORT TEXANS

1. Bonnie Parker, criminal.
2. John Tower, U.S. senator.
3. Audie Murphy, war hero.
4. Ima Hogg, philanthropist.
5. Bill Clements, governor.
6. Bill Shoemaker, jockey.
7. Davey O'Brien, 1938 Heisman Trophy winner.
8. Calvin Murphy, Houston Rocket. Second-shortest player in the NBA.

SOURCE: *Anne Dingus and Victoria Loe, "Tiny Texas," **Texas Monthly**, December 1979.*

HISTORICAL SHIPS

1. The New Spain fleet of 1554, sunk off Padre Island, is believed to be the earliest verified shipwreck site in the Western Hemisphere. There were at least three ships in the fleet, and the underwater archeological site has yielded coins, vessels, and other artifacts.

2. La Salle's ship *Amiable* was wrecked on the Texas coast in 1685. Timber from its ruins was used to help build Fort St. Louis.

3. The *U.S.S. Hatteras,* a Civil War ship, was sunk off Galveston by the *C.S.S. Alabama.* It has never been raised. Also off Galveston, near Pelican Island, is the wreckage of the *U.S.S. Westfield,* a second Civil War vessel, and a third is believed to be buried in Buffalo Bayou in Houston.

4. The bark *Elissa,* moored at Galveston, is a three-masted, square-rigged sailing ship, one of the last of her kind. The *Elissa* regularly worked in and out of the Port of Galveston in the 1880s.

5. The battleship *Texas,* which served the United States in both world wars, is now its own state park, moored next to the San Jacinto Battleground.

SHIPS OF THE NOT-SO-SHIPSHAPE TEXAS NAVY

1. *Liberty,* a former privateer, was lost when Texas couldn't pay a repair bill shortly after the ship had carried a wounded Sam Houston to New Orleans for treatment.

2. *Invincible,* a former slave trader, was taken by Mexican raiders, who wrecked it on a sandbar.

3. *Independence,* a former U.S. cutter, was also lost to the Mexicans.

4. The *Brutus* disappeared in a storm.

5. *Zavala,* a steam packet, rotted for lack of funds to repair it and was eventually sold for scrap.

6. The *San Jacinto* was wrecked in 1840.

7. The schooner *San Antonio* saw a mutiny in 1842; later it vanished during a storm.

8. Another schooner, the *San Bernard,* fell apart because it wasn't kept up properly.

9. The *Wharton,* a brig, suffered the same fate.

10. The *Archer,* also a brig, was inspected by the U.S. Navy in 1846, after Texas had become a state, but was declared unfit for duty.

11. The *Austin,* a sloop and flagship, was the only Republic of Texas ship that was approved by the U.S. Navy. Its crew was not, however; the Republic's usual lack of funds prevented the hiring of real sailors.

CONTRIBUTOR: *Kathryn Davenport, San Antonio.*

GREAT TRAINS
1. *Sunset Limited,* Southern Pacific (Los Angeles–New Orleans).
2. *Sunbeam,* Southern Pacific (Dallas–Houston).
3. *Texas Chief,* Santa Fe (Chicago–Galveston).
4. *Texas Special,* Katy, Frisco & Wabash (Chicago–St. Louis–San Antonio).
5. *The Ranger,* Santa Fe (Chicago–Galveston).
6. *Texas Zephyr,* Burlington (Denver–Fort Worth–Dallas).
7. *Sam Houston Zephyr,* Burlington (Houston–Fort Worth–Dallas).

8. *Texas Rocket*, Rock Island (Houston–Dallas–Fort Worth–Chicago).
9. *Choctaw Rocket*, Rock Island (Memphis–Amarillo).
10. *Texas Eagle*, Missouri Pacific (Washington D.C.–Dallas–San Antonio).
11. *Texas Eagle*, Texas & Pacific (Dallas–El Paso).
12. *Orleanian/Houstonian*, Missouri Pacific (Houston–New Orleans).
13. *Southerner*, Texas & Pacific, Missouri Pacific (El Paso–Fort Worth–Dallas–St. Louis–New Orleans).
14. *Flying Crow*, Kansas City Southern (Kansas City–Port Arthur).

CONTRIBUTOR: *John T. Patterson, Waelder.*

ODD RAILROAD LINES

1. Abilene Southern.
2. Angelina & Neches River.
3. Belton.
4. Moscow, Camden, & San Augustine.
5. Pecos Valley Southern.
6. Point Comfort & Northern.
7. Quanah, Acme, & Pacific.
8. Rockdale, Sandow, & Southern.
9. Roscoe, Snyder, & Pacific.
10. Weatherford, Mineral Wells, & Northwestern.

CONTRIBUTOR: *Edward Choate, Coleman.*

BUMPER STICKERS THAT SAY YOU'RE TEXAN

1. Eat More Beef.
2. Longhorns and Longnecks, No Place But Texas. (Popular variations include Aggies, Longbeds, and the Shah.)
3. Honk If You Love Jesus.
4. Foat Wuth, I Luv Yew.
5. I'm Mad Too, Eddie.
6. Drive 70, Freeze a Yankee.
7. Secede.

6. The Armadillo World Headquarters, the Austin beer garden and nightclub that featured every kind of music from jazz to punk and that fostered the development of progressive country-rock. It died in 1981 at age 10, razed to make way for a high-rise hotel.

FAMOUS LAST WORDS

1. Stephen F. Austin, "Father of Texas": "Texas is recognized. . . . Did you see it in the papers?" Said on his deathbed, 1836.

2. Sam Houston, president of the Republic of Texas, governor of the State of Texas: "Texas! Texas! Margaret!" On his deathbed, 1863. (Margaret was his wife.)

3. William Longley, gunfighter: "I see a lot of enemies out there, and mighty few friends." Said before he was hung in 1877.

4. Black Jack Ketchum, outlaw: "I'll be in hell before you start breakfast, boys. Let 'er rip!" Said before he was hung in 1901.

5. Lyndon Baines Johnson, 36th president of the United States: "Send Mike immediately!" Spoken over his bedroom phone to a secret service agent, 1973.

THREE SUICIDES

1. George Parr, son of Archie Parr, succeeded his father as the "Duke of Duval County." The millionaire Parrs had tremendous influence in a fifteen-county South Texas area and wielded considerable power in national as well as state politics. George Parr was convicted of tax evasion in 1934 and served time in prison, but after being pardoned by President Harry S. Truman he was promptly elected county judge, a position he had held before his trial. In 1948 Jim Wells County, part of the Parr stronghold, sent in the late amended return that enabled Lyndon Johnson to win the hotly contested U.S. Senate race with Coke Stevenson. Nine years after the Box 13 affair, Parr was found guilty of using the mails to defraud, but his sentence was overturned on appeal. In 1973, he was convicted a second time of tax evasion; while the case was on appeal he fatally shot himself at his ranch.

2. Anson Jones, last president of the Republic of Texas, was highly unpopular among Texans during his brief tenure in office because of his apparent reluctance to have Texas annexed by the U.S. Still, after Texas joined the Union, Jones expected legislators to name him to the U.S. Senate; he was passed by in favor of the more popular Sam Houston and Thomas J. Rusk. Sorely disappointed, Jones retired to his plantation and brooded over his misfortune till 1858, when he took his own life by shooting himself. (Ironically, his political rival Rusk, despondent over the death of his wife, had killed himself the previous year.)

3. Robert Howard, creator of the famed comic book character Conan the Barbarian, racked up sales of fantasy fiction second only to those of J. R. R. Tolkien. He lived all his life in Cross Plains, a shy boy who was intensely devoted to his mother. He lived vicariously through his characters: savage cavemen who lived in a dark, brutal world of fierce beasts and voluptuous women, or mystical swordsmen and sorcerers who moved through eerie, dreamlike worlds. He made a healthy salary, especially for a man working in a rural Texas town during the Great Depression. In 1936, though, Robert's mother fell ill; told that she was near death, he took a gun, went to his car, and shot himself in the temple. He was buried with his mother.

TEXANS WHO WERE BURIED NOT ON THE LONE PRAIRIE

1. Blues singer Blind Lemon Jefferson, Wortham Negro Cemetery.
2. Cattle baron Samuel Burk Burnett, Oakwood Cemetery, Fort Worth.
3. Outlaw John Wesley Hardin, Evergreen Cemetery, El Paso.
4. Father of Texas Stephen F. Austin, State Cemetery, Austin.
5. Faith healer Pedro Jaramillo, Jaramillo Family Cemetery, Los Olmos.
6. TV cowboy Dan Blocker, Masonic Cemetery, DeKalb.
7. Hero Sam Houston, Oakwood Cemetery, Huntsville.
8. U.S. Speaker of the House Sam Rayburn, Willow Wild Cemetery, Bonham.
9. Olympic gold medalist Babe Didrickson Zaharias, Forest Lawn Memorial Park, Beaumont.

10. Rebel Walter Williams (the last Confederate veteran), Mount Pleasant Cemetery, Franklin.
11. Sculptor Pompeo Coppini, San Fernando Cemetery, San Antonio.
12. Storyteller J. Frank Dobie, State Cemetery, Austin.

SOURCE: *Charles Steger, Longview.*

BURIED TREASURES: CACHES THAT ARE LOST BUT NOT FORGOTTEN

1. The Treasure of Castle Gap, Pecos County, buried in 1866. Said to be some 6 wagon loads of gold and silver bullion and jewels from the personal fortune of the ill-fated Emperor Maximilian of Mexico. The wagon train was waylaid and burned by its own hired guards.

2. El Muerto Springs Treasure, Presidio County, buried sometime in the 1860s. Bandits allegedly buried 20 mule loads of riches from church and bank robberies, including gold, silver, and jeweled images. (A mule load, incidentally, is about six fifty-pound bars.)

3. Rock Pens Treasure, McMullen County, buried in the 1840s. According to the deathbed confession of a man who was supposedly involved, 31 mule loads of "Mexican church loot" are buried in or near some rocks "laid around like a pen." Although these rock pens have been located, the loot remains undiscovered.

4. San Cajo Hill Treasures, McMullen County, buried at various times from the Spanish era through the 1850s. At least five stores of treasure—mostly gold coins—are associated with a hill called San Cajo (or Caja). There is no such saint, and the name may well be a corruption of *sin caja,* Spanish for "without box," an apt description of a number of impromptu funerals in and around the hill.

5. The Cannon Full of Gold, Neches River, buried in 1836. When Mexicans retreating from the Battle of San Jacinto were caught by Texans at a crossing on the Neches, a fight ensued during which several Mexican soldiers were spotted rolling a cannon into the river from a high bluff. Forty years later a man who claimed to be the son of one of these soldiers came to Texas to search for the cannon, which he said was packed from breech to muzzle with gold.

6. Santa Anna's Paychests, San Jacinto Battlefield, April 21, 1836. Dozens of rumors abound about the fate of the loaded paychests for Santa Anna's army, which were not found after the Battle of San Jacinto. One rumor says that the chests were dragged to a boggy area on the battlefield, where they sank.

7. The Singer Treasure, Padre Island, 1861. The Singer family, who operated a large ranch on Padre Island, were Union sympathizers. When they were forced to leave Texas after its secession they supposedly hid $80,000 in gold under a millstone near the ranch headquarters. After they returned in 1867, the site had been wrecked by a hurricane, and the burial spot was never found.

8. Fort Belknap Treasure, Young County, 1880s. A bandit buried some $18,000 in gold coins in a beanpot as far down as "the depth of a wagon rod" along a creek within half a mile of the abandoned Fort Belknap, between Graham and Newcastle.

9. Harp Perry's Silver, Llano County, 1834. His 1200 pounds of silver bars, molded inside pieces of cane, are supposedly hidden on a high hill north of the old smelter on Packsaddle Mountain.

10. Jim Bowie's Treasure, Llano, Mason, Menard, or McCulloch counties, 1830s. Over 100 treasures ranging from a cave full of gold and silver to 3 mule loads of silver are associated in one way or another with James Bowie. Most of the stories are probably mythical or overblown, with two possible exceptions. Twenty loads of silver on Brady Creek, buried in late 1835 or early 1836, may not be his, but 3 mule loads on Calf Creek have been linked to him by an eyewitness. The treasure, at any rate, has never been found.

CONTRIBUTOR: *C.F. Eckhardt, Seguin.*

ECCENTRIC CHARACTERS

1. John V. Singer, younger brother of the sewing machine inventor, sailed to Texas with his family in 1847 and was wrecked off Padre Island in a storm. The family all survived and made it ashore, salvaging supplies and food from the boat and living in makeshift dwellings à la Swiss Family Robinson. Singer made money by running a salvage service from the many wrecks off the island; later he ran cattle, but he rarely left his rustic home. In 1860, because of their Union sympathies, the family was kicked out of Texas by Confed-

24

erate authorities, leaving behind $80,000 in gold, silver, and coins. After the war, Singer returned for his treasure, but he never found it.

2. C. W. Post first came to Texas in the 1880s. Having developed several new cereal foods, including Post Toasties and the drink Postum, Post next turned to developing a model city with ideal health care. The city of Post, in what is now Garza County, had everything from a sanatorium to a hotel. Post laid the town out in perfectly identical blocks and built a large house on each for every one of his 1200 colonists. In his own little kingdom he was free to indulge in his favorite hobby, experimentation. He imported strange new strains of crops, tested Rube Goldberg–style machinery designs, and once tried to induce rain by exploding dynamite in his colonists' fields.

3. Howard Hughes would have been called crazy if he hadn't been so rich. He owned and ran Hughes Tool and Hughes Aircraft and, at various times, three airlines, a film company, and a multitude of Las Vegas casinos and hotels. In addition to his business interests he also produced motion pictures and set several aviation records. Eventually, though, he became a complete recluse; his last known photograph was taken in 1961. He lived alone in a Las Vegas penthouse and in various other secret places in the world and what he did for the rest of his life is a mystery; supposedly he spent all his time watching movies, taking drugs, and being finicky about his food. He broke his self-imposed silence just once, in 1972, to deny that he had authorized an autobiography, actually written by Clifford Irving, that was proved to be a hoax. When Hughes died in 1976, he was horribly emaciated; the cause of his death was never determined. After his funeral a profusion of wills sprang up and a fierce contest began over what state—Nevada or Texas—would get to claim him as its legal resident and collect millions in inheritance taxes.

4. Hondo Crouch, one of Texas' best-loved characters, owned, ran, and popularized the little hamlet of Luckenbach. He was dubbed the "Crown Prince of Luckenbach," and he came up with the town's motto: "Everybody's Somebody in Luckenbach." Hondo was a man of many talents: besides being sheriff, chief of police, and mayor of the town, he was a philosopher, journalist (pen name: Peter Cedarstacker), whittler, storyteller, actor, and prankster (he once blew up an outhouse during a theater performance). His fame and the subsequent fame of Luckenbach led various artists, notably Jerry Jeff Walker, to tape several albums there. Hondo hosted a world's fair at Luckenbach, one of many catchall celebrations he

held that always included chili cook-offs (his own specialty was armadillo chili) and cow-chip throwing and tobacco-spitting contests. Hondo's trademarks were his red bandana, battered pickup truck, and grizzled beard. He died in 1976.

5. Stanley Marsh 3 is Texas' greatest living eccentric. The Amarillo resident, a capitalist whose family has been involved in oil, cattle, banking, and television, is fond of outrageous clothing and weird hats. He uses only oversized stationery. At his home, Toad Hall, he raises exotic animals such as zebras and yaks. Once he attended a society wedding with a dwarf who was dressed as Aunt Jemima; another stunt was his appearance at a trial while carrying a bucket of cow manure. A patron of the unusual arts, Marsh has commissioned such oddities as ten Cadillacs buried nose-down in cement, a giant ramp leading to the middle of nowhere, and what he calls the "World's Largest Phanton Soft Pool Table."

STANLEY MARSH 3's FAVORITE THINGS

Stanley Marsh 3 is a character (see previous list).

1. My favorite cause is lost.
2. My favorite tape is Scotch.
3. My favorite sound is an echo.
4. My favorite space is empty.
5. My favorite people are twins.
6. My favorite image is mirrored.
7. My favorite word is identical.
8. My favorite act is disappearing.
9. My favorite stare is blank.
10. My favorite walk is a meander.
11. My favorite song is "Don't Fence Me In."
12. My favorite talent is my own.
13. My favorite way home is halfway.

EXOTICA

1. Camels were imported into Texas twice in the 1850s by the U.S. War Department, in the belief that they would be handy animals to use during Indian Wars on the plains because of their ability to go for long periods without food or water. Some 75 camels were imported and used largely as pack animals by the military before the project was dropped.

2. The train wreck stunt was a publicity idea thought up by the Missouri, Kansas, & Texas Railroad. The stunt involved two giant steam locomotives rushing toward each other at 100 miles an hour to demonstrate their speed. The thousands of spectators who watched the event from a huge field near Waco certainly got a thrill: the two engines crashed and the boilers exploded, killing two people and injuring hundreds. The man who dreamed up this little stunt, by the way, was named Crush.

3. Highways are paved with gold not in the mythical cities of Cibola but in Montague County, some five miles south of Ringgold on U.S. 81. Several stretches of the highway in that area were paved with material containing gold, although the value per ton was minuscule and not worth the cost of extraction.

THREE CANDIDATES FOR A NEW STATE SONG

Know how we got stuck with "Texas, Our Texas" as our state song? It was the winner of a statewide contest in 1929. That gives you some idea why it's so bad. So why do we keep it? There are plenty of great songs about Texas; below are the top choices for a new Lone Star anthem.

1. The words to "The Yellow Rose of Texas" were probably written sometime during the late 1830s or early 1840s. The yellow rose supposedly refers to Emily Morgan, a mulatto slave girl who lived in Texas during the revolution and who, legend says, was part of the loot Santa Anna collected as he swept through with his armies. Not much is known about Emily, but romanticists say that it was through her deliberate seduction that Santa Anna was, ah, amorously engaged when Sam Houston's armies descended upon the snoozing Mexican forces at San Jacinto and completely surprised them. Whatever the truth, Emily lives on in "The Yellow Rose of Texas." No one knows who the real lyricist was; he is thought to be a Negro, though, since the second line originally ran

"No other darky knows her, nobody else but me." The verse was first set to music in 1858; the composer is also unknown.

2. "The Eyes of Texas," official song of the University of Texas, was written in 1903 as a prank. Colonel William L. Prather, then the president of UT, was fond of exhorting students to always do their best because, as he said, "ladies and gentlemen, the eyes of Texas are upon you." During a University Glee Club performance that Prather attended, performers sang, to the tune of "I've Been Working on the Railroad," a verse by student John Lang Sinclair that began with Prather's favorite injunction. "The Eyes of Texas" is better known in the state than the national anthem, and it's a whole lot easier to sing.

3. "Deep in the Heart of Texas," written in 1941 by June Hershey and Don Swander, was not a success until its creators added the hand-clapping at the end of each phrase. Together, the two earliest recordings of the song sold over a million copies. "Deep in the Heart of Texas" has been performed in numerous motion pictures including *Heart of the Rio Grande,* with native Texan Gene Autry, who sang it; *Thirty Seconds Over Tokyo; How to Marry a Millionaire;* and *Teahouse of the August Moon,* in which it was sung by Glenn Ford, Eddie Albert, and Marlon Brando. Wouldn't it be nice to have a state song that you wouldn't have to remember the words to—you could just clap along?

STATE SYMBOLS, MEANINGFUL AND OTHERWISE

1. State bird: mockingbird.
2. State tree: pecan.
3. State motto: "Friendship."
4. State flower: bluebonnet.
5. State song: "Texas, Our Texas."
6. State dish: chili.
7. State grass: sideoats grama.
8. State gem: topaz.
9. State stone: palmwood.

ODD STATE PARKS

1. Acton State Park in Hood County is a mere 0.006 acre. It is the site of the cemetery plot of Davy Crockett's second wife, Elizabeth Patterson Crockett, who came to Texas eighteen years after her husband died in the Alamo.

2. The Battleship *Texas* is actually considered a state park in itself, and it is moored within another state park, the San Jacinto Battleground State Park. The *Texas* served in both world wars.

3. Texas State Railroad Historical Park, Anderson and Cherokee counties. The State of Texas built a railroad around the turn of the century to serve the state ironworks in Rusk; eventually the rail ran from Rusk to Palestine. Now it is run as a tourist attraction in the spring and summer.

4. Eisenhower Birthplace State Park. The 34th president of the U.S. was born in Denison; the park is a mere 3 acres. In contrast, the Lyndon B. Johnson State Park is 710 acres. But then Eisenhower always considered himself a Kansan.

MEANINGS OF COLORS IN THE TEXAS FLAG

1. Red: courage.
2. White: liberty.
3. Blue: loyalty.

CAPITOL FACTS

1. It is the largest of all the state capitol buildings and, at 390 feet high, is taller by 7 feet than the U.S. Capitol, after which it is modeled.

2. The statue atop the dome is supposed to represent the Goddess of Liberty; it faces south because, in 1888, 23 years after the Civil War, anti-Union feeling still ran high. The statue holds not a torch but a five-pointed star.

3. The Capitol is constructed completely of native materials; the granite, limestone, wood, and copper are all from Texas.

4. The state built a railroad from Burnet to Austin solely for the purpose of transporting the stone for the capitol.

5. The state gave the builders of the capitol three million acres of land in the Texas Panhandle in exchange for their work.

6. At the time it was completed, the Texas Capitol was thought to be the seventh largest building in the world. It covers three acres of ground.

SOURCE: *Texas Department of Highways and Public Transportation.*

RANCHES THAT COVERED A MILLION ACRES

1. The King Ranch. The most famous ranch in the world once contained 1,200,000 acres, and today it still covers 825,000 acres in South Texas. Santa Gertrudis cattle were developed on the King Ranch.

2. The XIT. It covered 3,050,000 acres when it was established in 1885. The Panhandle land, covering ten counties, was given by the State of Texas to a corporate syndicate in exchange for the construction of the State Capitol.

3. The JA. Owned by legendary cattleman Charles Goodnight in partnership with John Adair, it covered 1,335,000 acres at its peak. It, also, was in the Panhandle.

4. The Matador. A lower Panhandle ranch, it covered 1,500,000 acres. At various times the ranch also owned land in two other states, Canada, and Brazil.

SOURCE: *Southwest Collection, Texas Tech University.*

AND DON'T FORGET THE BAR N GRILL: FUNNY RANCH NAMES

Most of these ranches were named for their brands, and some are still operating today.

1. Four Sixes.
2. Frying Pan.
3. Rocking Chair.
4. Hashknife.
5. Two Buckle.
6. Dinner Bell.
7. Mashed O.
8. Shoe Nail.
9. Anvil.
10. ¿Quien Sabe?
11. Diamond Horse.
12. T-Anchor.

GOOD PLACES TO NAME YOUR POISON

1. The Jersey Lilly in Langtry was saloon, courthouse, and home to Judge Roy Bean. He named it—and the town—after British actress Lillie Langtry, a noted beauty of the era for whom he professed undying affection. Texas' most famous saloon is half the reason that Judge Roy was widely known as the "Law West of the Pecos." He always dispensed drinks to plaintiff, defendant, jury, and counsel before a trial, and rarely left the Jersey Lilly for any reason at all. He died there in 1903.

2. The Acme Saloon was the best-known saloon in El Paso—if not on the entire Mexican border—for decades. It was the site of many brawls and ruckuses, but it is best remembered as the place where Constable John Selman murdered John Wesley Hardin in 1895.

3. Rosa's Cantina, though not strictly a saloon, was made famous by Marty Robbins in his classic song "El Paso." The first verse goes, in part, "Nighttime would find me in Rosa's Cantina / Music would play and Felina would whirl . . ." Several Rosa's Cantinas actually existed from time to time in El Paso, but which one the song is based on doesn't matter; what does is that Robbins's song has as much to do with preserving the legend of the smoky, rowdy, masculine saloon as any Long Branch or Silver Dollar ever did.

31

4. Scholz Garten in Austin is the oldest saloon in the state still serving liquor. The German-style beer garden, completed in 1866, has been a hangout for generations of Austinites, from governors and millionaires to students and cowboys and just plain folks. It is on the National Register of Historic Places.

LADIES WHO MADE THE WEST WILD: EUPHEMISMS FOR PROSTITUTES

1. Fallen angels.
2. Soiled doves.
3. Fancy women.
4. Cyprians, after Cyprus, where people worshiped Aphrodite, the goddess of love.
5. Sage hens.
6. Girls of the line.
7. La Grange chickens.

EDIBLE INVENTIONS

1. The margarita, a happy accident, was supposedly created in 1942 by Pancho Morales, an El Paso bartender. Asked to make a drink that he hadn't heard of before, Morales fudged by substituting tequila. Olé!

2. Dr Pepper, a less stimulating but no less popular drink, was first mixed up in 1885 by Charles Alderton, a Waco pharmacist. Though long popular only in the South, today it is the third best-selling soft drink in the U.S.

3. Fritos were introduced in 1932 by Elmer Doolin of San Antonio. Many have tried, but none have succeeded, in duplicating the success of his original corn chip.

4. Barbecue is a Texas creation, regardless of what anyone from either of the Carolinas thinks, and so, for that matter, are chicken-fried steak, nachos, chili, and fajitas.

TONY VALLONE'S FAVORITE DISHES

Restauranteur Tony Vallone owns Tony's in Houston.

1. *Galantine de six oiseaux,* a pâté consisting of a partridge cooked in a pheasant cooked in a duck cooked in a goose cooked in a capon cooked in a turkey.

2. Breast of chicken Nonna, cooked with cognac, cream, sherry, tomatoes, and spices.

3. Praline mousse.

4. Herbed *paillard* of beef, spiced with shallots, parsley, basil, butter, salt, and pepper.

5. Veal sautéed with leeks.

6. Strawberry-raspberry soufflé.

ARCHITECTURAL PLAGIARISM

1. The White House, La Porte. Built by former governor Ross Sterling, it is an exact but three-fifths life size replica that faces onto Galveston Bay.

2. Boot Hill Cemetery, Tascosa. When a man named Bob Russell was shot dead, while drunk, by a murderous storekeeper, his wife Lizzie picked out his gravesite and named it. It became the permanent residence of many an outlaw who died with his boots on.

3. The City of Castroville. The joke's on us. Castroville isn't a small Texas town; it's a French-Alsatian village transported from Europe. Where else do you find tombstones marked in five languages?

4. Dutch windmill, Victoria. Now that wind power has become fashionable again, it's worthwhile to see the city's authentic Dutch windmill, built in 1859.

5. Tomb of the Unknown Soldier, Fort Worth. Go to the Pioneers' Rest Cemetery, find Ripley Arnold's tomb on the east side, and nearby you will find the Tomb of the Unknown Soldier — of the Indian wars.

CONTRIBUTOR: *Randolph Polk, Fort Worth.*

FAMOUS REPLICAS

1. Globe Theatre, Odessa.

2. XIT giant windmill, Littlefield.

3. Butterfield Overland Stage, Six Flags.

4. Fort St. Louis, Six Flags.

5. Old Fort Bliss, Fort Bliss, El Paso.

6. The Alamo, Alamo Village, Brackettville.

7. Oval Office, LBJ Library, Austin.

WEIRD MUSEUMS

1. El Campo Big Game Trophy Museum. Includes world-record animal trophies.

2. Fire Museum, Grand Prairie. Documents a century of Texas firefighting.

3. Jay Gould Private Railroad Car, Jefferson. An 88-foot car with four staterooms and amenities such as a butler's pantry, bar, and bath; specially made for the millionaire industrialist.

4. Dutch Windmill Museum, Nederland. The only city in Texas that ought to have this museum.

5. Beer Bottle World, New Braunfels. Over 14,000 different beer bottles — next to a beer garden, of course.

6. Odessa Meteorite Museum. Site of the U.S.'s second largest meteor crater, formed over 20,000 years ago.

7. Old Clock Museum, Pharr. More than five hundred clocks from different countries.

8. Jail Museum, Port Lavaca. The old Calhoun County jail, complete with iron bars.

9. Buckhorn Hall of Horns, San Antonio. Houses not only an astonishing array of horns — the kind deer have, that is — but also collections of rare marine creatures, exotic birds, and antique firearms.

10. Hertzberg Circus Collection, San Antonio Public Library. Includes such oddities as Tom Thumb's wedding cake.

11. Music Box Gallery, Sulphur Springs Public Library. More than two hundred music boxes from all over the world.

12. Private Bird Collection of Robert L. More, Sr., Vernon. Some ten thousand eggs from 750 species of birds.

13. World's Smallest Museum, Weslaco. Tiny one-room hole-in-the-wall houses antique telephone collection.

SOURCE: *Texas Historical Commission.*

CHURCHES WITH MORE THAN 21,000 MEMBERS

1. First Baptist, Dallas.

FIVE OF DR. W. A. CRISWELL'S FAVORITE BIBLE VERSES

Dr. W. A. Criswell is the pastor of First Baptist Church in Dallas.

1. Isaiah 40:8. "The grass withers, the flower fades, but the word of our God shall stand forever." Dr. Criswell's favorite verse.

2. John 3:16. "For God so loved the world that he gave his only begotten Son, that whosoever believed in Him should not perish but have everlasting life."

3. John 14:6. "Jesus said to him, 'I am the Way, the Truth, and the Life; no man comes to the Father except by me.'"

4. Job 19:25. "I know that my Redeemer lives, and at the last days he shall stand upon the earth."

5. Psalm 27:1. "The Lord is my light and my salvation; whom shall I fear? The Lord is the strength of my life; of whom shall I be afraid?"

LYNN ASHBY'S FAVORITE PUNS

Lynn Ashby, humor columnist with the *Houston Post,* notes that only very smart people like puns.

1. The wife of a distinguished classics scholar planned a very special cake for him. It was carefully decorated with quotations from Greek poets. Unfortunately, it tasted terrible—proving once again that we can't have archaic and eat it, too.

2. A snail goes to buy a Volkswagen. The deal is made, but the snail insists that the name "Volkswagen" be stricken and that a large "S" be put in its place. The dealer agrees, but asks why. "When I'm zooming down the highway," the snail explains, "I want folks to say, 'Look at that S-car go.'"

3. The chief of a tribe on a South Seas Island became extremely ill. The witch doctor was called in, and after due deliberation he prescribed a hot toddy for treatment. One was sent for, and the chief drank it, but nothing happened. He remained terribly ill. The witch doctor, now in a bit of trouble since his cure wasn't working, tried another medical trick. This time he prescribed a new treatment. "The chief is ill because the gods are angry," he said. "We must placate them. We have to toss virgins into the volcano. But not just any virgins," he added. "They have to be fat." This was done. Plump maiden after plump maiden was dutifully tossed into the volcano. Again nothing happened. The chief remained ill. At this point, the tribe rose up in anger and hauled the witch doctor to the edge of the volcano. As he was being pushed into the bubbling inferno, he yelled back a last medical suggestion: "If fat virgins don't succeed, try hot rye again."

4. A military alliance was being formed between China's Premier Hua and E.A. Muffet, the leader of the anti-Ayatollah Khomeini rebels in the Iranian province of Kurdistan. Elmer Little, an American living with the Kurdish people, was instrumental in arranging the Sino-Iranian conference where the pact would be signed. However, because of Elmer's extensive travel schedule, he was unable to attend the conference and so Little missed Muffet meeting his Kurds and Hua.

5. A long time ago in England, King George was having trouble collecting his taxes. It seems that the peasants were not paying their fair share. To remedy the situation, King George decided to build a portable torture rack to go around the countryside to use on peasants. The royal carpenters constructed a very modern, but bulky, torture rack. It was so bulky that no horse or horses could

pull it. King George solved this problem by importing two large elephants from India. The very day after the elephants arrived they were hitched up to the torture rack. They started down the road into the countryside when a peasant saw it and asked another peasant what it was. The second peasant replied, "That's a rambling rack for George's tax and an elephant engineer."

ORGANIZATIONS WE'RE NOT SURE WE'D JOIN (EVEN IF WE WERE ADMITTED)

1. Texas Pond of the International Order of the Blue Goose.
2. Texas Branch of the Huguenot Society of the Founders of Manakin in the Colony of Virginia. (Whew.)
3. Texas Society of the Nomads of Avrudaka.
4. Lone Star Chapter of the Telephone Pioneers of America.
5. Texas State Song Association.
6. And, last but not least, the Texas Turkey Federation.

TOP SIX HAIR TONICS IN TEXAS

1. Four Roses: most selected and most sold. Pro: makes your hair shine like a West Texas sunset. Con: overdose can make your eyes water for days.

2. Ballentine: preferred by the young *machito*. Pro: a surprisingly pleasant smell. Con: attracts lint.

3. Butch wax: favorite among the waxes. Pro: incredible staying power; a good application can last a month. Con: often used as a lubricant on metal.

4. Vitalis: especially popular among the up-and-coming. Pro: adequate staying power and good sheen ability. Con: scent is not likely to attract young ladies.

5. Brylcreem: the old standby. Pro: good creamy texture. Con: dull.

6. Crisco: used in an emergency. Pro: instant eye appeal. Con: stains pillows.

CONTRIBUTOR: *Jerry Treviño, San Antonio.*

REFLECTIONS FROM THE CIRCLEVILLE PHILOSOPHER

H. B. Fox is the Circleville Philosopher; his column appears in newspapers throughout Texas.

1. The most cosmopolitan rural community in Texas: Circleville. There are more folks in Circleville who've been to New York than there are folks in New York who've been to Circleville.

2. The most satisfied community in Texas: Circleville. The Circleville Chamber of Commerce warns all industrialists planning on locating a plant here to bring their own labor. We folks here are already working as much as we intend to.

3. The community with more swimming pools per capita than Highland Park in Dallas or River Oaks in Houston: Circleville. And this doesn't count stock tanks. We have ten times more of those than Dallas or Houston does.

4. The community with the most astute political observers: Circleville. No election has ever gone to suit us.

5. The best handling of the scare tactics of the far-out environmentalists who're always finding things that are bad for you: a rancher near Circleville. After drinking happily from his well for twenty years he got talked into having the water tested. The report from the state health department came back and said, "Contaminated. Unfit for human consumption." "That sure taught me a lesson," he said as he downed a dipperful. "I'll never have that well tested again."

JACK HEIFNER'S EIGHT QUALIFIED DON'TS FOR TEXANS VISITING NEW YORK CITY

Jack Heifner, a playwright, lived in Texas for 22 years and has been in New York for the last 12.

1. Don't ask for chicken-fried steak or a Mexican combination plate at Sardi's (unless you want to be rudely treated).

2. Don't yell "Hook 'em, Horns," on 42nd Street (unless you want to be attacked by the ladies of the evening).

3. Don't expect a Broadway producer to be excited about your idea for a musical called *Amarillo!* starring your niece who twirls flaming batons (unless you can write a check for a million to back the show).

4. Don't tell a cab driver *he* has a funny accent (unless you want a knuckle sandwich).

5. Don't ask to see the statue of Lincoln when you visit Lincoln Center (unless you want to be embarrassed).

6. Don't pay cash if some guy tries to sell you the Brooklyn Bridge (unless you are absolutely sure it will fit across your pool).

7. Don't waste your time taking a Dallas Cowboy cheerleader to visit the New York Public Library (unless she has a book report due for class and can't find her copy of *Scruples*).

Flora and Fauna

THE ORIGINAL TALL TEXANS

1. *Tyrannosaurus rex,* the fiercest of the fierce, stood twenty feet tall and sported a mouthful of sharp, glistening teeth. Its head was four feet long. One of its footprints, the size of a child's swimming pool, is preserved at Dinosaur Valley State Park near Glen Rose.

2. *Glyptodon,* a nightmarish ancestor of the armadillo, was about eight feet long. It protected itself with a heavy armored shell not unlike its descendant's and a massive clublike tail.

3. Saber-toothed cats included the enormous *Homotherium serus,* much larger than the modern tiger, and a smaller cousin, *Dinictus felina.* Both favored meals of baby mastodon.

4. The shovel-tusked mastodon was a huge monster with tusks five feet long and a foot wide, but it was a benign vegetarian. It was a naturalized Texan, its ancestors having originated in Africa and crossed to North America by means of a land bridge. One of its relatives was the equally large but likable long-jawed mastodon.

5. Several giant ground sloths, including *Mylodon, Megalonyx,* and *Eremotherium,* roamed Texas. Though some of them weighed up to two tons, they were so slow and ponderous that they didn't stand a chance when pitted against early Indians and other carnivores. Such easy prey died out early.

6. Two prehistoric rhinos were *Teleoceros* and *Aphelops,* the former an aquatic fellow with a small horn and the latter a hornless plains-dweller.

7. *Camptosaurus,* a plant-eater some twenty feet long, was the basic creature that springs to mind when one thinks of the word "dino-saur"—small-headed, long-necked, flabby, and dumb-looking.

8. *Typothorax,* a scavenger, was rather like a giant horned toad. Covered with scaly armor, it had a thick, heavy, spiked tail handy for battering luckless foes.

9. *Trilophosaurus* was a genial herbivore that looked like an over-grown lizard.

10. *Phytosaur,* which resembled a crocodile but looked even meaner, had a snout two feet long. It was carnivorous.

11. *Eupelor* was a prehistoric amphibian similar to the alligator. Its bulky head was roughly 18 inches square. It fed largely on small fish.

12. *Edaphosaurus,* a mammallike reptile, was a vegetarian and had a two-foot-high fin on its back for protection against heftier meat-eaters.

13. *Pterodactyl* was larger than some airplanes. The huge bird, which had a fifty-foot wingspan and a neck ten feet long, was a prehistoric vulture that lived on dinosaur carcasses.

SOURCE: *Texas Memorial Museum.*

LIKELY CANDIDATES FOR STATE ANIMAL

1. Armadillo.
2. Longhorn.
3. Horned toad.
4. Roadrunner.
5. Rattlesnake.
6. Tarantula.
7. Scorpion.
8. Javelina.
9. Buffalo.
10. Coyote.
11. Bald eagle.

FAMOUS ANIMALS (NON-EQUINE)

1. Lyndon Baines Johnson's dogs, Him and Her, two likable beagles. Remember the flap when Lyndon picked Him up by the ears? Two other LBJ dogs were Blanco, a collie, and Yuki, a mutt; the late president always claimed that Yuki was his favorite.

2. Monkey, a bull, was the progenitor of the new Santa Gertrudis breed developed by the Klebergs of the King Ranch. The hefty Santa Gertrudis, a cross between Brahman and Shorthorn, was the first breed of cattle in the western hemisphere and the first developed anywhere in over a century.

3. Old Rip, a horned toad, was put inside the cornerstone of the Eastland County Courthouse when it was built in 1897. Thirty-one years later the courthouse was torn down, and there was Rip, a little the worse for wear but nonetheless alive. He was exhibited to thousands of impressed spectators.

4. Bevo, the University of Texas mascot, a longhorn.

5. Reveille, the Texas A&M mascot, a collie.

6. Old Yeller and Savage Sam, two tough Texas mongrels created by author Fred Gipson.

7. Ham, the chimp on NASA's suborbital Mercury flight in 1961.

8. Bruno, Judge Roy Bean's pet bear.

9. Old Blue, any good ol' boy's hunting dog.

10. The jackalope, which, though it has spread to Oklahoma and other neighboring states, is a species native to Texas.

FAMOUS ANIMALS (EQUINE DIVISION)

1. Assault, a Triple Crown winner, came out of the King Ranch stables and was trained by the famous Max Hirsch. Assault took the Kentucky Derby, the Preakness, and the Belmont Stakes in 1946.
2. Cass-olé starred in the 1980 movie version of Walter Farley's classic horse novel, *The Black Stallion*. The stallion is the pet of a San Antonio doctor's daughter.
3. Widow-Maker was Pecos Bill's horse.
4. Saracen, Sam Houston's horse.
5. Buttermilk, Dale Evans's horse.
6. White Flash, Tex Ritter's horse.
7. Punkin, Bob Wills's horse.

MOST COMMON BREEDS OF DOGS REGISTERED WITH THE CITY OF DALLAS

Although mutts are the majority of the 38,000 dogs registered in Dallas, the ten most popular breeds are:

1. Poodle.
2. German shepherd.
3. Terrier (including Cairn, Yorkshire, and so on).
4. Cocker spaniel.
5. Dachshund.
6. Doberman pinscher.
7. Chihuahua.
8. Schnauzer.
9. Labrador retriever.
10. Collie.

SOURCE: *Environmental Health and Conservation Department, City of Dallas.*

UNUSUAL CATTLE BREEDS

1. Ankina.
2. Barzona.
3. Black Maine-Anjou.
4. Blonde D'Aquitaine.
5. Chianina.
6. Gelbvieh.
7. Marchigiana.
8. Pinzgauer.
9. Romagnola.
10. Tarentaise.

SOURCE: *Texas Cattle Raisers, Fort Worth.*

VICTOR EMANUEL'S LIST OF BIRDS FOUND IN THE U.S. ONLY IN TEXAS

Victor Emanuel leads nature tours in Texas and Mexico and has been birding for more than thirty years.

1. White-tailed hawk. This noble raptor of the tropical savannah is found from South Texas to Argentina.

2. Chachalara. Strange turkey-size bird that inhabits brush country and produces a raucous chorus at dawn.

3. Jacana. Bizarre, colorful, and tropical shorebird that walks on floating vegetation.

4. Ringed kingfisher. The largest member of its family in the New World.

5. Great kiskadee. Large, colorful flycatcher of South Texas.

6. Golden-cheeked warbler. Nests nowhere but in the Hill Country— the only bird that nests only in Texas.

7. Altamira oriole. A large bird with striking orange and black plumage.

EIGHT GOOD PLACES TO GO BIRDING

1. Smith Woods (High Island).
2. Bolivar Flats (the western tip of the Bolivar Peninsula).
3. Aransas National Wildlife Refuge.
4. Laguna Atascosa National Wildlife Refuge.
5. Santa Anna National Wildlife Refuge.
6. Bentsen Rio Grande State Park.
7. Big Bend National Park.
8. Guadalupe Mountains National Park.

CONTRIBUTOR: *William J. Graber III, Beaumont.*

ENDANGERED SPECIES UNIQUE TO TEXAS

1. Attwater's greater prairie chicken *(Tympanuchus cupido attwateri).*
2. Harter's water snake *(Natrix harteri).*
3. Cascade Cavern salamander *(Eurycea latitans).*
4. Texas blind salamander *(Typhlomolge rathbuni).*
5. Houston toad *(Bufo houstonensis).*
6. Fountain darter *(Etheostoma fonticola),* a fish.
7. Comanche Springs pupfish *(Cyprinodon elegans).*
8. Leon Springs pupfish *(Cyprinodon bovinus).*
9. Amistad gambusia *(Gambusia amistadensis),* a fish.
10. Big Bend gambusia *(Gambusia gaigei).*
11. Clear Creek gambusia *(Gambusia heterochir).*
12. San Marcos gambusia *(Gambusia georgei).*

SOURCE: *Texas Parks and Wildlife Department.*

THREATENED SPECIES NATIVE TO TEXAS

1. Golden-cheeked warbler *(Dendroica chrysoparia).*
2. Gray-banded king snake *(Lampropeltis mexicana alterna).*
3. Rock rattlesnake *(Crotalus lepidus).*
4. Trans-Pecos rat snake *(Elaphe subocularis).*
5. Rio Grande darter *(Etheostoma grahami),* a fish.

SOURCE: *Texas Parks and Wildlife Department.*

VENOMOUS TEXAS SNAKES

1. Western massasauga.
2. Western pygmy.
3. Western diamondback.
4. Canebrake rattlesnake.
5. Desert massasauga rattlesnake.
6. Banded rock rattler.
7. Mottled rock rattler.
8. Black-tailed rattlesnake.
9. Mojave rattlesnake.
10. Prairie rattler.
11. Western cottonmouth.
12. Southern copperhead.
13. Broad-banded copperhead.
14. Trans-Pecos copperhead.
15. Coral snake.

BIG-GAME HARVESTS, 1980–81

1. White-tailed deer, 260,383.
2. Wild turkey, 26,874.
3. Javelina, 22,229.
4. Mule deer, 4796.

SOURCE: *Texas Parks and Wildlife Department.*

UNUSUAL ANIMALS RAISED IN TEXAS

1. Giraffe.
2. Camel.
3. Zebra.
4. Ostrich.
5. Exotic deer (including chital deer from Southern Asia, fallow deer from Europe, and sika deer from China and Japan).
6. Exotic antelope (including gazelle, eland, impala, oryx, blesok, nilgai, and blackbuck—all African except the last two, which are Indian).
7. Llama.
8. Ibex (a wild goat).

SOURCE: *Exotic Wildlife Association, Kerrville.*

RARE ANIMALS AT THE SAN ANTONIO ZOO AND THEIR WORLD POPULATIONS

1. Whooping cranes, 121.
2. Golden lion tamarin, 350.
3. Snow leopard, 700–800.
4. Spurred tortoise, less than 100.
5. Ring-tailed lemur and ruffed lemur, found only on Madagascar; undetermined.
6. Maned wolf, 2,000–3,000.
7. Clouded leopard, population unknown; extremely rare.
8. Grévy's zebra, 15,000 in 1978; declining rapidly.
9. Père David's deer, 350.

SOURCE: *San Antonio Zoo.*

ANIMALS FIRST BRED IN U.S. AT THE SAN ANTONIO ZOO

1. Spurred tortoise.
2. New Guinea side-necked turtle.
3. Spiny-headed tree climber (a lizard).
4. Malayan water monitor.
5. Sinaloan milk snake.
6. European sand viper.
7. Giant pitta (a bird).
8. White rhinoceros.
9. Turkish viper.
10. American flamingo.
11. Dama gazelle.
12. Bare-headed rock fowl.

SOURCE: *San Antonio Zoo.*

ANIMALS THAT THE SAN ANTONIO ZOO HAS THE BIGGEST COLLECTIONS OF IN THE WORLD

1. Antelopes, including the lesser and greater kudu, Kirk's dik-dik, the scimitar-horned oryx, the addax, and the Nile lechwe.

2. Cranes, including the whooping, wattled, hooded, and sandhill, as well as six other varieties.

SOURCE: *San Antonio Zoo.*

ANIMALS THAT THE HOUSTON ZOO HAS THE BIGGEST COLLECTIONS OF IN THE WORLD

1. Boas and pythons, twenty varieties, including the rare Bismarck ringed python.

2. Touracos, ten species, of which eight have reproduced. These odd birds include the white-cheeked touraco, purple-crested touraco, and Gold Coast touraco.

RARE AND UNUSUAL ANIMALS AT THE HOUSTON ZOO

1. Cock of the rock, first bred in captivity in the Houston Zoo.

2. Brown pelican, which is endangered along the Texas coast.

3. Houston toad, a rare indigenous species which is in a captive breeding program at the zoo.

4. Vampire bats, seldom exhibited in captivity.

5. Spotted linsang, a relative of the civet, believed to be the only captive specimen in the world.

6. White-crowned mangaby, a monkey, probably the only pair in captivity.

7. Asian elephant male, rarely found in zoos anywhere.

A BOUQUET OF TEXAS WILDFLOWERS

1. Any variety of the bluebonnet is the state flower. The bluebonnet is also called wolf flower, buffalo clover, and *el conejo,* Spanish for "the rabbit," from the resemblance of the white tip on the petals of some varieties to a rabbit's tail.

2. Indian blanket, or "firewheel," is probably the best-known of Texas wildflowers; it covers the whole state.

3. Ocotillo, with its slender stalk and bright red flower, is also called "coach whip" or "flaming sword."

4. The Mexican hat resembles a sombrero in shape.

5. Agarita blooms in delicate yellow flowers. Indians used its stems to make dye, and its spring berries make good jelly.

6. Yucca can grow ten feet high. It produces huge, waxy white blossoms, and is also called "Spanish dagger."

7. Lavender foxglove, also called "fairy thimbles," can be dried and steeped to make tea.

8. Mountain pink was once used to treat fever and ague; hence its nickname, "quinine weed."

9. Horsement, which resembles a thimble, blooms in a variety of pastel colors; it is found all over the state.

10. Cenizo, also called "barometer bush," is sometimes mistaken for purple sage; there is no true sagebrush in Texas.

SOURCE: *Texas Department of Highways and Public Transportation.*

SENSITIVE NAMES FOR A PRICKLY SUBJECT: FUNNY NAMES FOR CACTUS

1. Cow's tongue.
2. Turk's head.
3. Red goblet.
4. Flapjack.
5. Long mama.
6. Twisted rib.
7. Glory of Texas.
8. Horse crippler.
9. Ladyfinger.
10. Dry whiskey (peyote).
11. Candy barrel.
12. Tom Thumb.

WILD, WILD WEEDS

An urban gardener might like these plants, but a rural one would grab his hoe.

1. Unicorn plant.
2. Buffalo burr.
3. Moon flower.
4. Silver leaf.
5. Sneeze weed.
6. Point loco.
7. Mexican poppy.
8. Paper flower.
9. Horsetail.
10. Plains larkspur.

CONTRIBUTOR: *Mrs. Robert G. Blackwood, San Angelo.*

LEGAL TEXAS GRASSES

1. Smutgrass.
2. Hairy grama.
3. Switchcane.
4. Red lovegrass.
5. Tanglebeard.
6. Splitbeard.
7. Bullnettle.
8. Broomsedge.

AGRICULTURAL RANKINGS IN THE U.S.

Texas is number one in:

1. Number of farms and ranches: 159,000.
2. Farm and ranch land: 138.4 million acres.
3. Cattle: 13.2 million head.
4. Sheep: 2.4 million head.
5. Goats: 1.4 million head.
6. Wool production: 19.1 million pounds.
7. Mohair production: 9.3 million pounds.
8. Cotton production: 5.5 million bales.
9. Watermelons: 46,000 acres harvested.
10. Spinach (for fresh market): 6100 acres harvested.
11. Pecans: 91 million pounds.

Number two in:

1. Sorghum: 136.1 million hundredweight.
2. Grapefruit: 9 million boxes.
3. Cantaloupe: 18,100 acres harvested.
4. Carrots: 16,100 acres harvested.
5. Green peppers: 10,300 acres harvested.
6. Cabbage: 14,400 acres harvested.
7. Onions: 29,500 acres harvested.

Number three in:

1. Oranges: 6.4 million boxes.
2. Rice: 23.5 million hundredweight.
3. Winter wheat: 138 million bushels.
4. Peanuts: 533 million pounds.
5. Total fresh market vegetables: 168,650 acres harvested.

Number four in:

1. Sunflowers: 84.6 million pounds.
2. Sugarcane: 883,000 tons.
3. Flaxseed: 45,000 bushels.
4. Bee colonies: 190,000.
5. Total vegetables harvested: 188,950 acres.

SOURCE: *Texas Department of Agriculture. Statistics as of September 1, 1980.*

RECORD CROP HARVESTS

1. Cotton: 5,628,000 bales, 1926.
2. Wheat: 7,310,000 acres harvested, 1947.
3. Corn: 180,000,000 bushels, 1976.
4. Rice: 27,462,000 hundredweight, 1968.
5. Sorghum: 233,520,000 hundredweight, 1973.
6. Soybeans: 20,930,000 bushels, 1979.
7. Sugarcane: 1,354,000 tons, 1976.
8. Sugar beets: 874,000 tons, 1968.
9. Oats: 1,932,000 acres harvested, 1921.
10. Peanuts: 533,025,000 pounds, 1979.
11. Barley: 441,000 acres harvested, 1958.
12. Flaxseed: 308,000 acres harvested, 1949.
13. Rye: 40,000 acres harvested, 1975.
14. Hay: 6,147,000 tons, 1979.
15. Guar: 52,000,000 pounds, 1975.
16. Eggs: 3,014,000,000, 1944.

SOURCE: *Texas Department of Agriculture.*

THE VERY FEW AGRICULTURAL PRODUCTS THAT ARE *NOT* PRODUCED IN TEXAS

1. Maple syrup.
2. Tobacco.
3. Pineapples.
4. Raspberries.
5. Currants.
6. Cranberries.
7. Bananas.

SOURCE: *Texas Department of Agriculture.*

Towns and Places

COUNTRY SINGERS WHO TOOK THEIR STAGE NAMES FROM TEXAS TOWNS

1. Vernon Dalhart (real name: Marion Try Slaughter). Supposedly he had worked in those two towns before he became a star.

2. Conway Twitty (real name: Harold Lloyd Jenkins). Actually, the first half of his assumed name came from Conway, Arkansas, but the last came from Twitty, Texas.

TOWN NAMES THAT CAME FROM PEOPLE'S NAMES SPELLED BACKWARDS

1. Notla, Ochiltree County.
2. Reklaw, Cherokee and Rusk counties.
3. Sacul, Nacogdoches County.
4. Remlig, Jasper County.

HARD-TO-PRONOUNCE TOWN NAMES

1. Boerne. Pronounced as if spelled "Burney."
2. Nacogdoches. Just ignore the "g."
3. Gruene. If you live here and are jealous, you turn Gruene with envy.
4. Buda. The Buddha would know it's "byooda."
5. Kountze. "Koonts" counts.
6. Palacios. Its horribly Anglicized pronunciation is "puh-LASH-us."
7. Lamesa. Equally awful Spanish: "luh-MEE-suh."
8. Mexia. Pronounced "muh-HAY-uh." Which reminds us of the joke about the two businessmen who passed through Mexia and stopped for a cup of coffee. Arguing over the pronunciation of the town name, they hailed the waitress and asked, "Say, how do you pronounce the name of this place, anyway?" And she said, "Day-ree-Queen."
9. Refugio. Pretend the "g" is an "r."
10. Knippa. Very sneaky: the "k" is not silent.
11. Quitaque. Another weird one. It's "KIT-uh-kway."
12. Kosciusko. Gesundheit.

ACKNOWLEDGMENTS TO: *Lynn King, Vega; Michael O. Baskin, Laurel, Maryland.*

SILLIEST TOWN NAMES

1. Baby Head.
2. Jot Em Down.
3. North Zulch.
4. Personville.
5. Punkin Center.
6. Okra.
7. Noodle.
8. Uncertain.
9. Tarzan.
10. Zippville.

BEST TOWN NAMES

1. Lutie.
2. Lazbuddie.
3. Running Water.
4. Rural Shade.
5. Seven Sisters.
6. Sublime.
7. Veribest.
8. Wizard Wells.
9. Circleback.
10. Dimple.

SIX TEXAS TOWNS NAMED FOR WOMEN

1. Bronte, named in honor of English novelist Charlotte Brontë.

2. Buda, named for a widow who ran a hotel there in 1880. The name is a corruption of the Spanish *"viuda,"* meaning widow.

3. Hetty, named for Hetty Green, wife of multimillionaire Edward H. Green. She was known as the "Witch of Wall Street" because she turned a $16 million inheritance into over $100 million but remained a miser all her life.

4. Marfa, named by the wife of a founder for the heroine of a Russian novel.

5. Panna Maria, which means "Virgin Mary," was so named by Polish settlers in 1854. The town is the oldest Polish settlement in Texas.

6. San Angelo was originally San Angela and was named for a Mexican nun. The federal government altered the spelling.

CONTRIBUTOR: *Virginia L. Smith.*

WORST STREET NAMES IN DALLAS

1. Proton Road. Neutron, Beta, and Gamma roads are nearby.

2. Star Trek Lane. In the same area are North Star Road and Two Worlds Street.

3. Test Tube Street. Two blocks to the west are Beaker and Flask.

4. St. Landry Drive. Everyone knows that the Dallas Cowboys are blessed by someone above, but this is just too much.

5. Ewing Avenue. Its name has been sullied by the fictional family of CBS's *Dallas*.

6. Microwave Avenue. Much too trendy. Electronic Street and Telephone Way pale in comparison.

7. Dilido Road. A glance at its sign while driving past tends to blur the letters.

8. Bye-Bye Lane. A street of unfriendly people, no doubt.

9. Elbow Street. Maybe there's lots of room on it, or else it takes a sudden bend.

CONTRIBUTOR: *Charles Edward Turner II, Dallas.*

BEST STREET NAMES IN DALLAS

1. Hyperbolic Street. Really. We're not exaggerating.
2. Cinderella Lane. For the rags-to-riches set.
3. Monetary Drive. It's just a few blocks east of Dividend, Profit, and Currency.
4. Nonesuch Road. There really is such a road.
5. Fabrication Street. It's not.
6. Kool Avenue. Named after the cigarette. Who wouldn't want to live on Kool?
7. Humoresque Drive. Located in the Singing Hills area.
8. Dazzle Drive. More flair than Flair Street, classier than Classic Drive.

SOURCE: *Charles Edward Turner II, Dallas.*

UNBELIEVABLE SAN ANTONIO STREET NAMES

A single subdivision in northwest San Antonio boasts the following street names:

1. Gomer Pyle.
2. Ben Casey.
3. Ben Hur.
4. Charlie Chan.
5. Gary Cooper.
6. Cary Grant.
7. Errol Flynn.
8. Danny Kaye.
9. Ernie Kovacs.
10. Lon Chaney.
11. John Wayne.
12. Dean Martin.
13. Mike Nesmith.
14. George Burns.
15. Edie Adams.
16. Desilu.

SUNDRY NAMES FOR FORT WORTH

1. Cowtown.
2. Panther City.
3. Bird's Fort.
4. Birdville.
5. Fort Town.
6. Camp Worth.
7. Out Where the West Begins.

PLACES NAMED FOR ROYALTY

1. Bastrop was founded by Baron Felipe Enrique Neri de Bastrop, a native Hollander who moved to Texas in the early nineteenth century.

2. Galveston was originally Galvez Town, named after Count Bernardo de Galvez, a Spanish soldier born in 1746. He fought Apaches in Mexico, supported American independence during the Revolution, and ordered the first survey of the Texas coast.

3. Bexar County was named for the San Antonio de Bexar presidio, the center of Spanish defense in Texas, which in turn was named for a son of the Duke de Bexar of Spain.

4. New Braunfels was named for Prince Carl of Solms-Braunfels, a German who came to Texas in 1844 to settle colonists on a land grant purchased by the Adelsverein, an association of noblemen.

5. Telferner, a little settlement in Victoria County, got its name from that of an Italian count, Joseph Telfener, who held stock in the Texas & Pacific Railway. The railroad ran a line through the town. (The town's founders, as you may have noticed, misspelled the count's name.)

COUNTIES WHOSE NAMES ARE MISSPELLED

1. Dimmit County, named for Philip Dimitt, a hero of the Texas Revolution.

2. Motley, named for Dr. J.W. Mottley, one of the signers of the Texas Declaration of Independence.

3. Collingsworth, named for James Collinsworth, first chief justice of the Republic of Texas.

WEIRD MOUNTAIN NAMES

1. Shoe Peg Mountain, Uvalde County.
2. Contrabando Mountain, Brewster County. Had to be on the border, of course.
3. Casket Mountain, Jeff Davis County. Perhaps too risky a climb.
4. Baby Head Mountain, Llano County.
5. Hen Egg Mountain, Brewster County.
6. Smoothingiron Mountain, Llano County.
7. Tallow Face Mountain, Eastland County.
8. Straddlebug Mountain, Brewster County.
9. Boiling Mountain, Kinney County. It's hot in them thar hills.
10. Butcherknife Mountain, Brewster County.

TALLEST MOUNTAINS

1. Guadalupe Peak, Culberson County, 8751 feet.
2. Bush Mountain, Culberson, 8676 feet.
3. Pine Top Mountain, Culberson, 8676 feet.
4. Bartlett Mountain, Culberson, 8513 feet.
5. Mount Livermore (a.k.a. Baldy Peak, Mount Baldy), Jeff Davis County, 8382.
6. El Capitán, Culberson, 8078.
7. Mount Emory, Brewster County, 7835.

FUNNY CREEK NAMES

1. Asylum Creek.
2. Pole Cat Branch.
3. Tradinghouse Creek.
4. Bullhide Creek.
5. Cannonsnap Creek.
6. Yo Lo Digo Creek.
7. Mesmeriser Creek.
8. Starvation Creek.
9. Drunkards' Branch.
10. Hog Wallow Creek.
11. Talking John Creek.
12. Headache Springs.

COUNTIES WITH CURIOUS NAMES

1. Panola County is the only county with a name derived from an Indian word—*ponolo,* meaning cotton.

2. Midland County was so named because it was halfway between Fort Worth and El Paso on the Texas & Pacific Railroad line.

3. Delta County, which is roughly triangular, was named for its shape's similarity to the Greek letter.

4. Goliad County derived its name from an anagram of the Spanish name *Hidalgo,* minus the silent "h."

COUNTIES NAMED FROM SPANISH WORDS AND THE MEANINGS OF THEIR NAMES

1. Atascosa: boggy.
2. Bandera: flag.
3. Blanco: white.
4. Brazos: arms.
5. El Paso: the pass.
6. Frio: cold.
7. Lampasas: lilies.
8. Lavaca: the cow.
9. Llano: plains.
10. Matagorda: thick cane.
11. Nueces: nuts.
12. Palo Pinto: painted wood.
13. Presidio: fort.
14. Refugio: refuge.
15. Sabine: cypress.
16. Val Verde: green valley.

CITIES THAT HAVE FIVE MILITARY BASES

1. San Antonio (with Randolph, Kelly, Lackland, and Brooks Air Force bases as well as Fort Sam Houston).

CONTRIBUTOR: *Frank W. Latham, Jr., Waco.*

OTHER STATES THAT HAVE CITIES NAMED HOUSTON

None of these Houstons has more than five thousand people.

1. Delaware (where it's pronounced "Howzton").
2. Minnesota.
3. Mississippi.
4. Missouri (where the city is in Texas County).
5. Pennsylvania.
6. Arkansas.

BIGGEST CITIES IN TEXAS IN 1900 (AND THEIR CURRENT RANK)

1. San Antonio: population 53,300 (third).
2. Houston: 44,600 (first).
3. Dallas: 42,600 (second).
4. Galveston: 37,800 (twenty-seventh).
5. Fort Worth: 26,700 (fifth).
6. Austin: 22,250 (sixth).
7. Waco: 20,700 (fifteenth).
8. El Paso: 15,900 (fourth).

PORTS OF IMPORTANCE

1. Houston, third largest port in the U.S., handling 105 million short tons a year.
2. Beaumont, sixth largest port in the country, 49 million short tons.
3. Corpus Christi, seventh largest U.S. port, 47 million short tons.

TWELVE TOWNS THAT HOLD ANNUAL CHILI COOK-OFFS

1. Terlingua.
2. San Marcos.
3. Houston.
4. Victoria.
5. Schulenburg.
6. Plano.
7. Alice.
8. Floresville.
9. Beeville.
10. Comfort.
11. Corsicana.
12. Llano.

TOWNS THERE ARE MORE THAN ONE OF

1. Cottonwood (Callahan and Madison counties).
2. Lakeview (Hall, Terry, and Jefferson).
3. LaSalle (Calhoun, Jackson, LaSalle, Limestone).
4. Lone Star (Cherokee, Comal, Wise).
5. Monticello (Fort Bend, Titus).
6. Nopal (DeWitt, Presidio, Willacy).
7. Novice (Lamar, Coleman).
8. Oak Grove (Bowie, Denton, Ellis, Grayson, Tarrant, Wood).
9. Oak Hill (Milam, Rusk, Travis).
10. Pinehurst (Montgomery, Orange).
11. Shady Grove (Cherokee, Dallas, Hopkins, Upshur).
12. Shiloh (Denton, DeWitt, Limestone, Rusk, Williamson).

ACKNOWLEDGMENTS TO: *Jon P. Jehl, Corpus Christi.*

History and Politics

HOT DATES IN TEXAS HISTORY

1. One billion years B.C.: Major geological changes that will determine Texas' modern face begin to occur.

2. 1532, 1540: Alvar Nuñez Cabeza de Vaca and Francisco Vasquez de Coronado become, respectively, the earliest Europeans to push into the territory that will become Texas, starting three centuries of exploration, colonization, and development.

3. March 2, 1836: Delegates at a convention at Washington-on-the-Brazos adopt a declaration of independence, forming the Republic of Texas.

4. December 29, 1845: Texas gives up its status as an independent nation to become the 28th member of the United States of America.

5. February 1, 1861: The Texas Legislature overwhelmingly adopts a resolution to secede from the Union, joining the Confederacy in the Civil War.

6. January 3, 1959: Alaska joins the Union, knocking Texas from its long-enjoyed position as the biggest of the states. Hardly a red-letter day.

A SAMPLING OF HISTORICAL MARKERS

Not all Texas historical markers commemorate so-and-so's birthplace or what's-his-name's house. Other subjects found worthy of commemoration include:

1. Outlaws (Jesse James's last hideout, Archer City; the Dalton Gang's last raid, Longview).

2. Prehistoric animals (American mammoths, Amarillo; dinosaur tracks, Glen Rose).

3. Murders (assassination of John F. Kennedy, Dallas; Indian massacres, Leander and Barksdale, among others).

4. Fruit (Pecos cantaloupe, Pecos; red meat grapefruit, A&M Station, Weslaco).

5. Factories (gun caps, Fredericksburg; brooms, Round Rock).

6. Hanging trees (Goliad, Hallettsville).

7. Flagpoles (Goliad, Mobeetie).

8. Transportation (early streetcars, Bonham; the mule, Muleshoe).

9. Fences (drift fence, Dumas; barbed wire, Canyon).

10. Immigrants (Chinese farmers, Calvery; first Czech settlers, Nelsonville).

11. Geographic center of Texas (Brady).

12. Meteor crater (Odessa).

Source: *Texas Historical Commission.*

HYSTERICAL MARKERS

Historical markers whose importance is lost on us:

1. Hand-carved Carousel, Abilene.
2. Cattle Dipping Vat, Kingsville.
3. Steel Dust, Dallas.
4. Two-Wheel Fire Hose Reel, Hereford.
5. Town Without a Toothache, Hereford.
6. Falling Leaves, Jefferson.
7. Candy Kitchen, Lampasas.
8. Terminus of Mule-Drawn Streetcar, Lampasas.
9. Famous Picnic of 1906, Post.
10. First TV in Texas, Fort Worth.

SOURCE: *Texas Historical Commission.*

TOWNS WITH MORE THAN 50 HISTORICAL MARKERS

1. Austin, 177.
2. San Antonio, 129.
3. Galveston, 89.
4. Houston, 84.
5. Jefferson, 73.
6. Gonzales, 66.
7. Bastrop, 52.
8. Columbus, 52.
9. Victoria, 52.
10. El Paso, 51.

SOURCE: *Texas Historical Commission.*

UNEXPECTED TEXAS SITES ON THE NATIONAL REGISTER OF HISTORIC PLACES

1. Hanger 9, Brooks Air Force Base, San Antonio, Bexar County. Built in 1918, this hangar is considered the oldest remaining on any U.S. military base.

2. Paint Rock pictographs, Concho County. This is the largest archeological site in Texas.

3. Port Isabel Lighthouse, Cameron County. Built in 1852, it is probably the oldest functioning lighthouse on the Texas coast.

4. Quitaque Railway Tunnel, Floyd County. Over half a century old, it is one of the few railroad tunnels left in the state.

5. Kreische Brewery, La Grange, Fayette County. An Austrian immigrant built Texas' first brewery sometime in the 1850s.

6. Post Sanatorium, Garza County. Health care facility dates from 1912.

7. Lucas Gusher, Spindletop Field, Beaumont, Jefferson County. The gusher that shot up on January 10, 1901, marked the beginning of the modern petroleum industry. (In nearby Nacogdoches County is the site of the first producing well in the state.)

8. International Boundary Marker, Panola County. This granite post, 140 years old, is the last of the markers that indicated the boundary between the U.S. and the Republic of Texas.

9. Shafter Historic Mining District, Presidio County. From 1886 till 1926, this mine and smelter produced silver.

10. Carnegie Public Library, Tyler, Smith County. Built in 1904 with a grant from Andrew Carnegie, it is Texas' oldest functioning public library.

11. Texas & Pacific Railway Steam Locomotive 610, Fort Worth, Tarrant County. One of the last steam engines used on the old railroad, it dates to 1927.

12. Austin Moonlight Towers, Travis County. Twenty-one of these towers, built in 1895, are thought to be the only examples of an odd nineteenth-century lighting system.

13. Victoria Grist Windmill, Victoria County. Built in 1870, it was used for grinding corn.

14. Cass County Courthouse. The oldest continuously used courthouse in Texas, it was built in 1860.

15. Waco Suspension Bridge, McLennan County. It was the longest suspension bridge in the world when it was completed in 1870.

SOURCE: *Texas Historical Commission.*

OLDEST TEXAS HOUSES ON THE NATIONAL REGISTER OF HISTORIC PLACES

1. Los Nogales, pre-1765, Seguin, Guadalupe County. A small stucco cottage that was a station stop on El Camino Real (the King's Highway).

2. Oliphant House, circa 1820, Milam, Sabine County. A two-story log home, once part of a plantation-ferry-tavern complex.

3. Ellerslie Plantation, circa 1824, Brazoria, Brazoria County. A typical antebellum mansion with a steam-driven sugar mill.

4. McCroskey Log Cabin, circa 1824, Jones Creek, Brazoria County. The log house served as headquarters for a cotton plantation.

5. Jesus Trevino House, 1830, San Ygnacio, Zapata County. A long, stone house, the oldest in the San Ygnacio Historic District.

6. Mrs. Sam Houston House, circa 1830, Independence, Washington County. After Sam Houston died in 1863, his wife, Margaret Moffette Lea Houston, lived in this simple frame house.

7. Smathers-DeMorse House, 1833, Clarksville, Red River County. The first house built in a house-raising when the town was organized.

8. Asa Hoxey Home, 1833, Independence area, Washington County. A two-story plantation house built of logs.

9. James McGloin House, 1834, San Patricio, San Patricio County. A verandahed example of the Greek Revival style.

10. Braches Home, 1836, Gonzales County. A large two-story frame structure that once was a stagecoach stop.

11. Samuel May Williams House, built 1837–40, Galveston. A single-story home with sturdy Doric columns.

12. Michael B. Menard House (the Oaks), circa 1838, Galveston. Another Greek Revival house, this was the home of the founder of Galveston.

13. Turner-White-McGee House, circa 1840, Roganville, Jasper County. A typical example of frontier architecture.

14. French Legation, 1841, Austin, Travis County. It served as the home and headquarters of the French chargé d'affaires for the Republic of Texas.

SOURCE: *Texas Historical Commission.*

OLDEST TEXAS BUILDINGS: SPANISH MISSIONS

Spanish missions in Texas had three basic purposes: to convert the heathen Indians to Catholicism and to educate them; to establish Spanish footholds in the territory and ready it for widespread farming and ranching; and to form centers for defense between French Louisiana and Spanish Mexico. Below are seven missions that still stand today.

1. Mission San Antonio de Valero—the Alamo. Founded in 1718, the Alamo is a mission known round the world; it has, without a doubt, the most interesting history of any mission in Texas. Though its modest exterior and cool interior cannot convey the turmoil that its walls have seen, something about the Alamo—its austere and ghostly air—sets it apart in an emotional as well as a historical sense.

2. Mission Ysleta. Founded in 1682, Ysleta is the oldest mission in the state and the chief mission of the El Paso area. It ministered to the peaceable Tigua Indians, one of the few tribes still in Texas today.

3. Mission Nuestra Señora de la Purísma Concepción. Built in 1755 in San Antonio, Concepción was occasionally used as a fort during the Texas Revolution; it still serves as a church today.

4. La Bahía. More a presidio than a mission, La Bahía was used as a fort by Colonel James Fannin and his men, who dubbed it Fort Defiance. Originally built in Goliad in 1721, La Bahía has been totally reconstructed and restored.

5. Mission San Francisco de la Espada. Established in 1731, the "mission of the sword" is another of San Antonio's missions. Its irrigation system is believed to be the oldest in the United States.

6. Mission San José y San Miguel de Aguayo. The largest and probably the most beautiful of San Antonio's missions, San José, built in 1720, is especially noted for Rosa's Window, whose elaborate stone blossoms and tendrils seem almost real. The sculptor, Pedro Huizar, is said to have wrought the window's decorations for love of a girl named Rosa.

7. Mission San Juan Capistrano. Established in 1756 in San Antonio, San Juan was really only a small chapel. The ruins of a larger church remain nearby; it was never completed.

SIX FLAGS OF TEXAS

1. Spain, 1519–1685, 1690–1821.
2. France, 1685–1690.
3. Mexico, 1821–1836.
4. Republic of Texas, 1836–1845.
5. USA, 1845–1861, 1865–present.
6. Confederate States of America, 1861–1865.

CHIEF CHIEFS

1. Quanah Parker, last chief of the Comanche. Quanah—his name means fragrance—was the son of the famous Indian captive Cynthia Ann Parker and a minor chief, Peta Nocona. Born about 1852, Quanah was only eight when his mother was recaptured and his father killed during a battle with whites. He suffered taunts from his fellow tribesmen because of his mixed blood but proved himself a fierce fighter and a skilled hunter. When the chief of his band of Quahadi Comanche, Bear's Ear, died, Quanah, who was then only nineteen or so, assumed the chieftainship.

   Like many other tribes the Comanche were furious over the encroachment of the white man into Indian territory; the whites not only were killing off the buffalo for sport and commercial purposes but also were attacking the Indians regularly with far superior weapons. In 1874, stirred by the dire prophesying of the medicine man and warmonger Isatai, Quanah led one of the last Indian forays in Texas. Accompanied by 700 Cheyenne, Kiowa, and Comanche, he charged a small buffalo camp in Hutchison County at dawn. The camp, Adobe Walls, was occupied by only 29 people, who managed to stave off the war party. The attack was desultory at best, a last stab by a man who knew that his people were losing everything.

The following year the Comanche surrendered to the white men and permitted themselves to be resettled on federal reservations. Many prominent chiefs had died—Silver Medal, Iron Mountain, Big Red, Milky Way, Gray Leggings—and thus Quanah eventually was recognized as head of the tattered Comanche nation. Because he was half-white, he found himself an important personage still, if in a different way. He became nationally known, traveling to Washington many times to confer with the commissioners of Indian affairs; became reacquainted with his respected white relatives, who were willing to acknowledge him because of his political connections; and was befriended by such notables as cattleman Charles Goodnight. Though he took to wearing the white man's suits and hats, Quanah never cut his hair; he never learned to write, but he was known in both Indian and white worlds as assertive and intelligent. Two of his more colorful characteristics were his fondness for women—he acquired seven wives—and his introduction of peyote to the Comanche. He died in 1911.

2. Satanta, best-known chief of the Kiowa. Born about 1820, Satanta, or White Bear, was famed for his love of horses. He was a bold and fearless fighter, the possessor of a powerful medicine that permeated his famous war shield and protected him in battle. In his twenties he had already become a rival of the chief of his band, a fact that perhaps caused his utter arrogance. He was especially known for his daring and conspicuous raids, most of them against Texas settlements. One of his favorite ploys was to swoop down on a fort or camp in broad daylight and stampede all the horses, leaving the fuming soldiers behind.

After Texas became a state the whites fought harder and harder against the Indians; the many army posts that sprang up were yet another intrusion onto what the Indians considered their turf. Though Satanta was a fighter, he realized that the force of the whites would soon outweigh that of the Indians, and so he began to respond to the overtures of peace tendered by the whites. In 1867 he signed the Medicine Lodge treaty, but the peace didn't last long; each side felt that the other had reneged on the terms. As a result Satanta declared war, but soldiers under General Philip Sheridan captured him and released him only after he promised to remain on his best behavior and to accept relocation on a reservation. He did neither. The incident had only angered him further; he dispatched

NATIVE INDIAN TRIBES

1. Caddos (including the Hasinai, Caddo proper, and Wichita confederacies), who were spread across North, Northeast, and East Texas.

2. Karankawas (including the Atakapas, Arkokisas, and Bidais), across South Texas and the Gulf Coast.

3. Coahuiltecans, in South Texas and the Rio Grande Plains.

4. Tonkawas, in Central Texas.

5. Lipan Apaches, largely in West Texas and the Trans Pecos.

6. Comanches, from the Panhandle southward.

INDIAN TRIBES REMAINING IN TEXAS TODAY

1. Tiguas (El Paso).
2. Alabamas (Big Thicket).
3. Coushattas (Big Thicket)

OBSCURE INDIAN TRIBES

Most of which are long gone and can be spelled a dozen different ways.

1. Pampopa.
2. Patzaw.
3. Xarame.
4. Tamique.
5. Deadoses.
6. Cujanes.
7. Coapites.

HEROES OF THE ALAMO

1. William Barret Travis was commander of the Alamo at the age of 27. A native of South Carolina, he was also a lawyer. Travis is famed for drawing a line in the dirt of the mission grounds and saying to his men, "Those who are prepared to give their lives in freedom's cause, come over to me." All but one crossed the line.

2. James Bowie, age 41, shared command with Travis until he was stricken with typhoid-pneumonia. Even then he continued to fight; when Travis drew his famous line Bowie had his cot carried over. The famous Indian fighter left Texans the legacy of the Bowie knife.

3. Davy Crockett, allegedly born on a mountaintop in Tennessee, was the old man of the Alamo; in 1836 he was nearly fifty years old. The famous frontiersman had served in the Tennessee legislature and the U.S. Congress before coming to Texas to aid in the fight for independence.

4. James Bonham, like Travis, was a native South Carolinian and a lawyer. In fact, he went to law school with Travis. Dispatched during the siege to seek aid for the Texans trapped in the Alamo, Bonham returned through enemy lines to report to Travis and to lend support in the defense, though he knew the decision meant death.

PRESIDENTS OF TEXAS

1. David G. Burnet (March 16, 1836–October 22, 1836).
2. Sam Houston (October 22, 1836–December 10, 1838; December 13, 1841–December 9, 1844).
3. Mirabeau B. Lamar (December 10, 1838–December 13, 1841).
4. Anson Jones (December 9, 1844–February 19, 1846).

PEOPLE WHO HAVE BEEN GOVERNOR OF TENNESSEE, GOVERNOR OF TEXAS, AND PRESIDENT OF TEXAS.

1. Sam Houston.

ANTI-HEROES AND VILLAINS

1. Santa Anna has, for 150 years, been Texas' public enemy number one. A career military man, he is best remembered as the murderous general at the siege of the Alamo—at which time he was also president of Mexico. But his vilest act, bar none, was ordering the slaughter of James Fannin and the 400 other Texas fighters who surrendered at Goliad. Unfortunately, Santa Anna survived the Texas Revolution; he died in 1876.

2. Pancho Villa, born Doroteo Arango, was the best-known border bandit of them all. He and his henchmen, the Villistas, ruled the Rio Grande for almost twenty years; he was a well-known figure in El Paso. He frequently made raids against wealthy Mexican landowners and generously rewarded the many peons who helped him escape capture. As a result he became a somewhat unwitting social revolutionary. In 1916 Villa led the only enemy invasion of the U.S. mainland when he attacked a cavalry post at Columbus, New Mexico. His political power grew, but seven years later, he was ambushed and shot dead.

3. Juan Cortinas's reputation has always been somewhat eclipsed by Pancho Villa's, even though Cortinas not only came first but was far fiercer and much more dedicated to the welfare of his countrymen. He really was a Robin Hood; he hated the Anglos who were encroaching on Mexican lands and became a vigilante who sought justice for his people by sharing his loot with them. However, despite his principles, Cortinas was indisputably bloodthirsty; during his reign along the border in the 1860s he was involved in numerous skirmishes with Texas Rangers and cavalrymen that left some 250 people dead.

4. William Clarke Quantrill headed a band of Confederate guerrillas whose depredations in the name of loyalty to the South were beyond belief. He and his gang of bushwhackers, called Quantrill's Raiders, burned buildings and homes and looted them, often killing the occupants, on a regular basis. In 1863 Quantrill and his second-in-command, Bloody Bill Anderson, led an attack on the beleagured city of Lawrence in Bleeding Kansas. Among the raiders with him on that occasion were Cole Younger and Frank James as well as some 400 others, who cut down 150 men and burned the town in revenge for the territory's indecision over whether or not to permit slavery. Quantrill was killed by Union soldiers in 1865.

SCOUTS WHO WERE LOYAL, BRAVE, AND PROBABLY IRREVERENT

1. Jesse Chisholm, trader, interpreter, and guide, marked out many Texas cattle trails as well as the famous Chisholm Trail, which led from Wichita, Kansas, to Council Grove, Oklahoma. Millions of men and cattle traveled it.

2. Captain Billy Dixon was a buffalo hunter whose skill awed lesser marksmen. He once shot an Indian off his horse from seven eighths of a mile away. A scrappy fellow, he participated in many rescues of Indian captives and stranded trail parties.

3. El Turco, an Indian, began his ill-starred career working for explorer Cabeza de Vaca. Claiming to know of cities made all of gold and silver, he led the Spaniards in circles around the High Plains until, suspicious, they questioned him. He confessed he was lying, and they promptly killed him.

4. Charles Goodnight established, with Oliver Loving, the Goodnight-Loving Trail from Fort Belknap, Texas, to Fort Sumner, New Mexico. He also developed the Goodnight Trail from Alamogordo, New Mexico, to Granada, Colorado. His ranch, the JA, owned with John Adair, at one time covered a million acres. Goodnight is also credited with being one of the first to cross cattle and buffalo to get cattalo.

5. Oliver Loving, co-founder of the Goodnight-Loving Trail, also marked out the Shawnee Trail from Texas to Chicago and the Western Trail, heavily traveled highway from Texas to Kansas. In 1867, while leading a drive through New Mexico with Goodnight, Loving was attacked by Indians and badly hurt. Rescued, he was treated at a nearby fort, but gangrene set in. Aware that he was dying, he begged Goodnight to take his body home to Texas, saying he didn't want to be buried on foreign soil. Despite the hot sun and the considerable distance, Goodnight obliged.

6. William A. "Bigfoot" Wallace was an Indian fighter, a Texas Ranger, an expert tracker, and a hell of a storyteller. He guided buffalo hunting parties, scouted for the military, fought *banditos* along the border, and chased runaway slaves.

AUSTIN'S TWO UNCLE BILLYS

1. William "Uncle Billy" Barton, guide and Indian fighter, was one of the first settlers in Travis County, arriving in 1837 and settling near the cold springs that were later named for him.

2. William "Uncle Billy" Disch played baseball professionally before coming to Austin to coach at St. Edward's University and then, moving up to the big time, at the University of Texas. The UT baseball field was named for him.

FORGOTTEN BLACKS IN TEXAS HISTORY

1. John (last name unknown) was one of the 187 heroes who died in the Alamo.

2. Estevanico, or Black Stephen, was the body-servant of Cabeza de Vaca, and as such was probably the first black ever in Texas.

3. Sam McCulloch, a freedman who fought in the October 9 defense of Goliad in 1835, was the first soldier injured in the Texas Revolution.

4. Emily Morgan, a slave girl, is the subject of the song "The Yellow Rose of Texas."

5. Kiomatia, also a slave girl, accompanied Mrs. Jane Long, the "Mother of Texas," into the territory in 1821.

6. William Goyens, a freedman, was one of the first black businessmen. He arrived in Texas in 1820 and amassed a fortune from various operations including a hotel, a sawmill, and a smithy.

7. Richard "Uncle Dick" Seale founded the first Negro church in Texas, the Dixie Baptist Church in Jasper, built in 1850.

8. Jules Bledsoe, born in Waco in 1898, was the first baritone to sing the classic "Old Man River" (in a 1927 New York production of *Showboat*).

GREAT LADIES

1. Jane Long, the "Mother of Texas." Jane Herbert Wilkinson Long, born in Maryland in 1798, married Dr. James Long when she was seventeen. In 1819, her husband was named the head of a U.S. expedition into the Texas territory to extend its boundaries; Jane, with two small children, remained behind but soon changed her mind. With her two daughters, one three years old and one only two months, she booked passage up the Red River to overtake Dr. Long; her only other companion was a young slave girl named Kiomatia. During the trip her infant daughter died. She finally met James on the Sabine River, though he refused to permit her to continue with him and his men to Goliad. She went to Galveston Island, where she expected to find men for protection, but Jane and her charges found themselves all alone in a crude hut throughout the bitter winter. She was pregnant. Food and wood ran low; the women survived on raw oysters from the bay. Jane gave birth to another daughter shortly before Christmas. Months later, they were rescued by Texas soldiers who told Jane of her husband's death: he had surrendered to Mexican forces and, after imprisonment in San Antonio and Mexico, had been killed. Though history links Jane Long romantically with Ben Milam and Mirabeau B. Lamar, she never married again. She did stay in Texas, operating a boarding house. She died in 1880.

2. Susanna Dickenson, heroine of the Alamo. A native Tennessean, Susanna came to Texas with her husband in 1835 and settled in Gonzales. When the battle for Texas independence began, Almaron Dickenson enlisted as a lieutenant in the Texas artillery; at the advance of Santa Anna's troops he joined the ranks at the Alamo and, in an unusual move, brought his wife and baby daughter, Angelina, with him for safety. After the fighting was over, Almaron and 186 other men had died. Santa Anna spared the lives of Susanna and her baby; she led the pitiful, ragged survivors back home to Gonzales. On the way they met a contingent of Texas soldiers, who thus learned the news of the Alamo. Although several Mexican women and children were present in the Alamo, Susanna Dickenson, who was probably no more than eighteen years old, was the only Anglo woman present. She eventually remarried and lived in Austin till her death in 1857.

3. Cynthia Ann Parker, kidnap victim and mother of Quanah Parker, Texas' greatest Indian chief. In 1836 Cynthia Ann was only nine years old when she was captured in a Comanche raid on her family's home, Fort Parker, in what is now Limestone County. Her brother

80

John, another small child, and three adult women were also taken captive; her father, Silas, was one of many men killed. Rescue attempts proved futile and Cynthia Ann was given up for lost, but five years later a scouting party spotted her in a band of Comanche, though her Indian family refused to sell her. Two years later, traders on the Canadian River recognized the Indian woman as really white, but she refused to leave her Comanche home; she had married a chief, Peta Nocona, and had two sons, Pecos and Quanah. Then, in 1860, during a battle between state militiamen and her band, Cynthia Ann—now called Naduah—was taken captive again, this time by her native people. Her identity was confirmed when she recognized her white name. Though her husband was killed in the skirmish her two sons escaped, and she brought with her two-year-old daughter, Topsanah. Cynthia Ann went to live with an uncle and later a brother, but she could never readjust to the white man's world and never succeeded in her attempts to escape and return to the Indians. In 1864, her daughter died; Cynthia Ann died weeks later—some say of a broken heart. She was 37.

4. Elisabet Ney, sculptor. German-born Elisabet Ney studied art at Munich and later in Berlin in the 1850s, a considerable accomplishment for a German woman of that day. By her mid-twenties Elisabet had settled on sculpture as her preferred medium; she executed busts of such notables as Arthur Schopenhauer. Though she supposedly married a young Scottish doctor, Edmund Montgomery, in 1863, it is a matter of some doubt; at any rate, in a move way ahead of her time she insisted on using her maiden name all her life. Elisabet lived in Madeira for a while and then Italy, turning out busts of Bismarck and King William I of Prussia, among others. When she returned to Munich, to much acclaim, she was awarded a studio in the royal palace, but eventually the court grapevine spread rumors about her relationship with Dr. Montgomery and they decided to leave. In 1872 they emigrated to Texas. Elisabet devoted many years to raising her children and did not sculpt at all; neighbors regarded her as an eccentric or a witch. One story claims that when one of her children died of a sudden illness she threw the body into the fireplace and cremated it. In 1893 Elisabet was commissioned to sculpt statues of Sam Houston and Stephen F. Austin for the Chicago World's Fair; these two works are now exhibited in the State Capitol. Elisabet lived in Austin for the rest of her life, executing many more busts and statues and reveling in her fame. She died in 1907. Today her house is a museum of her works.

5. Clara Driscoll, the "Savior of the Alamo." Born in 1881, Clara Driscoll was educated in Europe. In 1903, when she was only 22, she bought the Alamo, intending to keep it from being razed; she not only saved it but restored it extensively. Without her there would be no Alamo today. Clara also wrote two novels as well as a musical comedy, *Mexicana,* that ran on Broadway. She served as president of a bank and as head of the Daughters of the Republic of Texas, and from 1928 to 1944 was Texas' Democratic National Committee delegate. She died at age 64.

6. Ima Hogg, philanthropist. Ima Hogg was the only daughter of James Stephen Hogg, the first native-born governor of Texas. Her father is said to have named her after the heroine in a poem; reputedly he was not aware of the unfortunate pairing of the names. Ima, who was educated abroad, was noted for her dedication to the arts; she served as president of the Houston Symphony League and was equally generous to it and to the Houston Museum of Fine Arts, to which she donated several major works. She used some of her great wealth, most of which came from family oil holdings, to establish a pioneering institution in child psychiatry. She restored her father's plantation house and donated it to Texas as a state park; she also restored many historic buildings in Winedale and gave them all to the University of Texas. For these acts she received UT's Distinguished Alumnus Award, becoming the first woman to be so honored. Her own huge River Oaks estate, the famous Bayou Bend, she donated to the Museum of Fine Arts. She lived to the ripe old age of 93.

7. Oveta Culp Hobby, publisher. Born in 1905 in Killeen, Oveta Culp Hobby began her distinguished career at age 21 when she was appointed parliamentarian of the Texas House of Representatives. A few years later, she met William Pettus Hobby, a former governor of Texas and a man many years her senior, who was head of the *Houston Post* (then the *Post-Dispatch*). Oveta began working for the *Post* after her marriage, moving up from assistant editor to book editor to executive vice-president. During World War II Oveta was named head of the Women's Army Corps; under her its ranks swelled from five thousand to two hundred thousand. She was awarded the Army's Distinguished Service Medal. In 1953 she became the first secretary of the new Department of Health, Education, and Welfare, and was the subject of a *Time* cover story. Her husband died in 1964, but Oveta still runs the *Post,* serving as editor and chairman of the board.

8. Lady Bird Johnson, former first lady and philanthropist. Born Claudia Alta Taylor, Lady Bird Johnson married Lyndon Baines Johnson in 1934; at that time the future president was merely a secretary to a congressman. Though she never branched out into politics as many politicians' wives did, Lady Bird was noted for her Southern graciousness and her dedication to conservation and beautification, particularly the spreading of native Texas shrubs and flowers; she is to a great extent responsible for the plantings of colorful wildflowers that brighten the sides of Texas highways. Lady Bird also has served as a regent of the University of Texas, her alma mater. Since her husband's death in 1973, she has lived in Austin, supervising the family's extensive holdings.

ACKNOWLEDGMENTS: *Neila Petrick, Dallas.*

FOOTNOTE WOMEN IN TEXAS HISTORY

1. María de Jesús de Agreda, religious mystic. Born in 1602 in Spain, María became wholly immersed in Catholicism by the age of 16. She claimed that when she fell into trances her soul floated out of her body and traveled to a strange and wild land where she preached the gospel to the natives. Her eerie pilgrimages continued for years. When her story was told to a priest who had worked with a tribe of Texas Indians, he was amazed; the tribe had told him, he said, of a mysterious woman dressed in blue who appeared to them and told them of Christianity. After this confirmation of her blessedness, María's fame spread; among her many visitors was King Philip IV of Spain.

2. Angelina, Indian heroine. Born in the late seventeenth century, Angelina was a young Hainai Indian girl who was taken in by Spanish missionaries because she seemed exceptionally bright. By her teens she had learned Spanish, French, and several Indian dialects and often served as a guide and interpreter for white men. Legend has it that she saved French explorer Francois de Bellisle from death at the stake by claiming him as her husband. Widely respected among her tribe, Angelina was instrumental in teaching them the fundamentals of Christianity; she herself lived most of her life in a mission. Angelina River and County were named for her.

3. Johanna Troutman and Sarah Dodson, the Betsy Rosses of Texas. Sarah Dodson is credited with sewing Texas' very first Lone Star flag. Made of red, white, and blue calico, it flew over Washington-on-the-Brazos, then the Texas capital, during the revolution. Johanna Troutman's flag, a single blue star on a field of white, bore the legend "Liberty or Death." It was raised over the Texas fort at Goliad and waved there until burned by the Mexican armies.

4. Pamela Mann, frontierswoman. During the Texas Revolution, Sam Houston's army took from Pamela Mann a yoke of strong oxen to pull two heavy cannon. Furious—and none too patriotic—Pamela overtook the army and belabored the soldiers until they returned her livestock. She later moved to Houston where she ran the Mansion House hotel; she was noted for her ability—and willingness—to evict personally any rambunctious or penniless customers. In 1839 she was sentenced to death for the piddling offense of forgery but was pardoned by President Mirabeau B. Lamar. Though she had a somewhat seedy reputation all her life, she moved in the best Texas society.

5. Angelina Belle Eberly, heroine of the Archive War. In 1842, because of the threat to Austin by approaching Mexican armies during the Mexican War, Sam Houston ordered the capital of Texas relocated from Austin to Houston. When a group of overzealous volunteer rangers swarmed upon Austin to remove the papers and parapher-nalia of state, a furious Angelina Eberly repelled them by firing off a cannon. The rangers took the papers, regardless, but a group of Austin vigilantes, inspired by the feisty Angelina, followed the group and retrieved the archives, which because of her stayed in Austin for good.

6. Sophia Suttonfield Porter, Confederate heroine. Sophia is best remembered for her bravery during the Civil War. Having learned of the approach of federal troops, she crossed the swollen Red River —no small feat for a wispy lady in her fifties—to alert Colonel James Bourland and his men. Sophia was married three times: her first husband left her and, after obtaining a divorce, she married the famous trader Holland Coffee, who was murdered by Indians, and then George Butts, who was shot down by William Clarke Quantrill. Sophia certainly never lacked excitement in her life.

7. Lucy Holcombe Pickens, "Queen of the Confederacy." Lucy grew up in Marshall and later married Francis Wilkinson Pickens, who in 1858 became U.S. ambassador to Russia; the czarina was god-mother to Lucy's first child. In 1860, when the family returned to the

U.S., Lucy's husband was elected governor of South Carolina. "Lady Lucy" became a staunch supporter of the Confederacy; she sold silver and jewels to finance Rebel troops, and she was the only woman whose picture ever appeared on Confederate money.

8. Lizzie Johnson, cattle queen. Lizzie began her career as a bookkeeper for several cattle dealers and thus learned the business herself. In 1871, at age 29, she registered her own brand and then went on to become the only woman ever to drive her own herd up the Chisholm Trail. She married at age 38 but always kept her business and money separate from her husband's. After his death, she became a miser, subsisting on very little; when she died, she left an estate valued at $250,000.

9. Sarah Borginnis, the "Great Western." Sarah was a tall Texan; reputedly she stood six foot two. During the Mexican War, the stout Sarah followed her husband, a soldier in then-General Zachary Taylor's infantry, and served the men as laundress, cook, nurse, gunsmith, and morale booster. She was said to have rivaled Sam Houston for toughness and tenacity, and her reputation as a fighter put the fear of God into the burliest of men. Her nickname, given to her by the soldiers she ministered to, indicates their respect for her.

10. Sally Scull, a native Texan, was probably born about 1820. She was a well-known rancher in Bee County. At the beginning of the Civil War Sally, a loyal Rebel, undertook a dangerous mission to keep the Confederacy supplied with guns and ammunition. Joining up with a band of Mexican mercenaries, she negotiated with Texas growers to haul cotton across the border and sell it in return for supplies. She made several such trips during the war. After the South fell, Sally returned to ranching and also dabbled in horse trading. She was married three times. Though it was never proved, her last husband was rumored to have murdered her; at any rate, she vanished, and her body was never found.

FIVE UNSUNG HEROES AND HEROINES

1. Unknown four-year-old girl who sacrificed her new blue dress to supply first-place ribbons for Texas' first rodeo in Pecos in 1883.

2. Unknown woman who died in 9500 B.C. or thereabouts and many years later became one of the oldest victims of male chauvinism when she was unearthed and christened "Midland Man."

3. Ann Whitney, a teacher massacred by Comanches while trying to protect her pupils at the Hamilton school in 1867.

4. Sheriff T. J. Faught of Snyder, who didn't believe in guns, astonishingly enough, and who used a wooden pool cue if a show of force was called for.

5. The mule, for having meat so tough and stringy that Indians wouldn't eat him—thus causing the decline of many tribes that wouldn't interfere with mule trains carrying supplies to forts.

CONTRIBUTOR: *A. Ruff, Bellaire.*

BATTLES ONLY TEXANS WOULD HAVE FOUGHT

1. Battle of the Alamo. Estimates of the number of Mexican troops at the siege vary from 1000 to 5000, depending on whether you're asking a Mexican, a Yankee, or a Texan. Whatever the number, Santa Anna's men grossly outnumbered the 187 men in the mission-turned-fort.

2. Battle of San Jacinto. This time the Texans, under Sam Houston, had 900 men, but Santa Anna had half again as many Mexicans. Still, Sam and his men conducted a complete rout of the enemy, catching them sadly unawares during siesta and effecting a total surrender in a mere eighteen minutes. Nine Texans died; the Mexicans lost 600.

3. Battle of Sabine Pass. This embarrassingly fruitless attempt by Union naval forces to invade Texas during the Civil War began when a detachment of eighteen ships carrying heavily armed troops stationed itself off Sabine Pass and sent two gunboats to check out the Texans' defenses. The boats headed up the channel to Fort Sabine, where they were met with a volley of fire from Lieutenant

Dick Dowling and his 42 men. The Texans quickly disabled one boat and grounded the other by luring it too close to shore. In 45 minutes Dowling and his handful of men had taken two federal ships without sustaining a single injury. Thus routed, the Northern fleet quickly headed out and never returned.

4. Second Battle of Adobe Walls. The first battle of Adobe Walls was a full-fledged attack on Indians by Kit Carson and his cavalrymen, but that victory was nothing compared to the courage of the participants of the second skirmish, fought ten years later in 1874. Just before dawn on June 27, the 29 members of a buffalo camp in Hutchinson County were jerked awake when the ridgepole of a tent snapped. While they were repairing it, hunters spotted a huge party of Indian raiders on a mesa overlooking the camp. The Indians numbered 200 to 700, according to various historians, but the well-armed whites held them off for five days, losing four men but doing considerably more damage themselves. When a rescue party finally arrived, the Indians had given up and gone home.

CIVIL WAR EVENTS NOT MENTIONED IN MOST TEXAS HISTORY BOOKS

1. The defeat and retreat of Henry Sibley's invading Texas army in New Mexico in 1862. He had tried to rout the federal troops there.

2. The execution of wounded Texas-German Unionists after the Battle of the Nueces River.

3. The mass hanging of forty suspected Unionists without trial in Gainesville, also in 1862.

4. The defeat of Texas Confederates at the first Battle of Palmito Hill, near Brownsville, in 1864.

5. Texas' execution of captured Union troops after the final land battle of the war at Palmito Hill in May of 1865. (No black Union soldiers in the fight were taken alive.)

CONTRIBUTOR: *Captain John M. Hutchins, Fort Hood.*

UNION CIVIL WAR GENERALS FROM TEXAS

1. Andrew J. Hamilton.
2. Edmund J. Davis (later a Republican governor).

CONTRIBUTOR: *Frank W. Latham, Jr., Waco.*

AIRCRAFT OF THE GHOST SQUADRON, CONFEDERATE AIR FORCE BASE

1. Curtiss P-40 Warhawk: a tough little American Air Corps fighter favored by Claire Chennault and his Flying Tigers.

2. Messerschmitt Bf 109: probably the most famous Nazi airplane of World War II.

3. F4U Corsair: the Japanese called it "Whistling Death."

4. Spitfire: doughty little plane used by the Royal Air Force to defend England from Nazi attacks. More Spitfires were produced than any other Allied warplane.

5. P-47 Thunderbolt: the largest and heaviest of single-engine warplanes but still capable of climbing amazingly high. It once appeared on the cover of *Life.*

6. P-51 Mustang: fought everywhere in World War II and later was used in the Korean conflict. Its cousins were the P-38 and P-47.

7. P-38 Lightning: a warplane, bomber, and night fighter used in every theater of war.

8. Heinkel He 111: glass-nosed Nazi bomber, one of only six known to exist.

9. P-39 Airacobra: the smallest flier of the war, it had a cannon built into its nose. Its relative was the P-63 Kingcobra.

10. F4F Wildcat: a sturdy fighter with an impressive combat record. Its sisters were the F6F Hellcat, the most frequently used carrier-based fighter, and the F8F Bearcat, noted for its ability to climb sharply.

11. B-25 Mitchell: a fleet of these bombers, commanded by Jimmy Doolittle, undertook an incredible attack on Japan in 1942.

12. B-26 Marauder: another tough bomber. The Confederate Air Force's plane is believed to be the only flyable Marauder left in the world.

13. B-17 Flying Fortress: the name alone evoked confidence. The CAF's two Fortresses are dubbed *Sentimental Journey* and *Texas Raiders*.

14. B-24 Liberator: a high-speed, long-range bomber. It participated in the 1943 raid on Nazi oil refineries.

15. SB2C Helldiver: its crewmen called it the "Big-tailed Beast."

16. SBD Dauntless: the Navy's standard carrier-based reconnaissance plane and dive bomber.

17. C-47 Skytrain: the usual air transport during the war, it also was used in Viet Nam.

18. B-29 Superfortress: this giant bomber's attacks on Japan's Pacific holdings and later on Japan itself hastened the Allied victory.

SOURCE: *Confederate Air Force, Harlingen.*

FAMOUS TEXAS SOLDIERS OF WORLD WAR II

1. Audie Murphy was the most decorated soldier of World War II. Born in Hunt County, he joined the Army on his eighteenth birthday. He fought in North Africa, Sicily, and Italy and was twice injured while fighting in France. In January of 1945, alone on a battlefield with a field telephone to direct artillery fire, Murphy killed or wounded fifty Germans with a machine gun. For his bravery he was awarded the Congressional Medal of Honor, Distinguished Service Cross, the Purple Heart, and every other single combat medal offered by the Army. When he came home he was a national hero. He went on to star in some three dozen movies, mostly westerns, although *To Hell and Back* was based on his own experiences in the war. Murphy died in a plane crash in 1971.

2. Chester Nimitz, admiral, was born in Fredericksburg in 1885. He graduated from the U.S. Naval Academy at age twenty. Early in his career, on one of his first commands, he ran a destroyer aground in Manila Bay and was court-martialed for it, but the incident didn't affect his rise in the Navy. He served in World War I and later was

instrumental in setting up the Naval ROTC. When the Japanese bombed Pearl Harbor, Nimitz was promoted to full admiral and became commander-in-chief of the Pacific Fleet. On September 1, 1945, he signed the agreement of Japanese surrender aboard the battleship *Missouri* in Tokyo Bay. He died in 1966.

3. Claire Chennault, organizer of the Flying Tigers, was born in Commerce in 1890. A skilled aviator and a World War I veteran, he retired in 1937 from the U.S. Air Corps and became an adviser to Chiang Kai-shek and the Chinese Air Force. He organized the Flying Tigers in 1941, and the group of American pilots made a name for themselves as fierce and courageous fliers. Their assistance to the Chinese included defense of the Burma Road. In 1943 the Tigers were officially named the 14th Air Force. Chennault, a major general, won many medals, including the Distinguished Flying Cross. He died in 1958.

AGGIES WHO WON THE CONGRESSIONAL MEDAL OF HONOR

1. Private First Class Daniel R. Edwards, class of 1912. In July 1918 in France, while returning to the front lines from the field hospital where he had been treated for wounds, he crawled into an enemy trench and killed four Germans. He captured four more.

2. Second Lieutenant Lloyd D. Hughes, class of 1943. During a 1943 bombing raid over Nazi oil refineries, Hughes's plane was hit twice. Though it caught fire, he continued the attack and was killed.

3. Lieutenant Thomas W. Fowler, class of 1943. While under fire at Anzio, he organized the survivors of two infantry platoons and led them through a minefield, then tended to the wounded. He was unhurt, but died ten days later in another battle.

4. Staff Sergeant George D. Keathley, class of 1935. Taking command when all company officers were killed in a Nazi counterattack near Rome, he treated the injured and crawled from body to body, recovering bullets. Mortally wounded by a grenade, Keathley nevertheless stood up and fired his rifle until he collapsed and died.

5. Lieutenant Turney W. Leonard, class of 1942. After all his infantry's officers died, he assumed command and led an attack. Though wounded, he directed tank fire, killed several snipers, and knocked

out a machine-gun nest. After losing part of his arm, he headed for the field hospital, but was never seen again.

6. Lieutenant Eli Whitney, class of 1941. During fighting in Germany in 1944, he killed nine Germans and captured 23 more, despite being wounded in the arm, shoulder, and eye.

7. Marine Sergeant William Harrell, attended 1939–41. While on watch at Iwo Jima, Harrell lost both hands in a grenade attack. Before he was hurt he managed to kill at least five Japanese soldiers, and, amazingly, was found alive the next morning after the fighting.

8. Major Horace S. Carswell, Jr., attended 1934–35. When the bomber Carswell was piloting was hit off the coast of Japan in 1945, he continued flying the plane so that his crew could escape. He died in the crash. Carswell Air Force Base near Fort Worth is named for him.

SOURCE: *Texas A & M.*

U.S. PRESIDENTS WHO WERE BORN IN TEXAS

1. Dwight David Eisenhower, 34th president of the U.S., was born in Denison, a small town near Sherman in Grayson County, on October 14, 1890. The family moved to Kansas shortly afterward.

2. Lyndon Baines Johnson, our 36th president, was born on his parents' ranch near Stonewall in rural Gillespie County on August 27, 1908.

U.S. PRESIDENTS WHO DIED IN TEXAS

1. John Fitzgerald Kennedy, shot to death on November 22, 1963, as his presidential motorcade moved down Elm Street in Dallas. The president, who had been traveling in an open car with his wife Jacqueline, was struck in the neck and head. He was rushed to Parkland Memorial Hospital and pronounced dead at 1:00 p.m.

2. Lyndon Baines Johnson, who died in the same place where he was born: the Johnson ranch outside Stonewall. He suffered a fatal coronary on January 22, 1973.

TEN PRESIDENTIAL CANDIDATES WHO WON TEXAS.

As Texas goes, so goes the nation.

1. 1944: Roosevelt (Democrat).
2. 1948: Truman (Democrat).
3. 1952: Eisenhower (Republican).
4. 1956: Eisenhower.
5. 1960: Kennedy (Democrat).
6. 1964: Johnson (Democrat).
7. 1968: Nixon (Republican).
8. 1972: Nixon.
9. 1976: Carter (Democrat).
10. 1980: Reagan (Republican).

GEORGE BUSH'S LIST OF THINGS NO POLITICIAN EVER WANTS TO HEAR

George Bush is vice president of the United States.

1. "I bet you don't remember me, do you?"
2. "You're him? I thought you were much younger."
3. "The stations want their money for that media buy right away, and we don't have it. Somebody will have to sign a note."
4. "The dinner's tomorrow night and we've sold only twenty tables."

SIX TEXANS WHO WERE NAMED U.S. AMBASSADORS

1. George Bush (to the UN).
2. Anne Armstrong (to England).
3. Henry Catto (to El Salvador).
4. Ed Clark (to Australia).
5. Robert Krueger (to Mexico).
6. Mirabeau B. Lamar (to Nicaragua).

CONTRIBUTOR: *Susan Glick, Houston.*

GOVERNORS WHO LEFT OFFICE PREMATURELY

1. Henry Smith (provisional colonial governor before Texas gained its independence), 1835: impeached because of disagreements with Texas' fledgling politicians.

2. Sam Houston, December 21, 1859–March 16, 1861: resigned because of Texas' secession from the Union.

3. Francis R. Lubbock, November 7, 1861–November 5, 1863: left to join the Confederate Army.

4. Pendleton Murrah, November 5, 1863–June 12, 1865: administration ended with the fall of the Confederacy.

5. Elisha Pease, August 8, 1867–September 30, 1869: a Reconstruction governor appointed under martial law, he resigned.

6. Richard Coke, January 15, 1874–December 1, 1876: resigned to enter the U.S. Senate.

7. James E. "Pa" Ferguson, January 19, 1915–August 12, 1917: impeached on several charges, most of which alleged that he misappropriated public funds.

8. W. Lee "Pappy" O'Daniel, January 17, 1939–August 4, 1941: resigned to enter the U.S. Senate.

9. Beauford H. Jester, January 21, 1947–July 11, 1949: the only Texas governor ever to die in office.

REPUBLICAN GOVERNORS

1. Edmund J. Davis, 1870–74. The most unpopular governor in Texas history.

2. William P. Clements, 1978–present. Self-made millionaire who stunned Democrats by defeating John L. Hill.

WOMEN WHO WERE POLITIC FIRSTS

1. Mrs. L. P. Carlisle, first woman officeholder in the state, appointed clerk of Hunt County, 1902.

2. Annie Webb Blanton, first woman to run for office in Texas after women got the vote, 1918.

3. Minnie Fisher Cunningham, foremost fighter for woman's suffrage in Texas, first woman to run for governor and for U.S. Senate.

4. Jessie Daniel Ames, first president of the Texas League of Women Voters, 1918.

5. Marguerite Reagan Davis, first woman presidential elector from Texas, 1918.

6. Edith Therrel Wilmans, first woman state legislator, elected on a Ku Klux Klan ticket, 1922.

7. Miriam A. "Ma" Ferguson, first and only woman governor of Texas and first woman elected governor in any state, 1925.

8. Emma G. Meharg, first woman secretary of state (under Ma Ferguson), 1925.

9. Margie Neal, first woman elected to the Texas Senate, 1926.

10. Sarah T. Hughes, first woman named a state court judge, 1935. First Texas woman appointed a federal judge, 1961.

11. Lera Thomas, first Texas woman to serve in the U.S. Congress, 1966. She finished her husband's term after his death.

12. Barbara Jordan, first black to serve in the state senate since the nineteenth century; first black woman elected to the state senate, 1966, first Texas woman elected to the U.S. Congress, first black woman from the South to serve in Congress, 1972.

CURIOUS DAYS OBSERVED BY THE TEXAS LEGISLATURE

1. Confederate Heroes Day, January 19.
2. Casimir Pulaski Day, October 11.
3. Poetry Day, October 15.
4. Father of Texas Day, November 3.

Crime and Law

YO-HO-HO AND A BOTTLE OF BEER: A TRIO OF FAMOUS PIRATES

1. Jean Lafitte, one of the best-known pirates of all, was a flighty, vain fellow; his brother, Pierre, was actually the brains of the team. The two sailed up and down the Gulf of Mexico for almost twenty years; by the late 1810s they were virtually the kings of Galveston. Though French-born, they often served as agents for the governments of Spain and Mexico, garnering a considerable amount of influence as a result. The Lafittes weren't all bad; once, during a severe hurricane, Jean moved out of his Galveston mansion and into a leaky ship to allow his home to be used as a hospital.

2. Louis-Michel Aury, famed as a blockade runner, was a lifelong rival of the Lafittes. He, too, was born in France, and by the time he was 25 had acquired his own ship as well as a reputation as a daring skipper—and as an unpopular one, since he was the subject of more than one mutiny. His men patroled the Gulf, looking for cargo-laden ships to plunder and always spoiling for a fight. Aury was

financially successful—one of his takes was worth over three quarters of a million dollars—but because of the Lafittes' power he was never able to establish himself along the Texas Coast.

3. William Black, a Confederate pirate, was a native of New Orleans. After being wounded at the battle of Shiloh, he turned to privateering, running the Union blockade at New Orleans to ferry cotton to England. He was successful many times, once escaping the clutches of the Northern soldiers by convincing them he was British. During an attempt to capture a Union ship, Black himself was captured; he was court-martialed for piracy and sentenced to death but, through his usual luck, was pardoned after serving a short term in jail. He became a landlubber and was one of the first Texas breeders of Angora goats.

OUTLAWS

1. John Wesley Hardin was the most famous Texas gunfighter of them all. He shot at least 40 men in his career, starting with a Negro when he was 15. Fleeing from Union soldiers who wanted to prosecute, he nipped the problem in the bud by simply shooting them, too. He perfected a deadly cross-hand draw, grabbing for each gun with the opposite hand and coming up with two guns blazing. At 21, he made the mistake of killing a sheriff, an act that set both the Pinkerton detectives and the Texas Rangers on his trail. Nabbed, he was tried, but pleaded his own case so eloquently that the jury decided on a prison sentence instead of hanging. He served 16 years, getting out only to be shot down in 1895 by Constable John Selman, who put a bullet into the back of his head. Hardin never had a chance to draw.

2. Sam Bass, stage- and train-robber, headed for Texas in 1874, when he was 23. He worked at cowpunching for a while, but quickly tired of honest labor and turned to crime. Though he never made more than $100 in any take from a stage, he was noted for the little nicety of returning one dollar to each passenger so each could eat a meal. Moving on up to train-robbing, he netted an astonishing $60,000 in his first holdup of the Union Pacific. He hit four more trains, but the pickings were slim after that; bored and greedy, he decided to turn to bank-robbing. At Cove Hollow, his famous hideout near Denton, he planned the heist in detail, unaware that a traitor was in his gang—Jim Murphy, who had infiltrated the band in exchange

for a sizable reward. In 1878, when Bass arrived in Round Rock to scope out the town, he was cut down by a hail of bullets from Texas Rangers.

3. Clay Allison, gunfighter, might have been a great one if it hadn't been for his love of booze; he was well known in every saloon in the Panhandle. He was really more of a hired gun than a true gunfighter; his run-ins with other fast draws were often resolved by his shooting his competitor dead immediately, before he could be challenged to a fair duel. One story says that he and a foe, both intoxicated, dug a grave, then fought in it to save the loser's friends some trouble (Allison won). Another tale claims that he ate dinner with an enemy while both kept their guns on the table, but later pulled a hidden gun and shot the fellow dead as he drank his coffee. Liquor did prove to be Allison's undoing; in 1882, while drunk, he fell off a wagon and was crushed under its wheels.

4. Black Jack Ketchum, killer and robber, always teetered on the edge of insanity. No one knows where he got his nickname, but it was a popular sobriquet of the day (though Ketchum claimed to be the original Black Jack). With his brother, Sam, Ketchum undertook a cross-country crime spree in the 1890s, robbing trains, stages, post offices, general stores, railroad ticket offices, and wealthy individuals. It is indicative of his reputation that when he once sought refuge with Butch Cassidy's gang at the famous Hole in the Wall, the outlaws would have nothing to do with him. He was finally caught after he killed two men in an argument over cards. He was hung in 1901 in Clayton, New Mexico.

5. William P. Longley, gunfighter and killer, was a man much in the shadow of John Wesley Hardin. They were contemporaries, but the reckless Hardin seemed to garner all the attention, diverting what Longley felt was his fair share of fame. Like Hardin, he was a teenager when he killed his first man, who, like Hardin's first victim, was black. Longley was rabidly opposed to freeing the slaves; he would sometimes shoot black men on sight, and his favorite hobby was robbing and roughing up the hated carpetbaggers and tax collectors. He had a short fuse; once he blew a man's head off when the poor fellow made a rude remark about Texans. He had some thirty notches on his gun—ten less than Hardin had. Arrested for murder, he was condemned to death—a sentence he bitterly resented. It wasn't so much the dying he minded; it was the fact that Hardin got only a prison term. He was hung in 1877.

6. Johnny Ringo, like many of his peers, was a drifter, cowpuncher, killer, and gunman, but of a lesser breed. He began his career as a minor desperado in the 1870s and claimed to have ridden with Hardin, Sam Bass, and the deadly Clanton gang. Ringo (real name: Ringgold) was hired to participate in the Hoo Doo War, a Mason County feud that began when a local rancher was lynched for rustling and his friends plotted revenge. In 1882, Ringo's body was found outside Tombstone, Arizona; he had been shot once in the chest. Some say he finally lost a fight; others claim he killed himself.

BAD WOMEN

1. Bonnie Parker, born in 1911 in Rowena, was half of Texas' most famous desperado couple. She met Clyde Barrow while visiting her husband in prison; when Clyde was released, she joined up with him and they hit the road, robbing the Abilene State Bank for starters. The daring duo reaped lots of press coverage because of Bonnie, who reveled in her fame. She once left behind in a motel room a photo of herself in a cocky pose, gun in hand, cigar in mouth, foot resting on the bumper of a getaway car. Tiny and golden-haired, she didn't look like a killer, but she and Clyde murdered at least nine people. On May 23, 1934, they were ambushed by a contingent of law officers who riddled them with bullets.

2. Belle Starr, the "Bandit Queen," moved with her family to Texas in 1862, when she was sixteen. Though she was brought up in a devout family, Belle was a black sheep. She somehow met Cole Younger, provided him with a hideout for a while, and bore him a child; then she took up with a minor outlaw, Jim Reed, who was later killed in a gunfight. Next Belle joined a band of horse thieves. One of them, half-breed Sam Starr, became her new lover. Sam, too, died in a gunfight, and two years later, in 1889, Belle was shot down by an unknown assailant. Like Bonnie Parker, Belle was nothing but a common criminal whom popular legend romanticized as a beautiful and daring adventurer. She was ugly as sin to boot.

3. Frenchy McCormick made a name for herself as the prettiest saloon-keeper in Texas. Her real name is unknown, though she acquired her nickname because of her Creole heritage. In Tascosa, which was called the Cowboy Capital of the Plains, she was much in demand as a gambler and monte dealer — but though she bestowed her favors on many, she waited to marry a rich suitor, thus getting her own

saloon. Her change in marital status didn't affect her popularity; men still flocked around her tables. When the Texas railroads expanded they passed Tascosa by, and it dwindled to a mere village. But Frenchy never left; even after the death of her husband, she stayed on in a ghost town. She died in 1941.

4. Chipita Rodriguez was the first and only woman ever legally hung in Texas. In November 1863, she was accused of stabbing a man whose body was found floating in a river near her cabin in San Patricio County. Though there was no direct evidence to link her to the crime, she was found guilty and sentenced to death. She was executed on a Friday the thirteenth, and her ghost is said to haunt the place where she died.

5. Juana Navarro (later Mrs. Horace Alsbury) was, according to Alamo heroine Susanna Dickenson, a traitor who left the Alamo and rendezvoused with Santa Anna to report the situation inside the fort. Juana claimed that she never left the Alamo and was inside when it fell, but no one ever backed up her story. Despite her feeble defense, she was awarded a pension from the Texas government.

6. Kathryn Kelly, wife of the infamous gunsel George "Machine Gun" Kelly, grew up in Fort Worth. She married George because she was thrilled to be associated with the shady underworld, though at the time he was nothing but a small-time hood. Reputedly she gave him his nickname, deciding that it sounded appropriately gangsterish. She pushed him into robbing banks, which he was fairly good at, and then, lusting for greater gain, convinced him to attempt the kidnapping of a rich oilman. The plan failed miserably; Machine Gun and his moll were nabbed immediately and both given life sentences. He died in prison; after her release, she disappeared, to go down in history as a two-bit shrew.

7. Candace Mossler's 1966 trial for murder was one of the nation's most lurid. The platinum blonde was tried with Melvin Lee Powers, her 24-year-old nephew, for the murder of her husband, a multimillionaire. Candy, 46, and Jacques Mossler, 69, lived in the elegant River Oaks section of Houston. In June of 1964, Jacques was staying in Miami, Florida, when Candy and Melvin arrived there separately. On the night of June 30, the elderly man was attacked and stabbed 39 times by an intruder in his hotel room. Despite discrepancies in Candy's statements, a Dade County jury acquitted the two of the crime—swayed, in part, by the dramatic technique of Percy Foreman, the colorful Houston lawyer. Spicy rumors about the nature of the relationship between middle-aged Candy and her handsome nephew also livened up the trial. Candy married again in

1972. Her young husband suffered a curious accident one night, somehow slipping and falling from the roof outside Candy's third-floor bedroom window; he was seriously hurt, and they were later divorced. In 1976 Candy died during a heavily drugged sleep.

BAD LAWMEN

1. Ben Thompson, city marshal and murderer, was born in 1843 in England. He eventually ended up in Austin, where he ran a saloon and faro parlor with Phil Coe (who was later killed by Wild Bill Hickok). In 1880 Thompson ran for city marshal and, because of his fearsome skill with a gun—he was said to have killed 32 men in his career—the crime rate dropped to an all-time low. In 1882, while gallivanting in San Antonio, Ben got into an argument with Jack Harris, owner of the Vaudeville Theatre, and shot Harris dead. He was tried but acquitted. Two years later he made the mistake of again visiting the Vaudeville Theatre; while he was there, Harris's friends gunned him down as he watched a show.

2. J.K. "King" Fisher, sheriff, murderer, and cattle rustler, came from Tennessee. He worked with a justice of the peace just long enough to learn how the cattle rustlers he helped to arrest plied their trade; then he switched sides. During the 1870s he was the scourge of the Texas border, a master rustler who drove huge numbers of cattle and horses across the Rio Grande to Mexico. He didn't take kindly to interruption; he supposedly killed a dozen men, most of whom had ignored the signs he posted on many trails reading "This is King Fisher's road. Take another one." He was fond of fancy clothes and partying and was enjoying both when he was murdered with Ben Thompson at San Antonio's Vaudeville Theatre.

3. Constable John Selman, killer of John Wesley Hardin, started off his unorthodox law career by joining a vigilante group that administered extralegal penalties, such as death, to any unfortunate rustlers whom they caught. On the side, though, Selman himself was a rustler; once he disposed of a good-sized herd by butchering it and selling it to the Army. Drifting to El Paso, he worked on developing a tough reputation—which wasn't terribly hard since he was a pretty good shot and mean as hell to boot. On August 19, 1895, after hearing that John Wesley Hardin had made threats against him, Selman walked up behind Hardin, who was playing dice in the Acme Saloon, and shot him twice in the back of the head.

Arrested, he claimed that Hardin had spotted him in the mirror over the bar and had started to draw—a lie, but the county jury didn't really care that Hardin was dead, and Selman was acquitted on his plea of self-defense. A year later, he was killed by Deputy U.S. Marshal George Scarborough.

4. Jack Helm, murderous captain of E. J. Davis's State Police, came to Texas after the Civil War; where he came from isn't known. He was one of the self-appointed "regulators" who took it upon themselves to settle the famous Sutton-Taylor feud (by deciding that the Suttons were in the right). He and his henchmen carried on a bloody campaign in DeWitt and other counties, killing 21 members of the Taylor faction, and then Helm killed two more while he headed the State Police. Dismissed from his job by Governor E. J. Davis, he continued his reign of terror after the Suttons elected him sheriff of DeWitt County. In 1873, though, he was killed when one of the Taylors, acting on a tip from family cousin John Wesley Hardin, ambushed him.

NOT-SO-BAD LAWMEN

1. Judge Roy Bean, the "Law West of the Pecos," lived in San Antonio for twenty years before moving to tiny Langtry to open the famous Jersey Lilly saloon. He started to call himself "Judge" even before the Texas Rangers made him a justice of the peace. The Jersey Lilly (named after English actress Lillie Langtry, as Bean also claimed the town was) was the only courthouse for miles around, and Bean soon developed quite a following. He was noted for his curious handling of cases. Once, trying an Irishman for the murder of a Chinese worker, he opened court only to face dozens of angry—and armed—friends of the defendant. He then ruled that he could find no law that specifically forbade "shooting a Chinaman." Another time, when an unidentified corpse was discovered with a gun and forty dollars on it, the judge fined the dead man forty dollars for carrying a concealed weapon. Bean rarely left his saloon-*cum*-courthouse, and he died there in 1903.

2. Pat Garrett, the man who shot Billy the Kid, worked in Texas as a cowboy and buffalo hunter before moving to Fort Sumner, New Mexico, in 1878. Two years later he became sheriff of the county, having won the post by virtue of a promise to track down and kill Billy the Kid, with whom he often gambled in area saloons. Garrett

kept the promise; in 1881 he crept up on the Kid at a hideout on a local ranch and ambushed him in the dark. The young outlaw died not knowing who shot him. Garrett enjoyed a fierce notoriety as the slayer of the dreaded Kid. While riding on the crest of his fame, he moved back to Texas and organized his own group of Rangers. Garrett himself met his death by ambush, shot dead by an angry tenant on his ranchland in 1908.

3. Frank Hamer, who halted Bonnie and Clyde's career, is probably the best-known Texas Ranger of all time. During his long tenure with the Rangers he patroled the border and chased off bandits, tracked down bootleggers and their stills, and set traps for smugglers. He also kept peace in the raucous oil-boom towns of the Panhandle and West Texas and was never above diving into a fight with both fists if the situation called for it. In 1934, when Governor Ma Ferguson pleaded with him to hunt down Bonnie and Clyde, Hamer had already been retired for two years, but he willingly took the job and trailed the desperate duo to Gibsland, Louisiana. He and his posse might be accused of overkill, since they used some two hundred bullets to stop the criminals' flight. For his actions Congress awarded him a special citation.

TEN HONORARY TEXAS RANGERS

1. John Wayne.
2. Jimmie Rodgers.
3. Chill Wills.
4. James Arness.
5. Erle Stanley Gardner.
6. Peter Hurd.
7. Dr. Edward Teller.
8. Clint Walker.
9. Audie Murphy.
10. Slim Pickens.

SOURCE: *Texas Rangers, Texas Department of Public Safety.*

TEXAS PEACE OFFICERS' FAVORITE 10-CODE CALLS

1. 10-22 (Disregard).
2. 10-24 (Assignment completed).
3. 10-42 (Tour of duty finished).
4. 10-44 (Permission granted).

CONTRIBUTOR: *A. Cooper, Big Spring.*

TEXAS PEACE OFFICERS' MOST DREADED 10-CODE CALLS

1. 10-0 (Caution).
2. 10-10 (Fight in progress).
3. 10-15 (Civil disturbance).
4. 10-16 (Domestic disturbance).
5. 10-32 (Man with a gun).
6. 10-41 (Tour of duty beginning).
7. 10-50 (Collision).
8. 10-55 (DWI).
9. 10-79 (Notify coroner).
10. 10-89 (Bomb threat).

CONTRIBUTOR: *A. Cooper, Big Spring.*

TEXAS TRAGEDIES: MURDERS

1. The John F. Kennedy assassination. The fourth assassination of a president of the United States occurred in Dallas on November 22, 1963, when John F. Kennedy was shot to death by a sniper as he rode through town in a motorcade. The president was rushed to Parkland Memorial Hospital, where he was pronounced dead of head wounds. Two days later, a man named Lee Harvey Oswald was arrested and charged with Kennedy's murder (as well as the

death of J. D. Tippit, a policeman killed during the assassination); Oswald, authorities contended, had shot the president with a rifle from the sixth floor of the Texas School Book Depository. On November 25, Oswald was shot and killed in the basement of the city jail by Jack Ruby, a Dallas nightclub operator. Ruby was later convicted of first-degree murder but, while awaiting a new trial by order of the Texas Court of Civil Appeals, he died of cancer.

2. The sniper on the tower. One morning in August of 1966 at·the University of Texas in Austin, Charles Whitman, an ex-Marine who was a superb marksman, lugged a footlocker containing three rifles, a shotgun, and two pistols to the 29th-floor observation platform of the UT tower and barricaded himself in. Whitman had already killed his wife and mother, and he proceeded to pick off more victims from his vantage point high above the campus. The panic was tremendous; people strolling on the streets below didn't know what was happening, and as they bent to help those who had fallen they themselves became targets of sniper fire. For ninety minutes Whitman continued to take aim, killing 12 people and wounding 31, before Austin police managed to work their way into the tower and shot him dead. The Texas sniper murders were at that time the largest mass murders in the twentieth century.

3. The Joan Robinson Hill–John Hill saga. In March of 1969, ponytailed socialite Joan Robinson Hill, a resident of Houston's expensive River Oaks area and a noted equestrian, died of a mysterious and horrible illness. The cause of her death was never satisfactorily discovered; it appeared to be a massive infection of some sort. Her husband, a handsome young doctor, was charged with having caused her death by somehow introducing into her body a deadly type of bacterium. He was brought to trial and defended by up-and-coming attorney Richard "Racehorse" Haynes, and the eventual outcome was a mistrial. Shortly afterward Hill was shot dead by a masked intruder who had lain in wait for him at his home. Suspicion immediately fell on Joan's father, the aging Ash Robinson, who was completely devoted to his daughter and not overly fond of his son-in-law, but he denied any involvement and there was nothing concrete to link him to the surgeon's death. Three people were arrested in connection with the case, though the confessed killer, an ex-convict, was later killed when he started a fight with a policeman in a bar. Two women involved in the case were tried and sentenced to prison.

4. The Houston murders. In August of 1973, Houston police got a call from Elmer Wayne Henley, 17, who told them that he had just shot a man named Dean Corll. His confession began an investigation into the most brutal crime in Texas' history. Henley and David Brooks, 18, told a hideous tale of procuring teenage boys for Corll, who would offer the unfortunate youths drugs and liquor and then, having lulled them into a mood of compliance, tie them up, sexually abuse and torture them, and kill them by strangling or shooting. Police discovered a total of 27 bodies in various sites; 17 of the corpses were found stacked one atop the other in a single boat shed Corll had rented. Many of the victims were runaways or hitchhikers, and as a result many of the remains were never identified. Corll's neighbors professed shock at the news of his grisly murders; the 33-year-old man, they said, loved children. At the time it was revealed, the Houston case, like the Whitman tragedy, was the largest multiple-murder case in the twentieth century.

5. Fred Carrasco, called "el Señor" by his criminal peers, was a convicted killer and a suspected narcotics wholesaler who was serving 25 years for murder at the Huntsville penitentiary when he headed up the longest siege in prison history. In August of 1974 Carrasco and two fellow convicts seized fifteen hostages—teachers, librarians, a guard, and four other prisoners— and held them while they shouted demands for arms and getaway vehicles. Carrasco, 34, was no stranger to brutality; he had reputedly killed some fifty men in a bloody series of gang and drug wars, and somehow his underworld connections had enabled him to obtain the weapons to undertake the siege. On the tenth day, prison authorities lured Carrasco out with promises not to interfere as he made his escape with hostages for security, but a gory shootout erupted. Two female hostages were killed in the exchange of gunfire; Carrasco and one of his collaborators also died.

6. The Cullen Davis cases. Late on the night of August 2, 1976, petite, blonde Priscilla Davis and her lover, Stan Farr, were returning to her mansion in a classy section of Fort Worth when a man dressed in black appeared from a hiding place and shot Priscilla in the chest. Farr was hit by four bullets and died instantly. Though hurt, Priscilla escaped the gunman and ran out the door; as he followed, trying to grab her, he encountered a couple returning from a date and shot the man, but the woman eluded him. When police arrived, they found the body of Priscilla's twelve-year-old daughter, Andrea, in the basement; she had died of gunshot wounds. Priscilla and another eyewitness both identified the man in black as multimillionaire Cullen Davis, Priscilla's estranged husband. He was

arrested and tried, but acquitted. Two years later, Davis was again arrested, this time on charges of hiring a hitman to kill Judge Joe Eidson, who was presiding over Davis's divorce from Priscilla. Represented by the flashy Racehorse Haynes, who had been his attorney for the murder trial as well, Cullen was again a defendant; this time the case ended in a mistrial.

7. The Judge Wood murder. In June of 1979, U.S. Judge John H. Wood, 63, was killed by a single bullet as he left his home to go to work one morning. He was the first federal judge to be murdered in more than a century. The killer has not yet been found, but he was suspected of being involved in the drug trade; Judge Wood was known as "Maximum John" because of the stiff penalties he handed out for narcotics crimes, and he was much feared by drug traffickers. When he was killed, Wood was preparing to preside over the trial of Jimmy Chagra, a flamboyant millionaire and professional gambler who was accused of conspiracy to import and distribute cocaine and marijuana. Two other crimes were linked to the Wood shooting. Chagra's brother Lee, a hell-raising El Paso attorney noted for his successful defense of reputed drug dealers, had been murdered in his office the previous December, and a month before that U.S. attorney James Kerr had narrowly missed being cut down by bullets as he was driving in San Antonio. Kerr often prosecuted drug cases.

ACKNOWLEDGMENTS TO: *Elmer Sackman, Parkland, Washington.*

THREE FAMOUS TEXANS WHO WERE MURDERED

1. Actress Sharon Tate, killed in August of 1969. Her murderers, who also stabbed or shot four other people, were later proved to be members of the eerie Manson family.

2. King Curtis, died in New York in 1971. The Fort Worth-born rhythm-and-blues singer was a fine saxophonist and had a band called Soul, Inc. He was stabbed to death after an argument over a woman.

3. William Marsh Rice, founder of Houston's Rice University, chloroformed in New York in 1900. His valet did it, in collusion with a crooked lawyer who wanted to get his hands on Rice's millions.

FAMOUS LAWYERS

1. Temple Houston. Sam Houston's son was the first celebrity lawyer. His trial tactics were as clever as his clothes were ragged. He once successfully defended himself on a murder charge.

2. John Wesley Hardin. The original criminal lawyer, gunfighter Hardin studied law while serving time in prison, and later practiced in El Paso.

3. Percy Foreman. He's the grand old man of Texas attorneys. Both his physical and professional stature are impressive. Two of his many famous clients were James Earl Ray and Candace Mossler.

4. Charles Alan Wright. A professor at the University of Texas law school, he is *the* expert in the nation on federal courts and the U.S. Constitution.

5. Leon Jaworski. The prominent Houston attorney was thrust into the national spotlight when he was appointed special prosecutor during the Watergate scandal.

6. Page Keeton. Venerable UT law school professor is one of the nation's experts on torts and products liability.

7. John L. Hill. The former attorney general of Texas was the man behind numerous landmark decisions.

8. Richard "Racehorse" Haynes. The flashy, successful Houston attorney is as much of a celebrity as many of his clients—one of whom was Cullen Davis.

9. Joe Jamail. The Houston lawyer is the outstanding personal-injury attorney in the state and the Southwest.

10. Madalyn Murray O'Hair. Gadfly atheist was responsible for the U.S. Supreme Court's decision to ban prayer in public schools.

ACKNOWLEDGMENTS TO: *Patrick D. Redman, William D. King, and Barbara Gibson, Austin.*

DAVID A. ANDERSON'S LIST OF FIVE IMPORTANT LEGAL DEVELOPMENTS IN TEXAS

David A. Anderson is a professor at the University of Texas School of Law.

1. Section 39 of the 1866 State Constitution (article VII). The most interesting (and probably the most important) legal development in Texas wasn't even a case. The amendment stated in part "the State of Texas hereby releases to the owner of the soil all mines and mineral substances that may be on the same." It was adopted long before anyone realized the importance of oil and gas and apparently was added as a favor to the landowner whose property included a salt mine called el Sal del Rey, which Texas had taken possession of in order to supply the Confederacy during the Civil War. Without this amendment, of course, the only oil millionaire in the state would have been the State of Texas itself.

2. *U.S.* v. *Texas* (1950). Texas audaciously claimed that because it retained all its public lands in its treaty joining the Union, it owned the floor of the Gulf — and all the minerals there — all the way out to the edge of the continental shelf. The U.S. Supreme Court disagreed and gave Texas nothing beyond the low-water mark. The Texas congressional delegation then got Congress to compromise in 1953, giving Texas the minerals for three leagues (10.4 miles) out, in accordance with the limit set by the old Spanish law.

3. *U.S.* v. *Texas* (1895). Equally audaciously, Texas claimed as its northern boundary the north fork of the Red River and attempted to create "Greer County" between there and the south fork. The U.S. Supreme Court held that the boundary *was* the south fork, and added insult to injury by holding that it was the *south* bank of the south fork.

4. *Sweatt* v. *Painter* (1950). The U.S. Supreme Court held unconstitutional an attempt by the University of Texas to maintain racial segregation by creating a separate law school for a black applicant named Heman Sweatt. The court ordered Sweatt admitted to the UT law school, and the decision became an important precedent in the school desegregation case *Brown* v. *Board of Education* four years later. Although the case involved only the UT law school directly, it in fact ended legal racial segregation in all higher education in Texas, and did so earlier and with less turmoil than in other southern states.

5. *Turner* v. *Big Lake Oil Company* (1936). The Texas Supreme Court repudiated an ancient legal doctrine that would have held oil companies strictly liable for damages caused by the escape of saltwater, gases, and other oilfield and refinery wastes. Under the *Turner* rule, a victim must prove that the waste escaped because of some negligent act by the oil company. The *Turner* rule is partially responsible for making the Houston Ship Channel what it is today.

JOHN HILL'S MOST INTERESTING CASES

John Hill, former attorney general of Texas, is now in private practice.

1. *Electronic Data Systems, Inc.* v. *Government of Iran.* $19.2 million judgment for breach of contract. Court found no evidence of bribery and set a precedent for suits under the Sovereign Immunity Act against Iran by Americans holding debts.

2. *Mrs. Suzanne Quick, et al.* v. *Lockheed Aircraft Corporation.* Combined judgments of $3 million for wrongful deaths caused from structural defects in Lockheed Electra aircraft. Forerunner of program to improve air-frame safety requirements set by Federal Aviation Administration.

3. *State of Texas* v. *Howard Hughes Estate.* $100 million judgment in Houston probate court for Texas, based on jury finding that Howard Hughes had never abandoned Texas as his home.

4. *Louisiana* v. *Texas.* Boundary dispute in which valuable offshore property was awarded to Texas.

5. *State of Texas* v. *Southwestern Bell Telephone Company.* Ratepayers saved more than $50 million as a result of judicial determination that intrastate rate hike was grossly excessive.

6. Duval County corruption prosecution. Resulted in Duval County cleanup.

7. *National Heritage Insurance Company* v. *Texas Department of Human Resources, et al.* Involved decision of who was the lowest and best bidder on the $2 billion Texas Medicaid contract.

8. *State of Texas* v. *Jurek.* Upheld the constitutionality of the Texas death penalty statute. Texas presented the lead argument for the states in U.S. Supreme Court.

9. *Mrs. Eva Heatges et al.* v. *Coastal States Refinery, et al.* More than $3 million judgments resulting from explosion of contaminated oxygen bottle.

10. *Tony Garrett* v. *Estelle.* Upheld the right of the state to prohibit televising of a legal execution.

11. *State of Texas* v. *Lester Roloff.* Established the right of the state to require licensing of the Roloff child-care facilities.

12. *Texas Manufactured Housing Industry* v. *Texas.* Upheld right of the state to require bonding, licensing, and standards for manufactured housing (mobile homes, etc.) in the public interest.

RACEHORSE HAYNES'S LIST OF REASONS NOT TO GO TO COURT AGAINST RACEHORSE HAYNES

Richard "Racehorse" Haynes is a noted Houston trial attorney.

1. Most of the time, if you are in error or if you lie, you will be found out.

2. Generally, you cannot hide from the truth.

3. More often than not, there is no escape from the witness stand except to tell the truth.

4. You will not get away with telling a half-truth.

5. Ordinarily, you can't speculate or guess.

6. If you lie under oath, your face will give you away.

7. You will have to tell it like it is or suffer the consequences.

8. It is said, and it is not denied, that Haynes can read minds.

9. You may be there a long time.

C H A P T E R ★ 6

Science, Medicine, and Business

MOST FREQUENT TRAUMA CASES HANDLED AT BEN TAUB GENERAL HOSPITAL, HOUSTON

1. Rape.
2. Industrial amputations.
3. Fractures.
4. Dog bites.
5. Lacerations.
6. Stab wounds.
7. Gunshot wounds.
8. Burns.
9. Auto and motorcycle accidents.
10. Aggravated assaults.

MOST FREQUENT COMPLAINTS AT TRIAGE AT BEN TAUB GENERAL HOSPITAL, HOUSTON

1. Abdominal pain.
2. Chest pain.
3. Shortness of breath.
4. Trauma.
5. Psychiatric disorders.
6. Alcohol-induced problems.
7. Terminally ill patients in crisis.
8. Seizures.
9. Overdoses.
10. Viral syndromes.

SOURCE: *Ben Taub General Hospital staff.*

MOST FREQUENT CASES HANDLED AT THE MINOR EMERGENCY CENTER NORTH, AUSTIN

1. Lacerations.
2. Sprains, especially ankle and wrist.
3. Strains, especially back and neck.
4. Contusions.
5. Fractures.
6. Sore throats.
7. Venereal disease.
8. Poison ivy reactions and other contact sensitivities.
9. Upper respiratory infections.
10. Bronchitis.
11. Pneumonia.
12. Ear infections.
13. Gastrointestinal infections.
14. Urinary tract infections.
15. Allergic reactions.
16. Insect bites.
17. Headaches.
18. Stress-related problems.

SOURCE: *the Minor Emergency Center North, Austin.*

DENTON COOLEY'S LIST OF EASY OPERATIONS WITH BIG REWARDS

Noted heart surgeon Denton Cooley says that the gratification comes from observing the patient's improvement and from the surgeon's own satisfaction of having accomplished something significant; the rewards are not monetary.

1. Cardiac transplantation.
2. Mitral valvuloplasty for stenosis, the repair of an obstruction in the mitral valve of the heart.
3. Closure patent ductus arteriosus, the repair of an embryologic defect between two arteries close to the heart.

DENTON COOLEY'S LIST OF DIFFICULT OPERATIONS WITH SMALL REWARDS

1. Palliative resection, carcinoma of the esophagus.
2. Replacement of infected artificial heart valve.
3. Coronary bypass operations after previous unsuccessful attempts.

FAMOUS HEALERS

1. Medar Jalot was, with the exception of witch doctors, the first physician in Texas, arriving here in 1714 as companion to the adventurer Louis de St. Denis. His practice was mostly limited to barbering St. Denis and dissecting dead Indians. He died after being thrown from a horse, since, being the only doctor for hundreds of miles, he was unable to receive proper medical care.

2. Pedro Jaramillo, a Mexican *curandero* of the late nineteenth century, was, he said, led by God to become a healer. He relied not on recognized treatments but on divine guidance and never charged a cent. He usually traveled South Texas on a mule, making house calls dressed in a serape and sombrero, and was always in great demand.

3. Michael DeBakey, perhaps the best-known surgeon in the world, is head of the Baylor School of Medicine. A pioneer in vascular

surgery, he did the first successful implant of an artificial left ventricle in 1966 and also introduced the use of Dacron as a substitute for human tissue in repairing blood vessels.

4. Denton Cooley, a native Houstonian, is famed for his incredible work in open-heart surgery. In 1969 he implanted the first artificial heart, and he has also conducted many successful heart transplants. Dr. Cooley founded the Texas Heart Institute, where he is chief surgeon.

NINE MEDICAL ADVANCES FIRST DEVELOPED BY NASA

1. Blood-pressure and heart-monitoring sensors so small that they can be inserted with a hypodermic needle rather than through surgery.

2. Remote-monitoring equipment that lets a single nurse keep a continual check on as many as 64 patients at once.

3. A suitcase-size emergency treatment kit for trained ambulance attendants.

4. Transducers which were first used to measure spacecraft splashdown impact, now incorporated into a device for precision-fitting of artificial limbs.

5. Easy-to-prepare meals adapted from space food techniques and now used by the elderly and other persons who have some difficulty with more tiring methods of preparation.

6. Procedures to control contamination now used in operating and recovery rooms.

7. Dry, spray-on electrode techniques that permit the taking of accurate electrocardiograms even on bumpy ambulance rides.

8. A switch operated by eye movement that allows a paralyzed patient to control a TV set, handle an automatic page turner, adjust bed position, turn lights on and off, and so on.

9. Wheelchairs that can be operated by voice command for quadriplegics.

SOURCE: *Space and Life Sciences Directorate, NASA.*

NINE EVERYDAY THINGS FIRST RESEARCHED BY NASA

1. Cookware that goes from freezer to oven without cracking and that can be easily cleaned.

2. Pressure-sensitive fasteners and closures.

3. Fire-retardant paint and flameproof materials.

4. Shock absorbers capable of softening a sixty-miles-per-hour shock into the equivalent of a five-miles-per-hour jiggle.

5. More reliable batteries that last longer and are easily recharged.

6. Semiconductors hardly bigger than a pinhead, containing as many as a thousand circuits.

7. Ball-point pens that write in any position.

8. Miniaturized tape recorders.

9. New polyurethane plastics that are stronger than earlier types, and better molding processes that strengthen conventional plastics.

SOURCE: *Engineering and Development Directorate, NASA.*

FEMALE ASTRONAUTS

These women, now in training at NASA, were the first female astronauts in the U.S.

1. Anna L. Fisher.
2. Shannon W. Lucid.
3. Judith A. Resnik.
4. Sally K. Ride.
5. Margaret R. Seddon.
6. Kathryn D. Sullivan.

SOURCE: *NASA.*

REQUIREMENTS FOR ASTRONAUT PILOT CANDIDATES

Qualifications for mission-specialist astronaut candidates are slightly less stringent.

1. Bachelor's degree from an accredited institution in engineering, mathematics, or biological or physical science.

2. At least 1000 hours of pilot-in-command time in high-performance jet aircraft.

3. Vision: 20/50 or better uncorrected; correctable to 20/20.

4. Blood pressure: preponderant systolic not to exceed 140; diastolic not to exceed 90.

5. Height: between 64 and 76 inches.

SOURCE: *NASA.*

QUOTABLE NASA QUOTES

1. "Houston, Tranquility Base here. The *Eagle* has landed." First words by men on the moon, 1969, Apollo 11.

2. "That's one small step for a man, one giant leap for mankind." Said by Neil Armstrong during the first walk on the lunar surface, 1969, Apollo 11.

3. "Houston, we've got a problem." From the near-disastrous Apollo 13 flight, 1970.

4. "Hey, I see the comet! Holy cow! There's the tail!" Comment from Skylab, 1973, after its crewmen spotted Kohoutek, which was a washout for earthbound humans.

5. "Confirm. Hatch Three is open." First comment after historic docking of Apollo and Soyuz, 1975.

6. "How do astronauts go to the bathroom?" The question most frequently asked of NASA's public information office.

SOURCE: *NASA.*

BANQUETS HELD IN SPACE TO CELEBRATE THE DOCKING OF APOLLO AND SOYUZ

Russian menu: 1. Ukrainian borscht.
2. Spiced veal.
3. Sausage.
4. Cake.
5. Fruit juice.

American menu: 1. Roast beef.
2. Potato soup.
3. Rye bread.
4. Cheese.
5. Strawberries.
6. Almonds.
7. Tea with lemon.

SOURCE: *NASA.*

FIVE THINGS THAT WERE *NOT* INVENTED IN TEXAS

1. Barbed wire, thousands of miles of which crisscross the Texas plains, was perfected in 1874 by one J.F. Glidden of Dekalb, Illinois. Two other Yankees, H.B. Sanborn and John W. Gates, went on to become the best-known barbed-wire salesmen in the state.

2. The Stetson, ten-gallon and otherwise, is the most famous of all Texas headgear. It was designed and manufactured by John B. Stetson, a Philadelphian who came up with the prototype of the cowboy hat while living in the Midwest in the 1860s. It did, however, take the Texas Rangers to realize the full range of the Stetson's uses; the hat could be used to fan a fire, scoop up water, flag down help, or do a hundred other things.

3. The Colt .45 was created by Samuel Colt, a native of Connecticut. (His first gun was actually .35 caliber.) Several years after the .45

was introduced, Colt conferred with Captain Samuel Walker of the Texas Rangers on improvements to the revolver; the resulting model, the Walker-Colt, became the Rangers' chief weapon.

4. Windmills, which Texas has more of than any other state, have been around for centuries. The famous Dutch windmill, though, is drastically different from the western variety; the European type was generally used to provide power for light industry, while its American cousin, designed by a Yankee named Daniel Halliday, was intended to pump underground water. Thus the windmill played a vital role in populating Texas; without it, barren areas could never have been settled. Besides watering stock, windmills provided supplies for steam engines, aiding railroad expansion. Ranching Texans patented variations on windmill design from the late nineteenth century on up to the fifties.

5. AstroTurf, the first artificial turf, was created by chemists at the Monsanto company in St. Louis. Though the company had been experimenting with artificial turf for years, the grass-green playing surface was first put to the test in 1966 in the Astrodome, which gave it its name.

EUREKA, Y'ALL: GREAT INVENTORS

1. Pecos Bill, legendary cowboy, was the father of modern cowpunching. Various biographers credit him with inventing the branding iron, the lasso, bulldogging, hogtying, broncbusting, the saddle, chaps, bandanas, spurs, and the corral. Of course, such talent is only to be expected from a man who could rope a cyclone.

2. Gail Borden, who lived in Texas off and on from 1829 to 1874, was a man of many interests. After publishing one of the first newspapers in the area and preparing the first topographical map of the region, he began tinkering with a variety of ideas, including a portable beach house for modest Galveston ladies and a large land-water vehicle that resembled a covered wagon. His most important invention though, was his patented process for condensing milk, which led to the creation of the Borden dairy company.

3. Howard R. Hughes, father of the famous billionaire, was the source of his son's wealth. One of the pioneers of the oil industry, the elder Hughes and a partner, Walter B. Sharp, were the first to realize the need for a drill bit that could go through hard rock. Hughes thus

designed one with revolving cutters and heavy steel teeth, a rock bit that became world-famous because it enabled oilmen to tackle formations that were otherwise impenetrable. (Sharp, incidentally, is credited with being the first person to come up with the idea of using drilling mud, as well as the first man to successfully fight an oil well fire.)

4. Jacob Brodbeck, a German native, came to Texas in 1846, when he was 25. He once tried to design a clock that wouldn't need winding, an idea that paled next to the project he launched—literally—in 1863: a flying machine. His model had a rudder, wings, a propeller, and landing gear, but Brodbeck was never able to persuade the good folk of San Antonio to provide financial backing for full-scale development. He was truly a man ahead of his time.

5. Jacob Pliska, a blacksmith in Midland, built an airplane two years after the Wright Brothers conducted their historic 1903 flight. The plane was made of steel and canvas, with an open cockpit and stationary landing gear, and Pliska flew it several times, once reaching an altitude of sixty feet. During his lifetime, though, he received little credit for his design.

6. George McCormick, Jr., an Aggie, was responsible for a multitude of improvements on railroad locomotives. His various inventions included a safety tie bar, a new boiler, and improved lubrication techniques. In 1940 he was named a Modern Pioneer by the National Association of Manufacturers for his many designs.

7. Robert Munger, born in little Rutersville, invented dozens of devices to improve cotton ginning. He patented his first design in 1878, when he was only 24. His ideas include pneumatic feed systems, a saw-sharpening tool, and a baling machine.

8. Ole Ringness, the son of a Norwegian immigrant, lived near Norse, Texas. A regular worker on his father's farm, he quickly tired of hauling the heavy, standard-design plow through the mud, and came up with a model of a disc plow and a disc harrow. While on his way to New York in 1872 to patent his designs, he was murdered.

119

TEXAS COMPANIES ON THE 1980 FORTUNE 500 AND THEIR RANK

Of the Texas-based companies on *Fortune*'s famous list of the biggest companies in the country, all but three moved up in 1980. Texas also added a company to the list; only nineteen appeared on it in 1979.

1. Shell Oil, Houston—13.
2. Tenneco, Houston—18.
3. LTV, Dallas—31.
4. Dresser, Dallas—98.
5. Texas Instruments, Dallas—104.
6. Diamond Shamrock, Dallas—151.
7. Pennzoil, Houston—170.
8. American Petrofina, Dallas—203.
9. Anderson Clayton, Houston—214.
10. Cooper Industries, Dallas—225.
11. Commonwealth Oil Refining, San Antonio—246.
12. Superior Oil, Houston—267.
13. National Gypsum, Dallas—280.
14. Campbell-Taggart, Dallas—285.
15. Hughes Tool, Houston—326.
16. Fairmont Foods, Houston—417.
17. Cameron Iron Works, Houston—426.
18. Tyler Corporation, Dallas—435.
19. Big Three Industries, Houston—438.
20. Gulf Resources & Chemical, Houston—448.

SOURCE: *Fortune magazine.*

BIGGEST BANKS AND THEIR ESTIMATED DEPOSITS

1. First City National Bank, Houston, $3.3 billion.
2. Republic National Bank, Dallas, $3.1 billion.
3. Texas Commerce Bank of N.A., Houston, $3 billion.
4. First National Bank, Dallas, $2.9 billion.
5. Mercantile National Bank, Dallas, $1.5 billion.

SOURCE: *Federal Reserve Bank of Dallas.*

COUNTIES THAT HAVE NO BANKS

1. Borden.
2. Glasscock.
3. Hartley.
4. Kenedy.
5. King.
6. Loving.

SIX POOR COUNTIES

(See previous list.)

OWNERS OF MORE THAN HALF A MILLION ACRES OF TEXAS

1. State of Texas – 6,400,000 acres.
2. United States of America – 3,293,000 acres.
3. University of Texas System – 2,100,000 acres.
4. Texas Pacific Land Trust – 1,274,000 acres.
5. Temple-EasTex, Inc. – 1,067,000 acres.
6. King Ranch – 825,000 acres.
7. Kirby Forest Industries – 585,000 acres.
8. St. Regis Paper Company – 570,000 acres.

SOURCE: *Jim Chiles, "Who Owns Texas?", **Texas Monthly**, June 1980.*

WEALTHIEST METROPOLITAN AREAS AND PER CAPITA ANNUAL INCOMES (1978)

1. Midland, $10,658.
2. Houston, $9398.
3. Dallas-Fort Worth, $8756.
4. Odessa, $8551.
5. Amarillo, $8530.
6. Wichita Falls, $8255.

SOURCE: *U.S. Department of Commerce.*

GREATEST OIL-PRODUCING COUNTIES

1. Yoakum.
2. Gaines.
3. Ector.
4. Scurry.
5. Hockley.
6. Gregg.
7. Pecos.
8. Andrews.
9. Refugio.
10. Crane.

SOURCE: *Texas Mid-Continent Oil & Gas Association.*

SEVEN MINERALS TEXAS NO LONGER PRODUCES

1. Gold.
2. Silver.
3. Copper.
4. Mica.
5. Mercury.
6. Molybdenum.
7. Peat.

MINERALS THAT TEXAS PRODUCES AN AWFUL LOT OF

1. Oil.
2. Natural gas.
3. Sulfur.
   (Texas is the nation's leading producer of the above three.)
4. Helium.
5. Magnesium.
6. Lignite.
7. Gypsum.
8. Sand.
9. Gravel.
10. Clay.
11. Salt.

SOURCE: *Bureau of Economic Geology, University of Texas at Austin.*

MINERALS YOU PROBABLY DIDN'T KNOW TEXAS PRODUCES

1. Asbestos.
2. Diatomite.
3. Pumice.
4. Tungsten.
5. Talc.
6. Graphite.
7. Marble.
8. Uranium.
9. And last but not least, guano.

GEMS FOUND IN TEXAS

1. Topaz.
2. Tourmaline.
3. Opal.
4. Amethyst.
5. Garnet.

BEST–SELLING BEERS

1. Coors.
2. Miller.
3. Anheuser-Busch.
4. Schlitz.
5. Lone Star.
6. Pearl.

SOURCE: *U.S. Brewers Association, Southwest Region, Austin.*

BREWERIES

1. Lone Star, San Antonio.
2. Pearl, San Antonio.
3. Shiner, Shiner.
4. Anheuser-Busch, Houston.
5. Falstaff, Galveston.
6. Schlitz, Longview.
7. Miller, Fort Worth.

SOURCE: *U.S. Brewers Association, Southwest Region, Austin.*

BUSIEST PHONE BOOTHS IN DALLAS

1. Love Field.
2. Greyhound bus station, downtown.
3. Continental bus station, downtown.
4. Big Tex Truckstop, Mesquite.
5. H. L. Green's department store, Main Street.
6. NorthPark Center.
7. T.G.I. Friday's, Greenville Avenue.
8. All 7-Eleven stores.
9. All Stop 'N' Go stores.
10. Shepp's Food stores.
11. SMU Student Center.

SOURCE: *Southwestern Bell, Dallas.*

BEST-SELLING BASKIN-ROBBINS ICE CREAM FLAVORS IN TEXAS

1. Chocolate.
2. Vanilla.
3. Strawberry.
4. Pralines 'n' Cream.
5. Chocolate Chip.
6. Chocolate Mint.
7. Jamoca Almond Fudge.
8. Peanut Butter 'n' Chocolate.
9. German Chocolate Cake.
10. Jamoca.
11. Pistachio Almond Fudge.

SOURCE: *Baskin-Robbins Division Office, Dallas.*

BEST-SELLING ITEMS IN THE 1980 NEIMAN-MARCUS CHRISTMAS BOOK

1. Red- and blue-enameled owl pin with rhinestones, $12.

2. Glass plate with Christmas tree design in relief, $10.

3. Original album *Christmas Love,* commissioned by Neiman-Marcus, $19.50.

4. Nickel-plated lockbox, eight by six inches, $13.50.

5. Porcelain pomander with potpourri, imported from Japan, $8.

6. Six-pack of dessert breads and cakes including banana nut and pineapple macadamia, $18.

7. Sixteen-ounce bar of milk chocolate wrapped up in gold paper as bullion, $8.

8. Two-pound fruit cake with individually wrapped slices, $15.

9. Boys' sweatshirt with "Neiman-Marcus" written over left breast, $15.

10. Bumblebee pin, 14-karat gold plated, with rhinestones, $12.50.

SOURCE: *Neiman-Marcus, Dallas.*

STANLEY MARCUS'S LIST OF THE BEST THINGS IN TEXAS

Stanley Marcus, former chairman of the board of Neiman-Marcus, is the author of *Minding the Store.*

1. The Astrodome.
2. San Antonio River development.
3. Fort Worth Fat Stock Show.
4. George Schrader, city manager of Dallas.
5. Houston's Galleria.
6. Fort Worth's Kimbell Art Museum.
7. Neiman-Marcus.
8. Pink grapefruit.
9. Angelo's Barbecue, Fort Worth.
10. Dallas–Fort Worth Airport.
11. Birdwell Library at Southern Methodist University.
12. North Texas Commission.
13. Dallas Trade Mart.
14. Pennzoil Building, Houston.
15. Dallas City Hall.
16. Rio Grande Valley.
17. Humanities Research Center, the University of Texas at Austin.

STANLEY MARCUS'S LIST OF THINGS THAT ARE LESS THAN TEXAS' BEST

1. Crime rate.
2. State Fair of Texas.
3. University of Texas politics.
4. Blue laws.
5. Texas steaks.
6. Dallas County Commissioners' Court.
7. Dallas school board.
8. Mustang Mania.
9. Baylor's censorship policy.

ROGER HORCHOW'S LIST OF EXCUSES OFFERED BY SUPPLIERS WHO FAIL TO DELIVER

Roger Horchow is president of the Horchow Collection.

1. The mold maker went to Europe.

2. The boat was infested with snails.

3. The government turned the electricity on only a few hours a day (this from India).

4. The Food and Drug Administration is testing the dishes for lead content.

5. Only one man can make it, and he doesn't want to make the same thing over and over again. He says it's boring.

6. Our order was too large (or too small) for the manufacturer to handle.

7. The fabric to make it was damaged.

8. Our inventory list says we should have them, but we can't find them in our warehouse.

9. The boat arrived and the goods weren't there.

10. We can't find anyone to help my mother paint them, so it'll be a while.

11. The ship sank (or, the ship missed the Port of Houston, or, the ship sailed with the cargo still on the dock).

12. The air shipment got lost in New York (or, there wasn't any room for it on the plane).

13. The factory closed for vacation (or, the factory burned down).

14. The package fell off the truck.

15. The rains came and nothing would dry.

16. The village was wiped out by fire (or monsoon).

17. She had a baby (or, his wife had a baby and he didn't come to work).

18. The train derailed.

19. The weavers (or potters, or dyers, etc.) joined the revolution.

20. The stock boy thought it had been shipped, but it hadn't.

21. The supplier forgot to order more (or, he couldn't get enough raw material to fill the order).

22. The shipment was delayed by a strike.

23. The shipment is being held up in customs.

24. The shipment was lost in the manufacturer's computer.

25. We sold the order to somebody else.

TEN ITEMS THAT GUARANTEED THEIR PRESENTERS A 49–CENT PLANE FARE ON TEXAS INTERNATIONAL FROM HOUSTON TO LAS VEGAS IN 1978

1. A 1949 penny.
2. A 1949 Texas or Nevada License plate.
3. $49 in Monopoly money.
4. A resume listing 49 jobs.
5. A high school diploma dated 1949.
6. A college blue book with a grade of 49 on it.
7. 49 poker chips.
8. A 49-pound barbell.
9. Proof that you were born in the 49th state.
10. A 49-foot-long paper clip chain.

SOURCE: *Texas International Airlines.*

SOME FAMOUS GUESTS AT SAN ANTONIO'S MENGER HOTEL

1. Sarah Bernhardt.
2. Pola Negri.
3. John Wayne.
4. Bing Crosby.
5. Bob Hope.
6. Roy Rogers.
7. Dale Evans.
8. Sidney Lanier.
9. Ulysses S. Grant.
10. Teddy Roosevelt.
11. Harry S. Truman.
12. Dwight D. Eisenhower.
13. Lyndon Baines Johnson.
14. Richard Nixon.
15. Ronald Reagan.

SOURCE: *the Menger Hotel.*

SITES OF CONRAD HILTON'S FIRST TEN HOTELS

1. Cisco.
2. Fort Worth.
3. Dallas.
4. Abilene.
5. Waco.
6. Marlin.
7. Plainview.
8. San Angelo.
9. Lubbock.
10. El Paso.

SOURCE: *Conrad Hilton, Be My Guest.*

TEN LITTLE INNS

1. The Country Place, Fayetteville.
2. The Yacht Club Hotel, Port Isabel.
3. The Tarpon Inn, Port Aransas.
4. The Luther Hotel, Palacios.
5. The Faust Hotel, New Braunfels.
6. Prince Solms Inn, New Braunfels.
7. The Limpia Hotel, Fort Davis.
8. The Nutt House, Granbury.
9. Excelsior House, Jefferson.
10. New Jefferson Inn, Jefferson.

SOURCE: *Richard West, "Funky Hotels," Texas Monthly, November 1979.*

HOUSE RULES AT THE TEXAS HOTEL, SAN ANGELO

1. No visitors in sleeping rooms, whether male or female. See your friends somewhere else.

2. No drinking parties in rooms at any time.

3. No grass, glue sniffing, etc. The police will be called and the tenant will be evicted.

4. Any extra garbage (i.e., beer cans) must be put in garbage cans by the tenant who produced it.

5. No loud talking or cutting up late at night. Other people are trying to sleep.

6. Rent must be paid on the proper date and in advance.

CONTRIBUTOR: *Dorothy Joseph, San Angelo (former manager of the Texas Hotel).*

FARRAH FAWCETT'S LIST OF THE MOST ROMANTIC HOTELS IN THE WORLD

Farrah Fawcett is a Texas-born model and actress.

1. Inverlochy Castle, Scotland.
2. Gritti Palace, Venice.
3. Club 13, Normandy.
4. Mauna Kea, Hawaii.
5. Villa Vera Racquet Club, Acapulco.
6. Le Bristol, Paris.
7. The Pierre, New York.

MAJOR CONVENTIONS HELD AT THE DALLAS CONVENTION CENTER, 1980

1. General Conference of Seventh-day Adventists, attendance 20,000.
2. Church of God General Assembly, 20,000.
3. International Trucking Show, 18,000.
4. Food Marketing Institute, 18,000.
5. Radiological Society of North America, 16,000.
6. National Home Center Home Improvement Congress, 16,000.
7. National Shoe Fair of America, 13,000.
8. Home Interior and Gifts Convention, 12,000.
9. National Baptist Sunday School and Training Congress, 10,000.
10. Black Congress on Health and Law, 8200.
11. Christian Booksellers Association, 8000.
12. Society of Petroleum Engineers of AIME, 8000.
13. Mary Kay Cosmetics, 8000.
14. Southwest Marine Industry Trade Show, 7000.
15. American Home Economics Association, 6600.
16. American Association of Respiratory Therapy, 6000.
17. National Cable Television Association, 6000.
18. International Specialty Advertising Association, 5500.

SOURCE: *Dallas Chamber of Commerce Convention and Visitors Bureau.*

SINGLE–DAY EVENTS THAT DREW THE LARGEST CROWDS AT DALLAS'S REUNION ARENA IN 1980

1. ZZ Top, 19,012 (sold out).
2. The Who, 19,012.
3. Parliament Funkadelic, 19,012.
4. Kenny Rogers, 18,999.
5. Dallas Mavericks vs. Los Angeles Lakers, 17,481.
6. Fleetwood Mac, 16,713.
7. Barkays, 16,207.
8. Commodores, 15,747.
9. NBA doubleheader: Dallas Mavericks vs. Philadelphia 76ers and Kansas City Kings vs. Houston Rockets, 15,574.
10. Barry Manilow, 15,553.
11. The Cars, 15,028.
12. Willie Nelson, 14,944.

SOURCE: *Reunion Arena.*

SIX TOURIST ATTRACTIONS THAT DRAW OVER 100,000 PEOPLE A YEAR

1. Six Flags Over Texas, 2,000,000-plus.
2. Astroworld, 1,800,000.
3. Tower of the Americas, 600,000.
4. Lyndon B. Johnson Library and Museum, 400,000.
5. Big Bend National Park, 200,000.
6. Confederate Air Force Museum, 120,000.

SOURCE: *Texas Tourist Development Agency. Note: Many tourist attractions that are free, such as the Alamo, do not keep records of attendance.*

LARGEST CROWDS IN THE ASTRODOME

1. Baseball: 50,908 on June 22, 1966, Astros vs. Dodgers.

2. Football: (professional) 54,261 on December 3, 1978, Oilers vs. Steelers.
   (college) 53,668 on October 29, 1977, TSU vs. Grambling.

3. Tennis: 30,472 on September 20, 1973, Billy Jean King vs. Bobby Riggs.

4. Boxing: 37,321 on February 6, 1967, Cassius Clay (Muhammad Ali) vs. Ernie Terrell.

5. Basketball: 52,693 on January 20, 1968, UH vs. UCLA.

6. Concert: 53,749 on July 19, 1975 during the Kool Jazz Festival.

7. Rodeo concert: 46,513 on February 29, 1980, Kenny Rogers.

8. Livestock show: 18,120 on February 26, 1977, Houston Livestock Show.

9. Religious meeting: 61,000 on November 22, 1965, Billy Graham revival.

SOURCE: *the Astrodome.*

Entertainment

TOP GROSSING MOVIES IN TEXAS IN 1980

1. *The Empire Strikes Back.*
2. *Kramer vs. Kramer.*
3. *The Jerk.*
4. *Airplane!*
5. *Smokey and the Bandit II.*
6. *Coal Miner's Daughter.*
7. *Private Benjamin.*
8. *The Blues Brothers, Urban Cowboy* (tie).
9. *The Electric Horseman.*
10. *The Shining.*

SOURCE: *National Association of Theater Owners, Dallas.*

MAJOR MOVIES MADE IN TEXAS

Nearly one hundred more had been or were being filmed in the state at the beginning of 1981. Dates represent the year a film was shot.

1. *The Warrens of Virginia,* 1923, San Antonio.
2. *Wings,* 1927, San Antonio area.
3. *The Rough Riders,* 1927, San Antonio area.
4. *Viva Zapata!,* 1952, Rio Grande City area.
5. *The Last Command,* 1955, Brackettville.
6. *Giant,* 1956, Marfa-Valentine area.
7. *The Alamo,* 1960, Brackettville.
8. *Two Rode Together,* 1961, Brackettville.
9. *State Fair,* 1962, Dallas.
10. *Hud,* 1963, Claude.
11. *Baby, the Rain Must Fall,* 1964, Wharton.
12. *Bonnie and Clyde,* 1967, Denton-Dallas area.
13. *Viva, Max!,* 1968, San Antonio.
14. *Hellfighters,* 1969, Houston.
15. *Brewster McCloud,* 1970, Houston.
16. *The Andromeda Strain,* 1970, Shafter.
17. *The Last Picture Show,* 1971, Archer City.
18. *Lovin' Molly,* 1972, Bastrop.
19. *The Getaway,* 1972, El Paso, Huntsville, San Marcos, San Antonio.
20. *The Thief Who Came to Dinner,* 1972, Houston.
21. *Benji,* 1973, McKinney.
22. *The Great Waldo Pepper,* 1973, Elgin, Lockhart, Floresville, Kerr-ville.
23. *Sugarland Express,* 1973, San Antonio, Floresville, Del Rio.
24. *The Texas Chainsaw Massacre,* 1973, Round Rock.
25. *Houston, We've Got Trouble,* 1974, NASA/Houston.
26. *Logan's Run,* 1975, Dallas, Houston, Fort Worth.
27. *Futureworld,* 1976, NASA/Houston.
28. *Outlaw Blues,* 1976, Austin.
29. *Semi-Tough,* 1977, Dallas.
30. *For the Love of Benji,* 1977, Houston.
31. *The Bad News Bears in Breaking Training,* 1977, Houston and El Paso.
32. *Capricorn One,* 1977, Galveston.
33. *Eyewitness,* 1977, Dallas.
34. *FM,* 1977, Houston.
35. *Tilt,* 1978, Corpus Christi.
36. *When You Comin' Back, Red Ryder?,* 1978, El Paso.
37. *The Whole Shootin' Match,* 1978, Austin.

38. *Resurrection,* 1979, Shiner and El Paso.
39. *Urban Cowboy,* 1979, Houston.
40. *The Lathe of Heaven,* 1979, Fort Worth and Dallas.
41. *Middle Age Crazy,* 1979, Houston and Dallas.
42. *Honeysuckle Rose,* 1979, Austin.
43. *The Code of Josey Wales,* 1979, Brackettville.
44. *The Long Riders,* 1979, Palestine.
45. *Roadie,* 1979, Austin.
46. *Hangar 18,* 1980, Big Spring.
47. *The Oldest Living Graduate,* 1980, Dallas.
48. *The Border,* 1980, El Paso.
49. *Raggedy Man,* 1980, Maxwell.
50. *Murder in Texas,* 1980, Houston.

SOURCE: *Texas Film Commission.*

STEPHEN HARRIGAN'S LIST OF MOVIES ABOUT THE ALAMO

Stephen Harrigan is a novelist (*Aransas,* 1980) and an Alamophile.

1. *The Birth of Texas* (1915). This movie was recently discovered by a University of Texas film researcher in the basement of a building where it had been mercifully hidden from public viewing for decades. The film was supposedly directed by D. W. Griffith, but was in reality the work of one of his second-unit functionaries. In the movie's most memorable scene, two Alamo defenders, mortally wounded, turn to each other and shake hands before expiring.

2. *The Last Command* (1955). Starring Sterling Hayden as Jim Bowie. This one features a great theme song ("Wouldn't you/Wanna do/Like Jim Bowie?") and a Santa Anna (J. Carrol Naish) who is a little on the skinny side. Bowie romances Anna Maria Alberghetti and has a knife fight or two before he ends up in the Alamo. His rival, Travis, is played by Richard (*I Led Three Lives*) Carlson, and a bearded Arthur Hunnicutt plays Davy Crockett. Upon his death, Crockett blows up a cache of gunpowder, a theme picked up by John Wayne five years later in *The Alamo. The Last Command* is the best movie about the Alamo ever made; unfortunately, it stinks.

3. *Davy Crockett* (1955). I don't know what it is about this movie, but it gets me every time. Maybe it's the way Georgie Russell (Buddy Ebsen) says his last words—"Give 'em what fer, Davy"—or that last lingering shot of Fess Parker swinging Ol' Betsy, swatting the Mexicans like mosquitoes. This is a movie of enduring stupidity.

4. *The First Texan* (1956). I have only the dimmest memory of this movie. Joel McCrea plays Sam Houston, unmemorably, and the Alamo itself is mentioned only in passing. Still, we do get to meet Davy Crockett, played by a tall actor with a big Adam's apple that caused us kids in the audience to guffaw during his brief appearance.

5. *The Alamo* (1960). Like *The Last Command, The Alamo* was filmed in Brackettville, Texas. It is unique among Alamo movies in that it has an authentic set. Most everything else about it is made up out of whole cloth, including Jim Bowie's atomic-powered blunderbuss. *The Alamo* has great music, including "The Green Leaves of Summer" and "The Ballad of the Alamo," which is the best song ever written about that institution next to "Across the Alley from the Alamo." [Runners-up: "Jimmy the Mexican Soldier (Who Died at the Alamo)" and "Please, Santa Anna (I Don't Wanna Go)," a takeoff of "Please, Mr. Custer"—S.H.] John Wayne, of course, plays Davy Crockett, and he walks around saying things like "Republic. I like the sound of the word." The insufferable Laurence Harvey is cast as the insufferable Travis, and Frankie Avalon, wearing a skunk-skin cap, is the Boy Who Got Away. As Bowie, Richard Widmark makes a strange squawking sound when he is bayoneted on his cot.

6. *Viva Max!* (1969). The Daughters of the Republic of Texas would not allow the makers of *Viva Max!* to film inside the Alamo itself, so they had to build a replica in Spain or someplace. This movie was made in the same vein as *The Russians Are Coming*. It stars Peter Ustinov as a modern-day Mexican general who decides to recapture the Alamo. It's not very funny, and the Daughters were right about it: it's a desecration of hallowed ground.

PRODUCERS AND DIRECTORS FROM TEXAS

1. Howard Hughes. The eccentric millionaire produced numerous films in the thirties and forties, including *Hell's Angels* (1930), *Scarface* (1932), and *The Outlaw* (1943). He fostered the careers of many starlets and dated many more: Billie Dove, Jean Harlow, Katharine Hepburn, Ava Gardner, Ginger Rogers.

2. King Vidor. The journalist-turned-director made such early movies as *The Big Parade* (1925); later films included *Stella Dallas* (1937), *Northwest Passage* (1939), *Duel in the Sun* (1946), and *The Fountainhead* (1949).

3. Edward Sedgwick. He directed mainly pedestrian films, such as *Ma and Pa Kettle Back on the Farm* (1950), for a period of forty years.

4. Edwin Carewe. One of the great directors of silent films, he was noted for the beauty of his work. His movies include *Ramona* (1928) and *Evangeline* (1929).

5. Robert Benton. The University of Texas graduate won an Academy Award for his direction of *Kramer vs. Kramer* in 1979. The film also won five other Oscars.

TEXANS WHO WENT HOLLYWOOD

A partial list of men and women, past and present, who traded Texas for Tinseltown.

1. Dan Blocker. Born 1927, DeKalb; died 1972. Television (*Bonanza*).

2. Carol Burnett. Born 1936, San Antonio. Television (*The Carol Burnett Show*) and film (*A Wedding*).

3. Cyd Charisse. Born 1923, Amarillo. Film (*Silk Stockings*) and dance.

4. Joan Crawford. Born 1903, San Antonio; died 1977. Film (*Mildred Pierce* won her an an Academy Award).

5. Bebe Daniels. Born 1901, Dallas; died 1971. Film (*The Maltese Falcon,* 1931 version). Early silent screen star.

6. Linda Darnell. Born 1921, Dallas; died 1965. Film (*Forever Amber*).

7. Shelley Duvall. Born 1949, Houston. Film (*The Shining*).

8. Dale Evans. Born 1912, Uvalde. Multitudinous westerns.

9. Farrah Fawcett. Born 1947, Corpus Christi. Television (*Charlie's Angels*) and film (*Somebody Killed Her Husband*).

10. Larry Hagman. Born 1931, Fort Worth. Television (*Dallas*).

11. Ann Harding. Born 1902, Fort Sam Houston. Film (*Biography of a Bachelor Girl*).

12. Martha Hyer. Born 1929, Fort Worth. Film (*The Sons of Katie Elder*).

13. Carolyn Jones. Born 1933, Amarillo. Television (*The Addams Family*).

14. Evelyn Keyes. Born 1925, Port Arthur. Film (*Gone With the Wind*).

15. Linda Lovelace. Born 1949, Bryan. Film (*Deep Throat*).

16. Mary Martin. Born 1913, Weatherford. Film (*Birth of the Blues*), television (*Peter Pan*), and stage.

17. Spanky McFarland. Born 1928, Dallas. Film (*Our Gang* comedies).

18. Ann Miller. Born 1923, Chireno. Film (*Reveille for Beverly*) and stage.

19. Tom Mix. Born 1880, El Paso; died 1940. One of the first western actors.

20. Fess Parker. Born 1925, Fort Worth. Television (*Daniel Boone*) and film (*Davy Crockett*).

21. Paula Prentiss. Born 1939, San Antonio. Film (*Where the Boys Are*) and television (*He and She*).

22. Debbie Reynolds. Born 1932, El Paso. Film (*Singin' in the Rain*).

23. Zachary Scott. Born 1914, Austin; died 1965. Film (*The Southerner*) and stage.

24. Ann Sheridan. Born 1915, Denton; died 1967. Film (*King's Row*). Known as "the Oomph Girl."

25. Jaclyn Smith. Born 1948, Houston. Television (*Charlie's Angels*).

26. Sissy Spacek. Born 1949, Quitman. Film (*Coal Miner's Daughter*).

27. Gale Storm. Born 1922, Bloomington. Film (*The Texas Rangers*) and television (*My Little Margie*).

LIZ SMITH'S FAVORITE TEXAS CELEBRITIES

Liz Smith is a native Texan and a columnist for the New York *Daily News.*

1. Ginger Rogers, actress/dancer.
2. Ann Miller, actress/dancer.
3. Fess Parker,* actor.
4. Kathy Crosby,* actress.
5. Word Baker,* theater director.
6. Eli Wallach, actor.
7. Tom Jones,* playwright.
8. Harvey Schmidt,* playwright.
9. Bob Benton,* film director.
10. John Bryson,* photographer.
11. Bill Yates,* cartoonist.
12. Elaine Steinbeck, widow of John.
13. Mary Martin, actress.
14. Lady Bird Johnson, former first lady.
15. Liz Carpenter, former press secretary to above.
16. Bud Shrake, sports writer.
17. Dan Jenkins, sports writer and novelist.
18. Tommy Thompson, writer.
19. Barbara Barrie,* actress.
20. Pat Hingle,* actor.
21. Walter Cronkite, veteran CBS newsman.
22. Dan Rather, CBS newsman.
23. Zachary Scott (died 1965), actor.
24. Lyndon B. Johnson (died 1973), former U.S. president.
25. Jayne Mansfield (died 1967),* actress.

*Classmates of Liz Smith's at the University of Texas.

SIX FLAGS PERFORMERS WHO MOVED ON TO TELEVISION

1. Betty Buckley, who plays Abby Bradford on *Eight is Enough.*

2. Jay Johnson, who plays the dual role of Chuck and Bob on *Soap.* He also hosted a game show called *Celebrity Charades.*

3. Dennis Burkley, a regular on *Sanford and Son.*

4. Laurie Stephenson, a performer on the daytime serial *Texas.*

5. Ralna English, featured singer on *The Lawrence Welk Show.*

6. Chris Grant, regular on *The John Davidson Show.*

7. Cissy King, long-time dancer and regular on *The Lawrence Welk Show.*

SOURCE: *Six Flags, Inc., Show Productions.*

FIFTEEN FAMOUS TEXAS SONGS

1. "San Antonio Rose."
2. "Streets of Laredo."
3. "Red River Valley."
4. "I'm an Old Cowhand From the Rio Grande."
5. "T for Texas."
6. "The Ballad of the Alamo."
7. "El Paso" (and later "El Paso City").
8. "Goin' Back to Houston."
9. "Galveston."
10. "Miles and Miles of Texas."
11. "Texas When I Die."
12. "London Homesick Blues."
13. "Is Anybody Goin' to San Antone?"
14. "San Antonio Stroll."
15. "Waltz Across Texas."

CONTRIBUTORS: *Frank W. Latham, Jr., Waco; J. Stephen Gilbert, Abilene.*

TEXANS IN THE COUNTRY MUSIC HALL OF FAME

1. Tex Ritter, elected 1964. Woodward Maurice Ritter was born January 12, 1907, at Murvaul in Panola County. He once intended to become a lawyer, but turned instead to entertainment. His first recording, "Rye Whiskey," was released in 1931; it was followed by dozens of other songs, including, "Life Gets Teejus, Don't It," "Hillbilly Heaven," "Jingle, Jangle, Jingle," "Boll Weevil," and "Wagon Wheels." In the early forties Ritter became the first artist to be signed by Capitol Records. He appeared on eight radio shows in the thirties, notably "Cowboy Tom's Roundup," and in 1936 made the first of more than eighty films, *Song of the Gringo*. Ritter, called "America's Most Beloved Cowboy," was only the second living person ever inducted into the Country Music Hall of Fame. He died in Nashville, Tennessee, on January 2, 1974.

2. Ernest Tubb, elected 1965. Tubb, nicknamed "Wash" as a child, was born in rural Ellis County on February 9, 1914. At thirteen he first heard a Jimmie Rodgers record, which convinced him to become a singer. One of the people who helped him succeed in his goal was Rodgers's widow. Tubb's career took off in 1943 with his recording of the classic "I'm Walking the Floor Over You," which sold three million copies. He joined the Grand Ol' Opry the same year. With his band, the Texas Troubadours, Tubb traveled as many as 100,000 miles a year; his total record sales are twenty million. He was the sixth person elected to the Country Music Hall of Fame.

3. Jim Reeves, elected 1967. Reeves was born in Panola County, the same county that produced Tex Ritter, on August 20, 1924. At ten he had his own radio show in Shreveport, Louisiana. He continued to play guitar and sing throughout high school, but on graduation from the University of Texas he signed with the St. Louis Cardinals. After two years of professional baseball, though, he injured a nerve and returned to music, first as a disc jockey and eventually as the master of ceremonies on the famed "Louisiana Hayride" radio show. He began recording, and with the success of "Mexican Joe" in 1953, started climbing. He joined the Opry in 1955. Some of his best-known songs are "Blue Canadian Rockies," "Tahiti," and "He'll Have to Go," which sold three million records and made him the number-one male singer in country and western music in 1960. His fame was equally great overseas. In 1964, as Reeves was returning from a business trip, his private plane crashed ten miles outside Nashville. He was 39.

4. Bob Wills, elected 1968. Born in tiny Kosse in Limestone County, Bob Wills never made it past the seventh grade. He left home at sixteen, picking cotton and preaching for a while before returning home to his music-minded family. There he resumed the fiddling he had first learned as a child and began to play dances and parties regularly. In 1926 he moved to Turkey, which became his adopted hometown, and four years later formed the core of the band that was to make him famous. Though the group had various names, it first became known as the Light Crust Dough Boys because of the group's promotional work for a flour mill (around which time the band also played for W. Lee "Pappy" O'Daniel, a future governor of Texas). By the mid-thirties Wills and his Texas Playboys were widely known and in great demand. Though Wills appeared in quite a few movies he was best known for his foot-stomping music. Two of his songs, "San Antonio Rose" and "Faded Love," are among the best country songs of all time. Other tunes written and associated with Wills include "Steel Guitar Rag," "Lone Star Rag," "Take Me Back to Tulsa," and "Big Balls in Cowtown." He wrote approximately five hundred songs. Wills died on May 13, 1975.

5. Gene Autry, elected 1969. Though Autry was born in Tioga, Texas, on September 29, 1907, he moved to Oklahoma as a small boy (a town there bears his name). Autry was the original "Singing Cowboy." In the late twenties he began his radio work in Tulsa and Chicago, among other places, and in 1934 moved on to Hollywood, making eight movies in his first year there. He remained the top western box office draw for seven years. At the same time his songs were nationwide hits: "That Silver-Haired Daddy of Mine," "Buttons and Bows," "Back in the Saddle Again," "Tumbling Tumbleweeds," and "Rudolph the Red-Nosed Reindeer," which sold five million copies. Autry went to war in 1941 as a pilot with the Air Transport Command. When he returned he undertook the *Melody Ranch* and *Range Rider* TV series. He currently owns the California Angels baseball team as well as several TV and radio stations.

COUNTRY AND WESTERN STARS

1. Willie Nelson. Born Abbott, Texas, 1933. He is probably the best-loved musician in the state, as is evidenced by the number of Texans who simply refer to him as "Willie." A member of the Nashville Songwriters Hall of Fame, he has written many beautiful songs, such as "Hello, Walls" and "Crazy," which are now classics, as well as the gold record "Blue Eyes Cryin' in the Rain." His albums include *Red-Headed Stranger, The Troublemaker,* and *Stardust,* and he has appeared in several films, including *The Electric Horseman* and *Honeysuckle Rose.*

2. Waylon Jennings. Born Littlefield, 1937. Once a member of Buddy Holly's band, the Crickets, Waylon went on to form his own group, the Waylors. He has recorded steadily for over twenty years. One early hit was "That's What You Get for Lovin' Me," and a later one was "Good-Hearted Woman," recorded with Willie Nelson. He and Willie also made *Wanted: The Outlaws,* which won a Country Music Association award for best album in 1977.

3. George Jones. Born Saratoga, 1931. Sometimes called the "King of Country Music," George Jones first had a hit in 1955. "White Lightnin'" and "She Thinks I Still Care" were number-one hits; other major songs include "Window Up Above," "Things Have Gone to Pieces," and "Take Me." He recorded the last with Tammy Wynette, to whom he was once married.

4. Roger Miller. Born Fort Worth, 1936. His most popular song was doubtlessly "King of the Road," but "Dang Me" ranks a close second.

5. Ray Price. Born Perryville, 1926. His many well-known songs include "Crazy Arms," "My Shoes Keep Walking Back to You," and "Pride."

6. Buck Owens. Born Sherman, 1929. With his band, the Buckaroos, he has scored many hits, such as "Love's Gonna Live Here" and "Together Again," both of which he wrote.

7. Johnny Horton. Born Tyler, 1929; died 1960. The man who sang "The Battle of New Orleans" and "Sink the Bismarck" died in a car wreck when he was 31.

8. Lefty Frizzell. Born Corsicana, 1928. He is best remembered for "Saginaw, Michigan," a number-one hit in 1964.

9. Hank Thompson. Born Waco, 1925. A performer who carried on the great tradition of the western band, Thompson has had dozens of hits, including "Honky-tonk Girl," "Six-Pack to Go," and the classic "Wildwood Flower."

10. Jimmy Dean. Born Plainview, 1928. His single "Big Bad John" sold more than two million copies.

11. Kenny Rogers. Born Houston, 1941. Early pop hits with the First Edition were "Just Dropped In" and "Something's Burning"; later countrified story-songs include "Lucille," "The Gambler," and "Coward of the County."

12. Tanya Tucker. Born Seminole, 1958. Twenty-three-year-old Tanya has been a recording star half her life, recording "Will You Lay With me (in a Field of Stone)?," "Here's Some Love," "San Antonio Stroll," and "It's a Cowboy-Lovin' Night," among others.

13. Barbara Mandrell. Born Houston, 1948. "Sleeping Single in a Double Bed," "Standing Room Only," and "(If Loving You Is Wrong) I Don't Want to Be Right" were all hits.

14. Jeannie C. Riley. Born Anson, 1945. She became a success with her 1968 hit, "Harper Valley PTA."

15. Freddie Fender. Born San Benito, 1937. Latin-flavored songs include "When the Next Teardrop Falls," "Wasted Days and Wasted Nights," "You'll Lose a Good Thing," and "Living It Down."

16. Johnny Rodriguez. Born Sabinal, 1951. His first recording was "Pass Me By," followed by the successful "You Always Come Back to Hurting Me" and many others.

KVET COUNTRY-RADIO'S TOP TEN OF 1980

1. "Lookin' for Love," Johnny Lee.
2. "I Believe in You," Don Williams.
3. "Drivin' My Life Away," Eddie Rabbitt.
4. "On the Road Again," Willie Nelson.
5. "My Heart/Silent Night," Ronnie Milsap.
6. "Lady," Kenny Rogers.
7. "Smokey Mountain Rain," Ronnie Milsap.
8. "Love Me Over Again," Don Williams.
9. "He Stopped Loving Her Today," George Jones.
10. "It's Like We Never Said Goodbye," Crystal Gayle.

SOURCE: *KVET, Austin.*

KLIF'S ADULT CONTEMPORARY TOP TEN OF 1980

1. "Woman In Love," Barbra Streisand.
2. "Sailing," Christopher Cross.
3. "Magic," Olivia Newton-John.
4. "Drivin' My Life Away," Eddie Rabbitt.
5. "Lady," Kenny Rogers.
6. "The Rose," Bette Midler.
7. "All Out of Love," Air Supply.
8. "Longer," Dan Fogelberg.
9. "Let Me Love You Tonight," Pure Prairie League.
10. "Lookin' for Love," Johnny Lee.

SOURCE: *KLIF radio, Dallas (KLIF has since switched to a country format).*

GREAT ROCK STARS

1. Buddy Holly, born Charles Hardin Holley in Lubbock in 1936, was an incredibly powerful influence on rock 'n' roll. Earnest and bespectacled, he hardly looked the type to change the course of modern music. By the time he was fifteen he already had a local reputation as a country singer; then, impressed by singers like Elvis Presley and Carl Perkins, he switched to rock but created his own special style. He began writing songs, many of which are classics today: "Peggy Sue," "That'll Be the Day," "Maybe, Baby," "Oh, Boy," "Rave On," "Not Fade Away," "Words of Love," and many more. With his group, the Crickets, he toured all over the U.S. and Europe. On February 3, 1959, only a year and a half after he cut his first single, Buddy died in a plane crash near Mason City, Iowa, while on the way to a concert. (Also killed in the wreck were native Texan J.P. Richardson, called the "Big Bopper," and Richie Valens.) Buddy Holly was only 22, but he was already a legend.

2. Janis Joplin, a native of Port Arthur, was born in 1943. She left home at seventeen and began singing in bars and coffee-houses in Houston and Austin, then drifted to San Francisco. There she joined up with a newly formed rock group, Big Brother and the Holding Company, who were in search of a singer. The next year the band appeared at the Monterey Pop Festival, and Janis's raw, throaty, urgent voice wowed the crowd and made her name. Three of her albums are *Cheap Thrills,* with Big Brother; *I Got Dem Ol' Kozmic Blues Again, Mama* with the Kozmic Blues Band; and *Pearl,* her last album, with the Full-Tilt Boogie Band. She was famed for her electric performances of songs such as "Ball and Chain," "Piece of My Heart," and "Me and Bobby McGee," but though she was a dynamo onstage, offstage she seemed to radiate a simultaneous vulnerability and defiance. In 1970, at age 27, Janis was found dead of a heroin overdose in Hollywood's Landmark Hotel.

3. Roy Orbison, born in 1936, came from the little town of Wink, where he formed his first group, the Wink Westerners, in high school. It was strictly a country band, but Orbison soon reformed it into a rock 'n' roll band, the Teen Kings, and in 1956 they recorded "Ooby Dooby" at Norman Petty's studio in Clovis, New Mexico (the same studio where Buddy Holly first recorded). "Ooby Dooby" was a hit, and Roy moved to Nashville. He took up songwriting for a while but in 1960 recorded "Only the Lonely," which took off and sold two million copies. With dark glasses and slicked-back hair,

Roy developed his own particular image, and, like Buddy Holly, he was as popular in England as in the U.S. His later hits included "Running Scared," "Crying," and his 1964 gold record, "Oh, Pretty Woman." After 1965, though, his success seemed to falter a bit; he retired from the limelight after his wife and two of his children died in separate accidents. But though he recorded erratically, he never gave up music completely, and in 1981 he won a Grammy for his duet with Emmylou Harris on "That Lovin' You Feelin' Again."

ROCK, POP, AND SOUL PERFORMERS

1. Kris Kristofferson was born in Brownsville in 1936. A Rhodes scholar, he wrote now-classic songs like "Help Me Make It Through the Night," "Sunday Mornin' Comin' Down," and "Me and Bobby McGee" before starting his own successful recording career. He also starred in a number of movies, including *Alice Doesn't Live Here Anymore.*

2. Stephen Stills, born in 1943, is a former member of the groups Buffalo Springfield and Crosby, Stills, Nash, and Young. The Dallas native now performs solo. Two of his best-known songs are "For What It's Worth" and "Love the One You're With."

3. Steve Miller, also born in Dallas in 1943, began his career at age twelve in a group called the Marksmen. Major hits include "The Joker," "Your Saving Grace," and "Living in the USA."

4. Boz Scaggs, born in 1944, also played in the Marksmen in his hometown of Dallas and later in the Steve Miller Band, then took off on a solo career. One top ten hit was "Lowdown" in 1976.

5. Sly Stone, yet another Dallasite, was born in 1944. Sly formed the Family Stone in 1967 (his brother Fred was a member), and they turned out a string of hits, starting with "Dance to the Music" and also including "Stand!," "I Want to Take You Higher," and "Everybody Is a Star."

6. Trini Lopez, born—yes, it's true—in Dallas in 1937, recorded hit singles of folk songs like "If I Had a Hammer" as well as footstompers like "La Bamba."

7. Meat Loaf is still another Dallas boy, born in 1947. His first album was *Bat Out of Hell,* and he also had a role in the cult film *The Rocky Horror Picture Show.*

8. ZZ Top is an El Paso band, and the names of some of the group's albums—*Rio Grande Mud, Tres Hombres,* and *La Grange*—reflect their roots. The band has been performing for over a decade.

9. Mike Nesmith was born in Houston in 1942. One of the original members of the Monkees, a pop group that had a TV show of the same name, Nesmith was the only member with any real talent. He continues to write and perform serious music today.

10. Seals & Crofts, from Sidney and Cisco respectively, were both born in Houston. Their songs "Summer Breeze" and "Diamond Girl" were gold records.

11. Mac Davis, a Lubbock native born in 1941, is best-known for "Baby, Don't Get Hooked on Me." He has also appeared in films, notably *North Dallas Forty.*

12. B.J. Thomas, born in Houston in 1942, recorded "Bring Back the Time" and "Eyes of a New York Woman," among others. His most frequently heard hit is "Raindrops Keep Falling on My Head."

13. B.W. Stevenson, whose hometown is Austin, was born in 1949. He released a successful recording of "Shambala," and his song "My Maria" hit the top ten in 1973.

14. Joe Tex was born in Rogers in 1933. He began his career by winning first prize in a talent contest and went on to regularly turn out soul hits and novelty songs like "One Monkey Don't Stop No Show."

15. Johnny Nash, once a regular on radio shows, scored a hit in 1972 with "I Can See Clearly Now." He was born in Houston in 1940.

16. Billy Preston, who started out as a gospel singer, is a native Houstonian, born in 1946. He has worked with a number of star performers, including Little Richard, Ray Charles, and the Beatles.

ONE-SHOT TEXAS BANDS

People who flashed in the pan and their short-lived hits.

1. The Bobby Fuller Four (from El Paso), "I Shot the Law."

2. ? (Question Mark) and the Mysterians (from the Valley), "96 Tears."

3. Sam the Sham (from Dallas), "Wooly Bully" and "Little Red Riding Hood" (with the Pharaohs).

4. Bubble Puppy (from Austin), "Hot Smoke and Sassafras."

5. Paul and Paula (Joshua and Brownwood, respectively), "Hey, Paula."

6. Dobie Gray (Brookshire), "The In Crowd."

7. Five Americans (Dallas), "Western Union."

8. Archie Bell and the Drells (Houston), "Tighten Up."

9. Mason Williams (Abilene), "Classical Gas."

10. Bloodrock (Dallas), "D.O.A."

MACK McCORMICK'S LIST OF TWENTY MAJOR FIGURES IN TEXAS BLUES

Mack McCormick, folklorist and cultural historian, is a specialist in regional American arts and their various creative centers. He was director of a Festival of American Folklife presented at Montreal's Expo '71 by the Smithsonian Institution and has produced documentary recordings such as *A Treasury of Field Recordings.*

1. Texas Alexander. A drifter with a moaning, trembling voice who sang blues and work songs straight out of the Texas prison farms where he served hard time.

2. Charles Brown. A leading figure in one of the later developments in the blues—a softened, plum-in-mouth vocal style that gained great popularity in the period after World War II.

3. Clarence "Gatemouth" Brown. A shape-shifting performer whose talents span several traditions. Now active in country music, but most notable for his forties recordings that crystallized a hard, staccato guitar sound and helped shape the era of rock.

4. Clifton Chenier. Chief exponent of Zydeco, a hybrid music acquired when French-speaking people from Louisiana found jobs in southeast Texas and created a bilingual, blues-tinged dance music heard in the French Town sections of several Texas cities.

5. Sam "Lightnin'" Hopkins. Certainly not the last of the great bluesmen, but a compelling entertainer on the rare occasions when he makes the effort.

6. Prince Albert Hunt. One in a long line of country fiddlers seduced by the blues, and possessor of a lilting, insinuating style that remains unique.

7. Blind Lemon Jefferson. The keystone—the single most influential figure in early recorded blues. A blind, burly, lustful street singer. He never begged with a tin cup, but had dollars stuffed in his pockets by crowds that quickly gathered on the street corners at which he would arrive in a touring car driven by a uniformed chauffeur.

8. Blind Willie Johnson. An ardent bluesman in the memory of those who knew him and, on recordings made fifty years ago, the most passionate of the guitar-evangelists. His fierce, cracking voice was joyous with songs of worship and praise that bring redemptive power to the present day.

9. Janis Joplin. A singer of astonishing force and beauty who gave back more than she took from the blues.

10. Scott Joplin. An itinerant pianist from Bowie County who played elegant blues—along with stomps, mazurkas, and waltzes—in the wandering years before he flowered into the genius of classic ragtime.

11. Leadbelly (Huddie Ledbetter). The misunderstood multiple murderer and penitentiary inmate whose later life was entangled with gross publicity gimmicks, social causes, and hopeless career ambitions, all of which tend to obscure the fact that he was at every point of his life a major blues singer and ballad master.

12. Mance Lipscomb. The Navasota songster whose repertoire and gifts evoked the era before the blues became dominant, a generous and gentle sharecropper who found a new life performing for young audiences in the sixties.

13. Alexander Moore. A champion of love and a romantic poet whose poignant songs observe that life has a habit of remaining unfinished.

14. The Santa Fe Group. An assortment of barrelhouse pianists who thrived in Houston's Fourth Ward and found steady work in lumber camps along the Santa Fe Railroad and in Richmond's across-the-tracks sporting district. They created a repertoire known only to themselves (Andy Boy, Rob Cooper, Black Boy Shine, etc.) but which remains hearable today from the last living exponent of the school: Robert Shaw.

15. John T. Smith (a.k.a. "Howling Wolf" and "Funny Paper" Smith). An undiscovered giant with a gift for assuming names and disguises; a wry, comic, cynical, and much-imitated performer who frequented Fort Worth, West Texas, and some dusty corners of Oklahoma.

16. Henry "Ragtime Texas" Thomas. An exuberant railroading hobo from East Texas whose recordings furnish our deepest look at the roots of the blues and the rich mingling of nineteenth-century traditions.

17. The Thomas Family. A Houston dynasty centered in the Fifth Ward whose members include composer George Thomas, pianist and child prodigy Hersal Thomas, singers Hociel Thomas and Sippie Wallace (the senior Texas artist, still an active performer in her eighties), as well as friends like Bernice Edwards and rivals such as Victoria Spivey, whose own career in film and records spanned fifty years.

18. Bessie Tucker. The most spellbinding of a group of tough, brawling women singers who sprang up in Dallas's Second Avenue district, their lives largely unknown apart from their records and the biographical hints they contain.

19. Aaron "T-Bone" Walker. A dynamic, enduring performer whose career stretched from Oak Cliff street singing to tours of foreign capitals, and whose influence has touched thirty years of guitar players.

20. Johnny "Guitar" Watson. Among the youngest of those mentioned; a contemporary survivor and innovator.

Mack McCormick notes: the inclusion of some of those listed above is intended to be arguable and provocative. The exclusion of others is inexcusable. Black Ace, Euday Bowman, Walter Brown, Albert Collins, Will Ezell, Peppermint Harris, William McCoy, Jack Teagarden, Cotton Thompson, Eddie Vinson, as well as ranks of others deserve appropriate notice, not to mention important transplants ranging from Jimmie Rodgers to Johnnie Taylor and visitors such as Robert Johnson whose masterworks were recorded entirely in Texas. However, even if the longest possible list were rendered—one which might run to eight hundred names—it would omit hundreds more who contributed to the casual, ninety-year flow of the blues.

TWENTY EARLY JAZZMEN

1. John Dickson "Peck" Kelley, piano. Born in Houston, circa 1900.
2. Henry "Buster" Smith, reeds and guitar. Born in Ellis County, 1904.
3. Walter John "Jack" Teagarden, trombone and vocals. Born in Vernon, 1905.
4. Eddie Durham, trombone and guitar. Born in San Marcos, 1906.
5. Oran Thaddeus "Hot Lips" Page, trumpet and vocals. Born in Dallas, 1908.
6. Herschel Evans, reeds. Born in Denton, 1909.
7. Albert J. "Budd" Johnson, reeds and vocals. Born in Dallas, 1910.
8. "Queen" Victoria Spivey, piano, organ, and vocals. Born in Houston, circa 1910.
9. Ernie Caceres, reeds. Born in Rockport, 1911.
10. Tyree Glenn, trombone, vibraphone, and vocals. Born in Corsicana, 1912.
11. Teddy Shaw Wilson, piano. Born in Austin, 1912.
12. Eugene Ramey, bass. Born in Austin, 1913.
13. Gus Johnson, drums. Born in Tyler, 1913.
14. George Holmes "Buddy" Tate, reeds. Born in Sherman, 1914.
15. Eddie "Cleanhead" Vinson, reeds and vocals. Born in Houston, 1917.
16. Arnett Cobb, reeds. Born in Houston, 1918.
17. Charlie Christian, guitar. Born in Dallas, circa 1919.
18. Mitchell Herbert "Herb" Ellis, guitar. Born in McKinney, 1921.
19. Jimmy Giuffre, reeds. Born in Dallas, 1921.
20. McKinley "Kenny" Dorham, trumpet and reeds. Born in Fairfield, 1924.

CONTRIBUTOR: *J.M. Braffett, San Marcos.*

DOUG RAMSEY'S LIST OF TWENTY IMPORTANT YOUNGER JAZZ ARTISTS

Doug Ramsey, a noted jazz critic, now lives in San Francisco.

1. William M. "Red" Garland, piano. Born in Dallas, 1923.
2. Marc Johnson, bass. Born in Denton, 1954.
3. Ornette Coleman, alto saxophone, violin, and trumpet; also a composer. Born in Fort Worth, 1930.
4. Jimmie Ford, alto sax. Born in Houston, 1927.
5. Cedar Walton, piano. Born in Dallas, 1934.
6. Harold Land, tenor sax. Born in Houston, 1928.
7. Booker Ervin, tenor sax. Born in Denison, 1930.
8. Dewey Redman, tenor sax. Born in Fort Worth, 1931.
9. Billy Harper, tenor sax and flute. Born in Houston, 1953.
10. Wayne Henderson, trombone. Born in Houston, 1939.
11. James Clay, tenor sax and flute. Born in Dallas, 1935.
12. Leo Wright, alto sax and flute. Born in Wichita Falls, 1933.
13. Luis Gasca, trumpet. Born in Houston, 1940.
14. John Hardee, tenor sax. Born in Houston, 1920.
15. David "Fathead" Newman, tenor sax, alto sax, and flute. Born in Dallas, 1933.
16. Don Albert, trumpet and bandleader. Born in New Orleans, 1908; based in San Antonio from 1929 on.
17. Joe Sample, piano. Born in Houston, 1939.
18. Wilton Felder, tenor sax and electric bass. Born in Houston, 1940.
19. Larry Coryell, guitar. Born in Galveston, 1943.
20. King Curtis (Curtis Ousley), tenor sax. Born in Fort Worth, 1935.

TWO TEXAS PIANISTS

1. Scott Joplin, the "King of Ragtime," was born in Texarkana. A composer and performer as well as a pianist, he wrote "Maple Leaf Rag" in 1899; the song sold one million copies. He also wrote the opera *Treemonisha*.

2. Van Cliburn, who grew up in Kilgore, won first prize in the International Tchaikovsky Piano Competition in 1958. The Juilliard graduate debuted with the Houston Symphony Orchestra in 1947 and that year won the first of his many awards, the Texas State Prize.

TWO TEXAS CHOREOGRAPHERS

1. Alvin Ailey, born in Rogers in 1931, started his acclaimed troupe, the Alvin Ailey American Dance Theater, in 1958.

2. Tommy Tune, born in Wichita Falls in 1939, has been a featured dancer not only in Broadway productions but in several films.

PLACES YOU WOULDN'T EXPECT TO HAVE SYMPHONY ORCHESTRAS BUT, NONETHELESS, DO

1. Amarillo.
2. Abilene.
3. Wichita Falls.
4. Lubbock.
5. Beaumont.
6. Irving.
7. Longview.
8. Marshall.
9. Richardson.
10. San Angelo.
11. Sherman.
12. Waco.

EIGHT PIPE ORGANS IN PUBLIC LOCATIONS

1. Scampi's Organ Palace, Austin.
2. Jefferson Theatre, Beaumont.
3. Fine Arts Theatre, Dallas.
4. Landmark Pizza and Pipes, Dallas.
5. Pipe Organ Pizza, Dallas.
6. Casa Mañana Theatre, Fort Worth.
7. Organ World Studio, Garland.
8. Scooby's Fun Factory, Houston.

CONTRIBUTOR: *Ira M. Williamson, Orange.*

CIRCUS FOLKS AND WILD WEST PERFORMERS

1. Bill Pickett, called the "Wonderful Negro," was one of the first rodeo stars. Born near Liberty Hill in the 1860s, he was part white, part black, and part Choctaw. He quit school to become a cowboy after the fifth grade, eventually signing up with a traveling Wild West show. His specialty was bulldogging; some even credit him with inventing the sport, and he always added a bit of bravado the crowd loved—biting the steer's lip as he wrestled it down. He died in 1932, and forty years later became the first black in the National Cowboy Hall of Fame.

2. Frank Buck, born in Gainesville in 1884, was an animal handler and importer. Though he began his career with Texas cattle, within ten years he was making expeditions to Africa, South America, and India, capturing rare animals for zoos, private collections, and Hollywood movies. He even appeared with some of his dangerous and exotic charges in several films. He also wrote a number of books about his exploits, notably *Bring 'em Back Alive*.

3. Mollie Bailey ran a circus that toured Texas for half a century. She married a showman, Gus Bailey, when she was eighteen, and shortly thereafter they bought their first tent, building up an entourage of thirty wagons (and later several railroad cars) and including acts by clowns, acrobats, dancers, horses, camels, and elephants. The Bailey Circus visited about a hundred Texas towns a year until 1918, when Mollie died.

4. Adolph Toepperwein, crack marksman, was born in Boerne shortly after the Civil War. He worked for a circus for many years before linking up with the Winchester Repeating Arms Company, serving as an exhibition agent and public relations man. He married a Yankee who was completely ignorant of guns, but trained her to be a top sharpshooter, too. Billed as the "Famous Toepperweins," the two toured the country for forty years, staging shows that drew large crowds. Adolph set many records, including a world record in 1907 when he shot, without a single miss, 8000 targets thrown in the air.

5. Jack Earle, a native of El Paso, began his circus career in the twenties when he wandered into a sideshow of the Barnum & Bailey Circus to see the freak billed as the "Tallest Man in the World." To his surprise, Jack discovered he was taller than the man in the booth, who was shortly out of a job. Jack thus succeeded to the title of Tallest Man, though in truth many others were documented as quite a bit taller than he was: the circus posters claimed he was eight feet, seven inches, but he was really a foot shorter.

Education, Arts, and Media

BIGGEST COLLEGES AND THEIR ENROLLMENTS

1. University of Texas at Austin, 43,100.
2. Texas A&M University, 30,250.
3. University of Houston, 29,650.
4. Houston Community College, 27,100.
5. Texas Tech University, 22,700.
6. San Antonio College, 20,650.
7. University of Texas at Arlington, 18,250.
8. North Texas State University, 17,300.
9. University of Texas at El Paso, 15,750.
10. Southwest Texas State University, 15,050.

CONTRIBUTOR: *Don Deal, Houston.*

UNIVERSITIES WITH ENDOWMENTS OF A QUARTER OF A BILLION DOLLARS OR MORE

1. The University of Texas, $1 billion-plus.
2. Rice University, $250,000,000.

TUITION AT FOUR PRIVATE COLLEGES, SPRING SEMESTER 1981

1. Rice, $2900 per semester.
2. SMU, $150 per semester hour.
3. Trinity, $125 per semester hour.
4. Baylor, $70 per semester hour.

FORMER NAMES OF FAMOUS COLLEGES

1. UT-Arlington was once Arlington College, then North Texas Agricultural College, then Arlington State College.

2. UT-El Paso, originally called the Texas College of Mines, later became Texas Western College.

3. Texas A&I University started out as South Texas Teachers College, then was named the Texas College of Arts and Industries.

4. Texas Woman's University used to be the College of Industrial Arts, then became the Texas State College for Women.

5. Texas Southern University was formerly Houston College for Negroes and later Texas State University for Negroes.

SELECTED TERMS OF AGGIE SLANG

1. Air krapper: an Air Force cadet.
2. Anchor clanger: a Navy cadet.
3. Crunchie: an Army cadet.
4. Jarhead: a Marine Corps cadet.
5. Non-reg: a civilian undergraduate student.
6. Ol' Army: the way it used to be.
7. Humping it: Assuming the position taken when giving a cheer, i.e., putting hands on knees and bending at the waist.
8. Day duck: a student who does not live in a campus dorm.
9. Hole: an Aggie's dorm room.
10. Moose: an undesirable date.

SOURCE: *Lexicon of the Texas A&M Student Handbook.*

ELEVEN FAMOUS AGGIES

1. John David Crow, Heisman Trophy winner, 1957.
2. Pinky Wilson, author of the Aggie war hymn.
3. Jack Pardee, former Washington Redskins coach.
4. Bill Yeoman, University of Houston coach.
5. A.R. "Babe" Schwartz, longtime state senator.
6. Billy Clayton, speaker of the Texas House of Representatives.
7. The late Olin "Tiger" Teague, longtime U.S. representative.
8. Bill Moore, former state senator.
9. Randy Matson, Olympic gold medalist and world-record setter in the shot put.
10. Reagan Brown, Texas commissioner of agriculture.
11. Edward M. "Buck" Schiwetz, artist.

SOURCE: *Texas A&M University.*

CLASSY FACTS ABOUT A&M

1. Largest enrollment: first-year chemistry, which 4600 students signed up for in the fall of 1980.

2. Smallest enrollment: bryology, a botany course on mosses, liverworts, and hornworts.

3. Most unusual class: veterinary acupuncture, probably the only such class held in an American university. Runners-up are nuclear reactor theory, nautical archeology, and Texas geography for big-city kids.

Source: *Texas A&M University.*

FAMOUS SMU ALUMNI

1. James Cronin, 1980 Nobel prizewinner in physics.
2. Governor William P. Clements.
3. Senator John Tower.
4. Congressman James Collins.
5. Sports personality Don Meredith.
6. Five football greats: Doak Walker, Kyle Rote, Forrest Gregg, Bobby Wilson, Raymond Berry.
7. Dorothy Malone, Academy Award–winning actress.
8. Jerry Heidenreich, Olympic gold medalist in swimming.
9. Lamar and Ray Hunt, corporate titans.
10. Bob Banner and Aaron Spelling, TV producers.
11. Powers Boothe, Emmy-winning actor.
12. Jack Heifner, playwright.
13. Robert Folsom, mayor of Dallas.
14. Robert Krueger, former congressman, ambassador, and U.S. coordinator for Mexican affairs.

Source: *SMU.*

THE SMU BOOKSTORE'S BEST-SELLERS OF 1980

1. *Garfield at Large,* Jim Davis.
2. *Free to Choose,* Milton and Rose Friedman.
3. *The Collected Stories of Eudora Welty.*
4. *The World of Paul Crume,* edited by Marion Crume.
5. *The Official Preppy Handbook.*
6. *The 40- to 60-Year-Old Male,* Michael E. McGill.
7. *Fabergé Eggs,* commentary by Christopher Forbes, photographs by Larry Stein.
8. *The Aging Game,* Barbara Anderson.
9. *Gödel/Escher/Bach,* Douglas Hofstadter.
10. *Cosmos,* Carl Sagan.

SOURCE: *SMU.*

TEXAS UNIVERSITIES THAT HAVE WON THE GE COLLEGE BOWL

1. Rice University, 1966.

FAMOUS UT ALUMNI

1. Lady Bird Johnson, former First Lady.
2. Walter Cronkite, venerable CBS anchorman.
3. Fernando Belaundé-Terry, president of Peru.
4. Sam Rayburn, late speaker of the U.S. House of Representatives.
5. Denton Cooley, heart surgeon.
6. Alan Bean, fourth man to walk on the moon.
7. Tom Landry, coach of the Dallas Cowboys.
8. Allan Shivers, former governor.
9. John B. Connally, former governor.
10. Dolph Briscoe, former governor.
11. Lloyd Bentsen, U.S. senator.
12. Joe R. Greenhill, chief justice of the Texas Supreme Court.
13. J.J. "Jake" Pickle, congressman.

14. Fess Parker, actor.
15. Eli Wallach, actor.
16. Farrah Fawcett, actress.
17. Barbara Barrie, actress.
18. Liz Smith, columnist.
19. Tommy Tune, choreographer and dancer.
20. Robert Benton, director.

SOURCE: *University of Texas at Austin.*

1980 BEST-SELLERS AT THE UNIVERSITY CO-OP, THE UNIVERSITY OF TEXAS AT AUSTIN

Fiction:

1. *Jailbird,* Kurt Vonnegut, Jr.
2. *Aransas,* Stephen Harrigan.
3. *The Covenant,* James Michener.
4. *Still Life with Woodpecker,* Tom Robbins.
5. *A Confederacy of Dunces,* John Kennedy Toole.
6. *The Second Coming,* Walker Percy.
7. *Firestarter,* Stephen King.
8. *Freddy's Book,* John Gardner.
9. *The Ghost Writer,* Philip Roth.

Nonfiction:

1. *The Joy of Cooking,* Irma S. Rombauer and Marion R. Becker.
2. *Cosmos,* Carl Sagan.
3. *From a Limestone Ledge,* John Graves.
4. *Drawing on the Right Side of the Brain,* Betty Edwards.
5. *Gödel/Escher/Bach,* Douglas Hofstadter.
6. *The Next Whole Earth Catalog,* edited by Stewart Brand.
7. *Roadside Flowers of Texas,* Mary M. Wills and Howard S. Irwin.
8. *Texas Statehouse Blues,* Ben Sargent.
9. *What Color is Your Parachute?,* Richard Bolles.

SOURCE: *University Co-op, University of Texas at Austin.*

ALL-TIME BEST-SELLERS PUBLISHED BY THE UNIVERSITY OF TEXAS PRESS

1. *The Book of Merlyn,* which had sold 125,000 copies by the end of 1980. It appeared on the *New York Times* best-seller list on October 9, 1977, and stayed there for 26 weeks. According to the newspaper, it was the first work of fiction from a university press to make the list in a quarter of a century.
2. *The Diabetic's Cookbook,* 96,500 copies (now out of print).
3. *Alcoholism,* 43,000 copies.
4. *Roadside Flowers of Texas,* 39,900 copies.
5. *Platero and I,* 36,000 copies.
6. *The Texas Rangers,* 35,000 copies.

SOURCE: *University of Texas at Austin.*

MOST REQUESTED COURSES AT THE UNIVERSITY OF TEXAS

1. Rock Music Since 1969.
2. Science and the Environment.
3. Business and Professional Speaking.
4. Descriptive Introductory Astronomy.

LEAST REQUESTED COURSES AT THE UNIVERSITY OF TEXAS

1. Indian Philosophy: the Upanishads.
2. Second-year Hindi.
3. Second-year Swahili.
4. Elementary Sanskrit.
5. Intermediate Ballroom Dance.

CURIOUS COURSE TITLES AT THE UNIVERSITY OF TEXAS

1. Scandanavian Family Conflicts (sociology).
2. Cowboys and Samurai (Oriental and African languages and literature).
3. Extraterrestrial Life: Are We Alone? (astronomy).
4. Gypsy Language and Culture (linguistics).
5. Born-Again Religion (sociology).
6. Artificial Intelligence (computer sciences).

SOURCE: *University of Texas at Austin.*

TEN ORIGINAL MANUSCRIPTS IN UT'S HUMANITIES RESEARCH CENTER

1. William Faulkner's *Absalom! Absalom!*
2. D.H. Lawrence's *Lady Chatterley's Lover.*
3. George Bernard Shaw's *Pygmalion.*
4. Aldous Huxley's *Brave New World.*
5. E.M. Forster's *Passage to India.*
6. Samuel Beckett's *Waiting for Godot.*
7. Joseph Conrad's *Victory.*
8. Ernest Hemingway's *Death in the Afternoon.*
9. Eugene O'Neill's *Mourning Becomes Electra.*
10. Sinclair Lewis's *Main Street.*

SOURCE: *Humanities Research Center, University of Texas at Austin.*

TWENTY AUTHOR COLLECTIONS AT UT'S HUMANITIES RESEARCH CENTER THAT ARE THE WORLD'S LARGEST

1. Hilaire Belloc, poet and essayist.
2. Elizabeth Bowen, novelist.
3. Graham Greene, novelist and playwright.

4. Lillian Hellman, playwright.
5. Burl Ives, songwriter and folksinger.
6. Robinson Jeffers, poet.
7. Oliver LaFarge, novelist.
8. D. H. Lawrence, novelist and poet.
9. T. E. Lawrence, soldier and writer.
10. Carson McCullers, novelist.
11. Edgar Lee Masters, poet.
12. Arthur Miller, playwright.
13. A. A. Milne, children's writer.
14. Christopher Morley, essayist and novelist.
15. Ogden Nash, poet.
16. George Bernard Shaw, playwright.
17. Dylan Thomas, poet.
18. Irving Wallace, novelist.
19. Evelyn Waugh, novelist.
20. T. H. White, novelist.

SOURCE: *Humanities Research Center, University of Texas at Austin.*

CURIOSITIES AT UT'S HUMANITIES RESEARCH CENTER

1. Sir Arthur Conan Doyle's eyeglasses.

2. Evelyn Waugh's walking stick.

3. Erle Stanley Gardner's complete study—from chairs to knick-knacks.

4. *The Book of Merlyn,* by T. H. White. The original manuscript of the fifth book of *The Once and Future King* was accidentally discovered in the HRC's archives.

5. The first photograph ever taken, by Niépce in 1826.

6. Edgar Allan Poe's desk.

7. Photographs of Alice Liddell, the real Alice of *Alice in Wonderland,* taken by Lewis Carroll.

8. Some of Harry Houdini's magic gear.

9. A collection of worthless stock certificates of the nineteenth and twentieth centuries.

10. Some thirty songs handwritten by Paul Anka.

11. A 1000-item collection of patent models from the U.S. Patent office, which till 1870 required a working model of any invention submitted for patent application. The items include such creations as a self-rocking chair.

12. The archives of the British Sexological Society from 1897 to 1940.

SOURCE: *Humanities Research Center, University of Texas at Austin.*

BOOKS MOST OFTEN REQUESTED FROM FOUR DEPARTMENTS OF THE HOUSTON PUBLIC LIBRARY IN 1980

Humanities:

1. *Transit of Venus,* Shirley Hazzard.
2. *The Covenant,* James Michener.
3. *Kane and Able,* Jeffrey Archer.
4. *The Spike,* Arnaud de Borchgrave.
5. *Earthly Powers,* Anthony Burgess.
6. *Answer as a Man,* Taylor Caldwell.
7. *The Fifth Horseman,* Larry Collins and Dominique LaPierre.
8. *The Ninja,* Eric von Lustbader.
9. *The Tenth Commandment,* Lawrence Sanders.
10. *Confederacy of Dunces,* John Kennedy Toole.
11. *Music for Chameleons,* Truman Capote.

Social Sciences:

1. *Occupational Outlook Handbook.*
2. *U.S. Government Manual.*
3. *College Blue Book.*
4. *Who's Who in America.*
5. *Vernon's Texas Civil Statutes.*
6. *Martindale Hubbel Law Directory.*
7. *Code of Federal Regulations.*
8. *Thy Neighbor's Wife,* Gay Talese.
9. *China Men,* Maxine Hong Kingston.
10. *The Brethren,* Bob Woodward and Scott Armstrong.

Fine Arts:

1. *Architectural Graphic Standards.*
2. *This Business of Music,* Sidney Shemel.
3. *Drawing on the Right Side of the Brain,* Betty Edwards.
4. *Apartment Book,* Rick Mitz.
5. *The Dome Builder's Handbook.*
6. *Scott Standard Postage Stamp Catalogue.*
7. *Bed and Bath Book,* Terence Conran.
8. *Shelley,* Shelley Winters.
9. *From Cannon to Campbell,* edited by Mickey Herskowitz.
10. *Donahue: My Own Story,* Phil Donahue.

Children's:

1. *Charlie and the Chocolate Factory,* Roald Dahl.
2. *Little House on the Prairie,* Laura Ingalls Wilder.
3. *The Hobbitt,* J.R.R. Tolkien.
4. *The Lion, The Witch, and the Wardrobe,* C.S. Lewis.
5. Various Nancy Drew books, Carolyn Keene.
6. *Encyclopedia Brown,* Donald Sabal.
7. *Where the Sidewalk Ends,* Shel Silverstein.
8. *Superfudge,* Judy Blume.
9. *Ramona and Her Father,* Beverly Cleary.
10. *The Black Stallion,* Walter Farley.

SOURCE: *Houston Public Library.*

SMALLEST PUBLIC LIBRARIES

1. Gorman Public Library, Eastland County, 575 volumes.
2. Balmorhea Library, Reeves, 650.
3. Irion County Library, 1050.
4. Murphy Public Library, Collin, 1500.
5. San Juan Public Library, Hidalgo, 1750.
6. Austwell Library, Refugio, 1800.
7. Shiner Public Library, Lavaca, 1900.

SOURCE: *Texas State Library.*

ODD BOOKSTORES

1. The Aldredge Bookstore, Dallas. Includes a wedding chapel.
2. The Wilson Bookshop, Dallas. Fine leather-bound books.
3. Frontier America, Bryan. The smallest bookstore in Texas—it's a post office box.
4. Detering Book Gallery, Houston. A beautiful converted mansion.
5. Ray S. Walton Books, Austin. Serves coffee to customers.
6. Limestone Hills Book Shop. Most historic bookstore—it was once attacked by Indians.

CONTRIBUTOR: *Trudi Watson, Napa, California.*

EIGHTEEN OUTSTANDING WRITERS

1. John Graves, essayist (*Goodbye to a River; Hard Scrabble*).

2. Larry McMurtry, novelist (*Horseman, Pass By; In a Narrow Grave*).

3. J. Frank Dobie, historian and folklorist (*Coronado's Children; Apache Gold and Yaqui Silver*).

4. Max Apple, novelist and short-story writer (*The Oranging of America; Zip*).

5. William Humphrey, novelist (*The Ordways; Home From the Hill*).

6. A.C. Greene, essayist (*A Personal Country*).

7. Benjamin Capps, novelist (*The Brothers of Uterica; The White Man's Road*).

8. Elmer Kelton, novelist (*The Time It Never Rained; The Wolf and the Buffalo*).

9. William Goyen, novelist (*The House of Breath*).

10. Shelby Hearon, novelist (*Painted Dresses; A Prince of a Fellow*).

11. Donald Barthelme, novelist and short-story writer (*City Life; Unspeakable Practices, Unnatural Acts*).

12. T.R. Fehrenbach, historian (*Lone Star*).

13. Walter Prescott Webb, historian (*The Texas Rangers*).

14. Roy Bedichek, naturalist (*Adventures With a Texas Naturalist*).

15. Michael Mewshaw, novelist (*Land Without Shadow; The Toll*).

16. Larry L. King, essayist and journalist (*Confessions of a White Racist*).

17. Vassar Miller, poet (*If I Could Sleep Deeply Enough; My Bones Being Wiser*).

18. Naomi Shihab Nye, poet (*Different Ways to Pray*).

SOURCE: *five Texas writers, one of whom appears on this list.*

BEST–SELLING BOOK BY A TEXAN (OTHER THAN THE BIBLE)

1. *Old Yeller,* by Fred Gipson, which, since it was first published in 1956, has sold three million copies, more than any other book by a Texan.

SOURCE: *The Handbook of Texas, Texas State Historical Association.*

FIVE RARE BOOKS EXHIBITED BY THE DETERING BOOK GALLERY AT THE 1980 SAN FRANCISCO BOOK FAIR, AND THEIR SALE PRICES

1. James Joyce, *Finnegans Wake.* London, 1939. Signed by the author. Buckram, enclosed in a cloth box. $1500.

2. William Caxton, *An Original Leaf From the Polycronicon Printed by William Caxton at Westminster in the Year 1482.* San Francisco, 1938. One of 297 copies printed. $600.

3. Geoffrey Chaucer, *The Works of Geoffrey Chaucer.* London, 1896. Bound in morocco. One of 425 copies. A magnum opus of the Kelmscott Press. $12,000.

4. Arthur Rackham, illustrations in *Undine* by De La Motte Fouque. London, 1909. One of 1000 numbered copies signed by Rackham, whose illustrations include fifteen color plates. $600.

5. Max Weber, *Woodcuts and Linoleum Blocks by Max Weber.* New York, 1955. One of 225 numbered copies printed from the original blocks and signed by Weber. $250.

SOURCE: *Detering Book Gallery, Houston.*

LONE STAR PLAYWRIGHTS

1. Preston Jones, probably the best-known for talent and Texan-ness. *A Texas Trilogy,* his most famous work, includes *The Last Meeting of the Knights of the White Magnolia, Lu Ann Hampton Laverty Oberlander,* and *The Oldest Living Graduate.* Jones died in 1979.

2. Donald Coburn. His touching play *The Gin Game* won the Pulitzer Prize for drama in 1978.

3. Jack Heifner, the author of the popular Broadway play *Vanities,* as well as *Patio/Porch.*

4. James McLure, an SMU graduate whose Texas-oriented one-acts include *Lone Star* and *Pvt. Wars.*

5. Marty Martin, an Austinite who wrote *Gertrude Stein, Gertrude Stein, Gertrude Stein.*

6. Larry L. King, the author of several books, who also wrote the script for *The Best Little Whorehouse in Texas.*

7. Tom Jones and Harvey Schmidt, two University of Texas alumni, who wrote the long-running play *The Fantasticks.*

EIGHT STORIES BY O. HENRY THAT ARE SET IN TEXAS

O. Henry (real name: William Sydney Porter) lived in Texas off and on from 1882 to 1898, mostly in Austin and Houston. He left the state involuntarily after being convicted of embezzlement at the bank where he worked.

1. "Hygeia at the Solito."
2. "A Fog in Santone."
3. "Bexar Script No. 2692."
4. "A Chaparral Prince."
5. "The Mirage on the Frio."
6. "A Houston Romance."
7. "The Legend of San Jacinto."
8. "Whisky Did It."

SOURCE: *O. Henry Museum, Austin.*

BOOKS COPYRIGHTED IN THE REPUBLIC OF TEXAS

1. *Topographical Description of Texas,* by George William Bonnell. It was published by Clark, Wing, and Brown in 1840 in Austin.

EIGHT FICTIONAL TEXANS

1. Hud, from Larry McMurtry's novel *Horseman, Pass By.*
2. Jett Rink and Bick Benedict, from *Giant* by Edna Ferber.
3. Old Yeller, from the book of the same name by Fred Gipson.
4. Pecos Bill, a product of tall-tale tellers.
5. Arthur "Goddam" Fenstemaker, from *The Gay Place,* a novel by William Brammer.
6. Peggy Sue, who gave her name to the Buddy Holly song.
7. Felina, of Marty Robbins's song "El Paso."
8. J. R. Ewing, from the television series *Dallas.*

WRITERS WHO HAVE WON PULITZER PRIZES

1. Allen Drury, *Advise and Consent,* 1960 (fiction).
2. Katherine Anne Porter, *Collected Stories,* 1966 (fiction).
3. Donald Coburn, *The Gin Game,* 1978 (drama).
4. Marquis James, *The Raven,* 1930 (biography).
5. Paul Horgan, *Great River,* 1955 (history).
6. William H. Goetzmann, *Exploration and Empire,* 1967 (history).

STOP THE PRESSES: NEWSPAPERS AND NEWS-PAPERPEOPLE WHO HAVE WON PULITZERS

1. *Alice Daily Echo,* to Mrs. Caro Brown for general reporting, 1955.
2. *Amarillo Globe-Times,* for meritorious public service, 1961.
3. *Lufkin News,* for meritorious public service, 1977.
4. *Dallas Times Herald,* to Skeeter Hagler for feature photography, 1980.
5. *Fort Worth Star-Telegram,* to Larry C. Price for spot news photography, 1981.

EARLY NEWSPAPERS

1. The *Gaceta de Texas,* the very first paper in the territory, appeared in May of 1813. It consisted of a single sheet printed front and back in Spanish. The gazette was created to report on the Gutíerrez-Magee expedition, a foray against Spain by several groups of Mexican soldiers whose ranks were bolstered by American adventurers. The expedition failed, and so did the *Gaceta,* which was published only once.

2. *El Mejicano,* produced by the editors of the *Gaceta,* appeared a month later. It also was a report on the expedition.

3. The *Texas Republican,* which began in 1819, was the first English-language paper in Texas.

4. The *Telegraph and Texas Register* was first published in San Felipe de Austin, an early capital of the Republic. The *Register* was forced to halt publishing at the advance of Santa Anna's armies; the Mexicans later seized the printing press and dumped part of it in Buffalo Bayou. Battered but unbowed, the *Register* moved to Columbia and in August of 1836 published the constitution of the Republic of Texas, allowing many Texans to see it for the first time. Later the paper relocated to Houston; it continued publishing till 1877.

BIGGEST NEWSPAPERS AND THEIR DAILY CIRCULATIONS AS OF MARCH, 1980

1. *Houston Chronicle,* 348,600.
2. *Houston Post,* 330,200.
3. *Dallas Morning News,* 287,000.
4. *Dallas Times Herald,* 249,900.
5. *Fort Worth Star-Telegram,* 240,600.
6. *San Antonio Light,* 122,600.
7. *San Antonio Express-News,* 76,600.

BEST HIGH SCHOOL NEWSPAPER NAMES

1. *Runeskrift,* Lanier High School, Austin.
2. *Le Raconteur,* Greenwood High School, Midland.
3. *World of AHS,* Andrews High School.
4. *Sharky Sparky Gazette,* Sabine Pass High School.
5. *Featherduster,* Westlake High School.
6. *Yowl of the Hounds,* Taft High School.

CONTRIBUTOR: *Thomas A. Prentice, Austin.*

FUNNIEST NEWSPAPER NAMES

1. The *Jefferson Jimplecute.* There are two explanations of how it got its name: one, that it resulted from a printer's error—quite a big error—or, two, that it is an acronym for "Join Industry, Manufacturing, Planning, Labor, Energy, Capital (in) Unity Together Everlasting." Weird.

2. *Decatur Wise Times.* OK, so Decatur's in Wise County. It's still a good name.

3. *Flatonia Argus.* Sharp-eyed folks at this newspaper, all right.

4. *Fort Worth Mind.* Think about it.

5. *Goliad Advance Guard.* Best historical newspaper name.

6. *Hondo Anvil Herald.* A refreshing change from the old *Times Herald* duo.

7. *Mexia Bi-Stone Weekly.* Surely, we thought, it's the Stone Bi-Weekly. But no.

8. *Madisonville Meteor.* Flash!

9. *Port Lavaca Wave.* Printing this paper is literally making *Waves.*

10. *Refugio Timely Remarks.* In weekly installments.

11. *Schulenberg Sticker.* Sometimes the truth hurts.

PUNNIEST NEWSPAPER NAMES

1. *Ferris Wheel.*
2. *Hart Beat.*
3. *Moulton Eagle.*
4. *Comanche Chief.*
5. *Alpine Avalanche.*

THREE EARLY MAGAZINES

1. *Texas Siftings* began publication in Austin in 1881 as a weekly humor magazine, edited by Alexander Sweet and managed by John Knox. Three years later the magazine moved to New York; there was even a European edition by 1887. The magazine was sold in 1895.

2. *Rolling Stone,* not to be confused with the current publication of the same name, was perhaps more legitimately a newspaper than a magazine. An Austin weekly, it lasted only from 1894 to 1895, and its chief claim to fame was that its editor, William Sydney Porter, wrote several celebrated short-stories under the name O. Henry.

3. *Pitchfork,* a humor magazine published in 1909 in Dallas, was composed largely of anecdotes and tall tales but was sprinkled with more serious articles. Edited by Wilford B. Smith, it continued for thirty years.

TOWNS WITH THE BEST RADIO CALL LETTERS

1. Odessa, with both KRIG and KOYL.
2. Mineola, with KMOO.
3. Pleasanton, with KBOP.

RADIO CALL LETTER QUIZ

Match the call letters of these stations with the cities they're in; there should be plenty of clues. Don't worry; you're bound to get number 12 right.

1.	KUT.	a.	Dalhart.
2.	KTAM.	b.	Dallas.
3.	KXIT.	c.	Lubbock.
4.	KPAS.	d.	Waco.
5.	KLBK.	e.	Dallas.
6.	KILE.	f.	Bryan-College Station.
7.	KRIO.	g.	Houston.
8.	KSMU.	h.	Midland.
9.	KDFW-TV.	i.	Galveston.
10.	KHOU-TV.	j.	Austin.
11.	KMID-TV.	k.	El Paso.
12.	WACO.	l.	McAllen.

RADIO CALL LETTERS THAT SPELL WORDS

1. KNIT, Abilene.
2. KNOW, Austin.
3. KEYS, Corpus Christi.
4. KELP, El Paso.
5. KILT, Houston.
6. KISS, San Antonio.
7. KITE, San Antonio.

MOST-POPULAR EXHIBITS AT THE MUSEUM OF FINE ARTS, HOUSTON

1. "Cézanne: the Late Work," January 25 to March 19, 1978. Attendance: 224,122.

2. "The Armand Hammer Collection: Four Centuries of Masterpieces," October 26, 1979, to January 20, 1980. Attendance: 159,331.

3. "Master Paintings From the Hermitage and the State Russian Museum," February 3 to March 16, 1976. Attendance: 112,900.

4. "Mark Rothko, 1903–1970: a Retrospective," February 8 to April 1, 1979. Attendance: 75,515.

SOURCE: *Museum of Fine Arts, Houston.*

TWO OF THE KIMBELL ART MUSEUM'S CLAIMS TO FAME

1. It is the last building designed by the great architect Louis I. Kahn, and it won the Honor Award of the American Institute of Architects.

2. It paid a record-setting price for an impressionist masterpiece by bidding $3.9 million for *Peasant in a Blue Smock,* by Paul Cézanne, at an auction of the Henry Ford collection by Christie's in 1980.

SOURCE: *Kimbell Art Museum, Fort Worth.*

LANDMARK ACQUISITIONS AT THE DALLAS MUSEUM OF FINE ARTS

1. Largest painting: William Conlon's *Slip Stream,* 9 feet by 10 feet 6 inches.

2. Largest sculpture: Mark di Suvero's *Ave,* 36 feet, 19 inches by 30 feet, 10 inches by 45 feet, 5 inches.

3. Smallest work of art: pre-Columbian gold cast armadillo from Panama, measuring only three eighths of an inch and displayed under a magnifying glass.

4. Most popular work: Frederic Edwin Church's *Icebergs.*
5. Most widely traveled work: Jackson Pollock's *Cathedral.*
6. First painting purchased: Childe Hassam's *September Moonrise.*
7. Most unusual work: an African nail fetish of the late nineteenth century, a small wooden figure thrust through with nails and other sharp objects, which purportedly served to alert and concentrate the spirit power in the fetish.

SOURCE: *Dallas Museum of Fine Arts.*

MICHAEL ENNIS'S LIST OF THE BEST ARTISTS IN TEXAS

Michael Ennis writes about art and other subjects for *Texas Monthly.*

1. Jim Love, Houston sculptor. His witty, semi-abstract sculptures convey a vast range of human emotions while commenting ironically on the conventions of modern sculpture.

2. Earl Staley, Houston painter. Brilliantly composed and colored paintings communicate broadly based humanistic themes.

3. David McManaway, Dallas sculptor. An assemblagist, he combines a great sense of color and form with haunting psychological insights.

4. Roger Winter, Dallas painter. One of the best realist painters anywhere. His simple street scenes are done with marvelous restraint.

5. James Surls, Houston sculptor. Large, semi-abstract, surrealistic wood sculptures combine tremendous energy, ambition, and originality.

6. Mac Whitney, Dallas sculptor. The best purely abstract artist in Texas. His huge steel sculptures have all the quirky expressiveness of small drawings.

7. Carlotta Corpron, Denton photographer. Pioneer Texas "art" photographer back when photographers weren't usually considered artists — and neither were women.

8. William Lester, Austin painter. A painter's painter. Did nature-theme abstractions back when abstract art was generally attributed to communists.

9. Charles Umlauf, Austin sculptor. A magnificent draftsman, he also creates abstract sculpture with the best of them. His "official" figurative sculptures for the University of Texas don't fully showcase his superior technical skills.

10. George Krause, Houston photographer. He has been highly honored for his work.

11. Philip Rentería, Houston painter. The most talented and original of Texas' many talented but not-so-original young abstract artists.

MOST FAMOUS BUILDINGS

1. The Alamo, cradle of Texas liberty, known around the world as the site of one of the most heroic battles of all time.

2. The Astrodome, the first fully enclosed domed stadium. When it was built in 1965, it was called the eighth wonder of the world.

3. The Texas School Book Depository, from the sixth floor of which Lee Harvey Oswald allegedly shot John F. Kennedy.

TALLEST BUILDINGS

1. Texas Commerce Tower, Houston: 1002 feet.
2. First International Plaza, Houston: 744 feet.
3. One Shell Plaza, Houston: 714 feet.
4. First International Building, Dallas: 710 feet.

BOONE POWELL'S LIST OF GREAT TEXAS BUILDINGS

Boone Powell is a noted architect with Ford, Powell & Carson in San Antonio.

1. Mission Concepción, San Antonio. Built in 1755. The most powerfully designed of the San Antonio missions.

2. The Stagecoach Inn, Winedale. A handsome early Texas inn, circa 1835. Beautifully restored by Ima Hogg.

3. Neill-Cochran House, Austin. 1853. Architect: Abner Cook. A wonderful Greek Revival house of early Texas, perhaps Cook's finest work.

4. Joseph Carlé House and Store, Castroville. Circa 1855. Early Texas with Alsatian influences. A set of very charming buildings on the square.

5. General Land Office, Austin. 1857. Architect: Conrad E. Stremme. One of the most interesting and original public buildings in the state.

6. State Capitol, Austin. 1888. Architect: Elijah E. Myers. A powerful symbol though not particularly original. The stonework is superb.

7. The Ashbel Smith Building, University of Texas Medical Branch, Galveston. 1889. Architect: Nicholas Clayton. A great building by the most important architect of nineteenth-century Texas. Known as "Old Red" to medical students and continually jeopardized by UT regents and narrowly focused school administrators.

8. Texas courthouses. As a collection they are the best group of buildings that the state produced. Those of the late nineteenth century are of the great period of public construction in the state. The best include courthouses of these counties: Bexar (San Antonio),

Caldwell (Lockhart), Coryell (Gatesville), Denton (Denton), DeWitt (Cuero), Ellis (Waxahachie), Hill (Hillsboro), Hood (Granbury), Hopkins (Sulphur Springs), Lavaca (Hallettsville), and Victoria (Victoria).

9. Bayou Bend, Houston. 1928. Architect: John Staub. The finest sumptuous house by the most prolific designer of estates for Houston's aristocracy. Classic Revival in Texas at its grandest.

10. Chapel in the Woods, Texas Woman's University, Denton. 1939. Architects: Ford and Swank. One of two great contemporary religious buildings in Texas.

11. Temple Emanu-El, Dallas. 1957. Architects: Howard Meyer and Max Sandfield. The other.

12. Kimbell Art Museum. 1974. Architect: Louis I. Kahn. Kahn's only building in Texas has provided a great museum and the finest contemporary design in the state. A true masterwork by a master of modern architecture.

C H A P T E R ★ 9

Sports

NONPAREIL ATHLETES

1. Mildred "Babe" Didrickson Zaharias, a Port Arthur native. In the 1932 Olympics she won gold medals in the 80-meter hurdles and the javelin, setting world records, and also won a silver medal in the high jump. Fifteen years later, the incredible Babe won seventeen golf tournaments in a row. She was named Woman Athlete of the Year six times.

TEXAS PLAYERS IN THE PRO FOOTBALL HALL OF FAME

1. Lance Alworth, wide receiver.
2. Sammy Baugh, quarterback.
3. Raymond Berry, end.
4. Forrest Gregg, tackle.

5. Lamar Hunt, owner.
6. Dick "Night Train" Lane, defensive back.
7. Yale Lary, defensive back.
8. Bobby Layne, quarterback.
9. Ollie Matson, halfback.
10. Y. A. Tittle, quarterback.
11. Clyde "Bulldog" Turner, center.

CONTRIBUTOR: *Robert D. Younts, Corpus Christi.*

TEXAS FOOTBALL GREATS WHO WEREN'T DALLAS COWBOYS

1. Sammy Baugh, a.k.a. "Slingin' Sammy." Great NFL quarterback and punter for the Washington Redskins.

2. Bobby Layne. Colorful and versatile All-Pro quarterback, mostly with the Detroit Lions.

3. Frank Ryan. Another brilliant NFL quarterback, Cleveland Browns.

4. Raymond Berry. Great receiver for the Baltimore Colts.

5. Don Maynard. Berry's successor as the pros' outstanding receiver, New York Giants.

6. Y. A. Tittle. The Giants' All-Pro quarterback.

7. Mean Joe Greene. Pittsburgh's most valuable theft from Texas.

8. Kyle Rote. Giants' captain and star end.

9. Doak Walker. Four-time All-Pro with Detroit.

10. Earl Campbell. Three-time leading rusher in NFL.

DALLAS COWBOYS' RING OF HONOR

1. Bob Lilly, defensive lineman and perennial All-Pro.
2. Don Perkins, running back.
3. Don Meredith, quarterback.
4. Chuck Howley, linebacker.

SOURCE: *Dallas Cowboys.*

DALLAS COWBOYS WHO BELONG ON THE PRECEDING LIST

1. Roger Staubach.

MOST COMMON PROFESSIONS OF THE 1980–81 DALLAS COWBOY CHEERLEADERS

1. Full-time student (12 members).
2. Secretary or receptionist (9).
3. Nurse or nursing student (3).
4. Flight attendant (2).

SOURCE: *Dallas Cowboys.*

DALLAS COWBOYS' WON–LOST RECORD (THROUGH 1980)

1. 1960, 0–11–1. At that time the worst record ever for an NFL team.

2. 1961, 4–9–1.

3. 1962, 5–8–1.

4. 1963, 4–10–0.

5. 1964, 5–8–1.

6. 1965, 7–7–0.

7. 1966, 10–3–1. Lost to Green Bay in the championship game.

8. 1967, 9–5–0. Defeated Cleveland in divisional play-offs; lost to Green Bay in championship.

9. 1968, 12–2–0. Lost to Cleveland in play-offs; defeated Minnesota in the Nothing Bowl.

10. 1969, 11–2–1. Lost to Cleveland in play-offs again; then lost to Los Angeles 0–31.

11. 1970, 10–4–0. Defeated Detroit and San Francisco in play-offs; lost to Baltimore in the Super Bowl.

12. 1971, 11–3–0. Defeated Minnesota, San Francisco, and Miami for 1972 Super Bowl title.

13. 1972, 10–4–0. Defeated San Francisco; lost to Washington in championship game.

14. 1973, 10–4–0. Defeated Los Angeles; lost to Minnesota.

15. 1974, 8–6–0. The year the Cowboys weren't in the play-offs.

16. 1975, 10–4–0. Defeated Minnesota and Los Angeles, but lost to Pittsburgh in the Super Bowl.

17. 1976, 11–3–0. Lost to Los Angeles.

18. 1977, 12–2–0. Defeated Chicago, Minnesota, and Denver to win their second Super Bowl.

19. 1978, 12–4–0. Stopped by Pittsburgh in the Super Bowl after beating Atlanta and Los Angeles.

20. 1979, 11–5–0. Lost to Los Angeles in divisional play-offs.

21. 1980, 12–4–0. Beat Los Angeles and Atlanta but fell to Philadelphia in the play-offs.

SOURCE: *Dallas Cowboys.*

ROGER STAUBACH'S LIST OF THE MOST MEMORABLE MOMENTS OF HIS CAREER

Roger Staubach, longtime quarterback of the Dallas Cowboys, still lives in Dallas.

1. My first Army-Navy game in November, 1962. We beat Army, 34–14.

2. The Cowboy's two Super Bowl victories, one in 1972 (24–3 over Miami) and the other in 1978 (27–10 over Denver).

3. Ending up my regular season career by knocking the Washington Redskins out of play-off contention, beating them 35–34.

HOUSTON OILERS' WON-LOST RECORD (THROUGH 1980)

1. 1960, 10-4-0. Won first AFL championship by defeating Los Angeles.

2. 1961, 10-3-1. Won second AFL championship against San Diego.

3. 1962, 11-3-0. Lost AFL title to the Dallas Texans in football's longest game: 77 minutes, 54 seconds.

4. 1963, 6-8-0.

5. 1964, 4-10-0.

6. 1965, 4-10-0.

7. 1966, 3-11-0.

8. 1967, 9-4-1. Lost to Oakland in AFL championship game.

9. 1968, 7-7-0.

10. 1969, 6-6-2.

11. 1970, 3-10-1.

12. 1971, 4-9-1.

13. 1972, 1-13-0.

14. 1973, 1-13-0.

15. 1974, 7-7-0.

16. 1975, 10-4-0.

17. 1976, 5-9-0.

18. 1977, 8-6-0.

19. 1978, 10-6-0. Beat Miami and New England in play-offs before losing to Pittsburgh in championship game.

20. 1979, 11–5–0. Defeated Denver and San Diego in play-offs, then lost out to Pittsburgh.

21. 1980, 11–5–0. With Pittsburgh out of the play-offs, Houston lost to Oakland in the first round.

BASEBALL GREATS

1. Tris Speaker. Greatest center fielder of his day; his lifetime batting average was .344.

2. Rogers Hornsby. His lifetime batting average of .358 is the highest in National League history.

3. Ernie Banks. Called 'Mr. Cub." Twice named Most Valuable Player; an All-star thirteen times.

4. Frank Robinson. Only man ever to be named MVP in both leagues.

5. Nolan Ryan. One of two pitchers to have thrown four no-hitters.

MAJOR LEAGUE BASEBALL PITCHERS WHO HAVE PITCHED NO-HITTERS

1. Nolan Ryan (four).
2. Ted Lyons.
3. Tex Carleton.
4. Burt Hooton.

CONTRIBUTOR: *Robert D. Younts, Corpus Christi.*

HOUSTON ASTROS' WON-LOST RECORD (THROUGH 1980)

1. 1962, 64-96.
2. 1963, 66-96.
3. 1964, 66-96.
4. 1965, 65-97.
5. 1966, 72-90.
6. 1967, 69-93.
7. 1968, 72-90.
8. 1969, 81-81.
9. 1970, 79-83.
10. 1971, 79-83. Key players traded to Cincinnati.
11. 1972, 84-69.
12. 1973, 82-80.
13. 1974, 81-81.
14. 1975, 64-97.
15. 1976, 80-82.
16. 1977, 81-81.
17. 1978, 74-88.
18. 1979, 89-73.
19. 1980, 93-70. Won western division in one-game play-off with Los Angeles. Lost five-game play-off to Philadelphia in a series of heart-breakers (four extra-inning games).

TEXAS RANGERS' WON-LOST RECORD (THROUGH 1980)

1. 1972, 54-100.
2. 1973, 57-105.
3. 1974, 84-76.
4. 1975, 79-83.
5. 1976, 76-86.
6. 1977, 94-68.
7. 1978, 87-75. Key players traded to Cleveland.
8. 1979, 83-79.
9. 1980, 76-85.

HOUSTON ROCKETS' WON–LOST RECORD (THROUGH 1980)

1. 1971–72, 34–48.
2. 1972–73, 33–49.
3. 1973–74, 32–50.
4. 1974–75, 41–41. (3–5 in play-offs).
5. 1975–76, 40–42.
6. 1976–77, 49–33. (6–6 in play-offs).
7. 1977–78, 28–54.
8. 1978–79, 47–35. (0–2 in play-offs).
9. 1979–80, 41–41. (2–5 in play-offs).
10. 1980–81, 40–42. (Lost championship to Boston.)

SAN ANTONIO SPURS' WON–LOST RECORD (THROUGH 1980)

The Spurs have never failed to make the play-offs since the team has been in San Antonio.

1. 1973–74, 45–39.
2. 1974–75, 51–33.
3. 1975–76, 50–34.
4. 1976–77, 44–38.
5. 1977–78, 52–30.
6. 1978–79, 48–34.
7. 1979–80, 41–41.
8. 1980–81, 52–30.

GREAT GOLFERS (Male)

1. Ben Hogan. Four-time winner of U.S. Open; won all four major tournaments.

2. Byron Nelson. U.S. Open and Masters winner; nineteen victories in 1945 alone.

3. Lee Treviño. Has won five major championships. The PGA's most colorful player.

4. Jimmy Demaret. Three-time Masters champ.

5. Jack Burke, Jr. Masters and PGA champion.

6. Lloyd Mangrum. U.S. Open victor (and war hero). Won eleven tournaments in 1948.

7. Ralph Guldahl. Back-to-back U.S. Open wins, 1937 and 1938.

8. Don January. Consistent winner on the pro tour for thirty years.

GREAT GOLFERS (Female)

1. Betty Jameson. Women's U.S. Amateur winner in 1939 and 1940. In LPGA Hall of Fame.

2. Mickey Wright. Over 80 wins in the LPGA; a member of its Hall of Fame. Now lives in Dallas.

3. Babe Zaharias. Texas' greatest athlete won seventeen consecutive tournaments in one year. In the LPGA Hall of Fame.

4. Betsy Rawls. Tour victories total 55. Also in the LPGA Hall of Fame.

5. Kathy Whitworth. Eight times the leading money winner of the LPGA. Over 70 tour victories. Another Hall of Fame entrant.

TRACK AND FIELD STARS

1. Bob Beamon. Achieved the incredible 29-foot, 2.5-inch long jump at the 1968 Olympic Games. Attended the University of Texas at El Paso.

2. Jim Hines. Olympic gold medalist and world-record sprinter from Texas Southern University.

3. Dave Roberts. Rice University graduate was once the world-record holder in pole-vaulting with a mark of 18 feet, 6.5 inches.

4. Fred Hansen. Another Rice alumnus who once held the world pole-vaulting record (then 17 feet, 4 inches).

5. Randy Matson, an Aggie from Pampa, was the first man to break 70 feet with the shot put, at one time holding world and Olympic records.

GREATS IN OTHER SPORTS

1. Cecil Smith, ten-goal (highest-ranking) polo player for 23 years in a row. He grew up in Austin.

2. Bill Shoemaker, a Fabens native, the jockey who has ridden more winning horses than anyone else.

3. A. J. Foyt, auto racer, the only four-time winner of the Indianapolis 500. Arguably the greatest auto racer of all time. His hometown is Houston.

4. Johnny Rutherford, auto racer. The Fort Worth resident has twice won at Indy.

5. Lloyd Ruby, auto racer. Numerous championships but never the big one. He hails from Wichita Falls.

6. Jack Johnson, fighter. Galveston native was the first black heavyweight champion, holding the title from 1908 to 1915.

7. George Foreman, fighter. Powerful heavyweight champion later roped into defeat by Muhammad Ali. A Houston native.

8. Kyle Rote, Jr., soccer player. America's major homegrown soccer star; he comes from Dallas.

9. Harold Solomon, tennis player. Moonball specialist of the pro tennis tour. A Rice graduate.

10. Wilmer Allison. Fort Worth native was a major tennis star of the thirties.

COLLEGES THAT WON NCAA CHAMPIONSHIPS

1. The University of Texas at El Paso is Texas' only NCAA winner in basketball. The school was called Texas Western College in 1966 when its team became the first ever to use no white players in the championship game. UTEP also has won eight NCAA track victories—five for indoor track in 1974, 1975, 1976, 1978, and 1980, and three for outdoor track, in 1975, 1979, and 1980—and was NCAA champ in yet a third sport, cross-country, in 1969, 1975, 1976, 1978, 1979, and 1980.

2. The University of Texas at Austin is the only NCAA baseball champ among Texas universities, with victories in 1949, 1950, and 1975. UT also won golf titles in 1971 and 1972.

3. Trinity University, with its 1972 victory, is the only NCAA tennis champ from Texas.

4. The University of Houston has won an incredible 13 NCAA golf championships: from 1956 through 1960; 1962; 1964 through 1967; 1969; 1970; and 1977.

5. North Texas State won the NCAA golf title four years in a row from 1949 through 1952.

COLLEGES THAT HAVE WON NATIONAL FOOTBALL CHAMPIONSHIPS

1. TCU, 1938 (picked by Associated Press).
2. Texas A&M, 1939 (AP).
3. Texas, 1963 (AP and United Press International), 1969 (AP and UPI), 1970 (UPI).

HEISMAN TROPHY WINNERS

1. 1938: David O'Brien, TCU (quarterback).
2. 1948: Doak Walker, SMU (halfback).
3. 1957: John David Crow, A&M (halfback).
4. 1977: Earl Campbell, Texas (running back).

TEXAS VICTORIES AT THE COTTON BOWL

1. 1937: TCU 16, Marquette 6.
2. 1938: Rice 28, Colorado 14.
3. 1941: A&M 13, Fordham 12.
4. 1943: Texas 14, Georgia Tech 7.
5. 1946: Texas 40, Missouri 27.
6. 1949: SMU 21, Oregon 13.
7. 1950: Rice 27, North Carolina 13.
8. 1953: Texas 16, Tennessee 0.
9. 1954: Rice 28, Alabama 6.
10. 1957: TCU 28, Syracuse 27.

11. 1962: Texas 12, Mississippi 7.
12. 1964: Texas 28, Navy 6.
13. 1968: A&M 20, Alabama 16.
14. 1969: Texas 36, Tennessee 13.
15. 1970: Texas 21, Notre Dame 17.
16. 1973: Texas 17, Alabama 13.
17. 1977: Houston 30, Maryland 21.
18. 1980: Houston 17, Nebraska 14.

TEXAS VICTORIES AT THE SUN BOWL

1. 1937: Hardin-Simmons 34, Texas School of Mines* 6.
2. 1944: Southwestern 7, New Mexico 0.
3. 1945: Southwestern 35, University of Mexico 0.
4. 1950: Texas Western* 33, Georgetown 20.
5. 1951: West Texas State 14, Cincinnati 13.
6. 1952: Texas Tech 25, University of the Pacific 14.
7. 1954: Texas Western 37, Mississippi Southern 14.
8. 1955: Texas Western 47, Florida State 20.
9. 1963: West Texas State 15, Ohio 14.
10. 1966: Texas Western 13, TCU 12.
11. 1968: UTEP 14, Mississippi 7.
12. 1977: A&M 37, Florida 14.
13. 1978: Texas 42, Maryland 0.

*The Texas School of Mines was renamed Texas Western College, which in turn was renamed the University of Texas at El Paso.

TEXAS VICTORIES AT THE BLUEBONNET BOWL

1. 1963: Baylor 14, LSU 7.
2. 1966: Texas 19, Mississippi 0.
3. 1968: SMU 28, Oklahoma 27.
4. 1969: Houston 36, Auburn 7.
5. 1973: Houston 47, Tulane 7.
6. 1975: Texas 38, Colorado 21.

THE THREE LEAST SUCCESSFUL COLLEGE TEAMS WHO APPEARED IN THREE OR MORE TEXAS BOWLS IN THE PAST THIRTY YEARS

1. Texas Tech, 1–5–0, leads the list of poor performers in Texas bowl games. The Red Raiders suffered losses to Wyoming (1956), Georgia (1964), Georgia Tech (1970), and North Carolina (1972), all in the Sun Bowl, and Nebraska (1976) in the Bluebonnet Bowl.

2. Alabama, 0–3–2, may be the most surprising member of this list. Yet while the team is a perennial football power, it has had little luck in Texas bowls. The Tide has lost to three different Southwest Conference teams in the Cotton Bowl: Rice (1954), Texas A&M (1968), and Texas (1973). In the Bluebonnet Bowl Alabama has at least managed ties: with Texas (1960) and Oklahoma (1970).

3. TCU, 2–4–1, has appeared in all three Texas bowls. In the Cotton Bowl TCU lost to Kentucky (1952) and Mississippi (1956), though the college did beat Marquette (1937) and Syracuse (1957) and tie Air Force (1959). In the Bluebonnet Bowl the Frogs lost to Clemson (1959); later, they made it to the Sun Bowl only to lose to Texas Western (1965).

CONTRIBUTOR: *Don Deal, Houston.*

SILLY NAMES FOR HIGH SCHOOL TEAMS

1. Itasca Wampus Cats.
2. Knippa Purple Rock Crushers.
3. Munday Moguls.
4. Big Spring Steers.
5. Taylor Ducks.
6. Hamlin Pied Pipers.
7. Hutto Hippos.
8. Killeen Kangaroos.
9. El Campo Ricebirds.
10. Amarillo Sandies.

SPORTS NICKNAMES

1. O. A. "Bum" Phillips, former Oilers coach.
2. Hugh "Bones" Taylor, former Oilers coach.
3. Frank "Pop" Ivy, former Oilers coach.
4. L. R. "Dutch" Meyer, TCU football coach.
5. Charles "Ki" Aldrich, TCU lineman.
6. Clyde "Bulldog" Turner, All-Pro center.
7. Raymond "Rags" Matthews, TCU end.
8. Mike "Pinky" Higgins, major league infielder.
9. Bill "The Shoe" Shoemaker, jockey.
10. Barton "Botchey" Koch, Baylor guard (football).
11. Clarence "Big Boy" Kraft, Texas League baseball player.
12. Byron "Buster" Brannon, athlete and coach at Rice and TCU.
13. John "Boody" Johnson, Waco High School star.
14. John "Snipe" Conley, Texas League pitcher.
15. Bill "Jitterbug" Henderson, Aggie sports star.
16. J. V. "Siki" Sikes, Aggie sports star.
17. Dick "Night Train" Lane, great pro defensive back.

TEXANS WHO HOLD WORLD FISHING RECORDS

1. David S. Cordill of Spicewood, who in 1977 caught the largest white bass on record below the Longhorn Dam. The bass weighed 5 pounds, 9 ounces.

2. Townsend Miller of Austin, who hooked a 50-pound, 5-ounce long-nose gar in the Trinity River in 1954.

3. Bill Valverde of Mission, whose record alligator gar weighed 279 pounds even. He caught it in the Rio Grande in 1951.

SOURCE: *Texas Department of Parks and Wildlife.*

RECORD-SETTING SHARKS

All these sharks were caught on rod and reel.

1. Bull shark, 497 pounds, 9 feet, 2 inches. Caught by Dale Harper of Houston in 1971 off Galveston.

2. Great hammerhead shark, 871 pounds, 13 feet, 7¾ inches. Caught by Mark A. Johnson of LaMarque in 1980, 18 miles southeast of the Galveston jetties.

3. Lemon shark, 357 pounds, 8 feet, 8¾ inches. Caught by L.J. Schaper, Jr., of Hitchcock, in 1980 east of the Buccaneer Field off Galveston.

4. Mako shark, 388 pounds, 9 feet, 1 inch. Caught by Robert Hada of Port Aransas in 1977 off Port Aransas.

5. Tiger shark, 837 pounds, 11 feet, 7 inches. Caught by Robert L. Derrick of Alta Loma in 1980, 35 miles southeast of Galveston.

SOURCE: *Texas Department of Parks and Wildlife.*

FIVE FRESHWATER FISHING RECORDS

The Texas Parks and Wildlife Department stipulates that entries in the freshwater division be caught on rod and reel only.

1. Largemouth bass, 14 pounds, 1.5 ounces. Caught by Jim Kimbell of Pittsburg, Texas, at Lake Monticello in 1980.

2. Channel catfish, 36 pounds, 8 ounces. Caught by Mrs. Joe L. Cockrell of Austin at the Pedernales River in 1965.

3. Flounder, 9 pounds. Caught by Catherine Pond of Austin at Lake Long in 1978.

4. Redfish, 26 pounds. Caught by Jack Kimbrough of Clute at Chub Lake in 1971.

5. Rainbow trout, 4 pounds, 12 ounces. Caught by Ron Sharp of San Antonio at the Guadalupe River in 1968.

SOURCE: *Texas Department of Parks and Wildlife.*

FOUR FISHING RECORDS HELD FOR OVER FORTY YEARS

1. Freshwater drum, 55 pounds. Caught by Asa Short of Fort Worth at White Rock Lake in 1924 by trotline.

2. Snook, 57 pounds, 8 ounces. Caught by Louis Rawalt of Corpus Christi off Padre Island in 1937 by rod and reel.

3. Jewfish, 551 pounds. Caught by Gus Pangarakis of Magnolia off Galveston in 1937 by rod and reel.

4. Sawfish, 736 pounds. Also caught by Gus Pangarakis off Galveston by rod and reel, two years later.

SOURCE: *Texas Department of Parks and Wildlife.*

BEST SPRING–FED SWIMMING HOLES

1. Lampasas City Pool. Bathhouse built around 1910.
2. Balmorhea State Park. Can't be beat for sheer size.
3. Fort Clark Springs. The fort is still there too.
4. Springs of San Felipe. Ice-cold, and near a nice park in Del Rio.
5. Crystal Springs. Near Maude. It's the Riviera of the Piney Woods.
6. Landa Park. New Braunfels. Choice of spring-fed or chemical pool.
7. San Marcos River. And all the college kids know it.
8. Roaring Springs. In Motley County. It's almost fifty years old.
9. Barton Springs. Austin. The most accessible.
10. Mountain Springs. Near Hillsboro. Complete with bathhouse. A genuine good ol' boy pool.

CONTRIBUTOR: *C. M. "Dink" Starns, Fort Worth.*

GOOD PLACES TO SCUBA DIVE

1. Lake Amistad. Twelve miles northwest of Del Rio on the confluence of the Pecos, Rio Grande, and Devil's rivers.

2. Lake Travis. Twenty miles northwest of Austin on the Highland Lakes chain of the Colorado River.

3. San Marcos River. Below Aquarena Springs to City Park in San Marcos; visibility 25 to 50 feet.

4. Park Chalk Bluffs. Relatively unknown spot on the Nueces River at Highway 55, fifteen miles from Uvalde; visibility up to 40 feet.

5. Jacob's Well. Near Wood Creek resort at Wimberly. A beautiful— and sometimes dangerous—cave dive.

6. Canyon Lake. Forty miles north of San Antonio on FM 306. A very clear lake.

7. Comal River. A beautiful site on Texas' shortest river, in New Braunfels's Landa Park. Visibility 30 feet; good underwater photograpy opportunities.

8. Gulf Coast. Various spots include the northernmost tropical reef in the Western Hemisphere (the Flower Gardens), sunken ships, and a railroad track.

CONTRIBUTOR: *V. Phillip Hosey, Austin.*

GEORGE BUSH'S FAVORITE JOGGING PATHS

George Bush is vice president of the United States.

1. Memorial Park, Houston.
2. Steve Prefontaine jogging course, Eugene, Oregon.
3. Three Rivers Stadium, Pittsburgh, Pennsylvania.
4. Naval Observatory, Washington, D.C.

RODEO PROS WHO WERE ALL-AROUND CHAMPS

1. Larry Mahan, Dallas, 1973. He won five previous titles while living in Oregon.

2. Phil Lyne, George West, Texas, 1971 and 1972.

TWO FAMOUS FLIERS

1. Wiley Post, born in 1898 in Grand Saline, was the first person to fly around the world solo. The 1933 flight in his plane *Winnie Mae* proved the usefulness of automatic pilot. In 1935, while on a pleasure trip with humorist Will Rogers, Post's plane crashed near Point Barrow, Alaska. Both men were killed.

2. Howard Hughes, movie producer and millionaire, was an accomplished aviator. In 1935 he set the world land speed record for a plane (352 miles per hour); in 1937 he set a new record for a transcontinental flight (7 hours, 28 minutes); and in 1938 he established a new round-the-world record (91 hours, 14 minutes). Hughes also designed, built, and flew (once) what was then the world's largest plane, the *Spruce Goose,* which had a wingspan of 320 feet. He is a member of the Aviation Hall of Fame.

STATE OF TEXAS REPRESENTATIVE TO THE XIII OLYMPIC WINTER GAMES TORCH RELAY TEAM (Lake Placid, New York, 1980)

1. Gene Deutscher, Fort Worth.

SOURCE: *Gene Deutscher, Fort Worth.*

FIVE LISTS WE ASKED FOR BUT DIDN'T GET

1. Eddie Chiles's reasons he's mad.
2. J.R. Ewing's role models.
3. Dale Evans's happiest trails.
4. Suggestive letter combinations that are banned on license plates by the Texas Highway Department.
5. What's right about Wichita Falls, by its mayor.